CAPTAINS

CAPTAINS

Tales from the Vicarage

Volume Seven
by Mike Walters

First published in Great Britain in 2018
by Tales From

© 2018 Tales From Ltd

Printed and bound by Page Bros Ltd

Jacket design by www.stonecreativedesign.com

ISBN 978-1-912249-02-2

Tales From Ltd
107 Jupiter Drive, Hemel Hempstead, Herts HP2 5NU
Registered company number: 9082738
www.talesfrom.com
info@talesfrom.com

CAPTAINS

CONTENTS

INTRODUCTION

Captaincy is not an exact science and, in football, to a large degree it remains an unquantifiable measurement of leadership. The skipper may lead his team from the tunnel onto the pitch, mark his mascot as closely as he would shadow an opponent defending a set-piece, wear an armband, shake hands in the centre-circle before kick-off and choose to attack the Rookery end in the second half. But then he becomes just another face in the cast of 22 players chasing the ball for 90 minutes, right?

After all, it is the manager or head coach who is architect of team selection, formation, tactics and substitutions. It is the boss who must front-up to explain a damaging defeat, or reel off a few platitudes when performances are attractive to supporters and sponsors alike.

But not everybody is qualified to wear an armband as an ornament of responsibility. From military brassards to stewards at a political rally or dinner ladies on playground duty at lunchtime, they are garters of authority, even if they are largely symbolic in football.

Yet captains are synonymous with moments in time, snapshots from history in which their rank thrusts them to the front pages of the archives.

Think of England winning the World Cup in 1966, and the most indelible image is of the captain, Bobby Moore, holding the Jules Rimet trophy aloft. Think of rugby's Webb Ellis equivalent, or golf's Ryder Cup – it is the captain who enjoys the privilege and adulation when the first waves of acclaim make landfall.

As William Shakespeare observed in *Twelfth Night*, some are born great, some achieve greatness, some have greatness thrust upon them. And if the great Bard had been around 400 years later, doubtless he would have added that some are lucky enough to captain Watford Football Club.

This volume, the seventh in the *Tales from the Vicarage* series, is essentially a tribute to 11 fine players who led the Hornets over half a century. It is neither a leaderboard of all those who have been assigned the captaincy, nor a slight on any worthy officers of the regiment who do not feature in these pages.

It is also fair to say the captains included here did not all expect the role to fall their way. For instance, Pat Rice – the man who led Watford into the top flight for the first time in 1982 – was signed specifically for his leadership qualities. On the other hand, Les Taylor, another crucial piece of the jigsaw during Graham Taylor's first magic carpet ride at Vicarage Road, only led the side out three times in 211 appearances – but one of those games happened to be the biggest occasion in the club's history.

This *Captains* XI does have at least one common denominator – in prosperity or austerity, each served Watford with distinction. In recent times uneducated elements in the media have portrayed Vicarage Road as the spiritual home of revolving doors, or a transit lounge for jobbing mercenaries, but the testimony of our witnesses suggests it is a club which cultivates a deep-rooted affection among its exemplars of influence.

As many of our venerable cast would attest, captaincy is often a triumph of intuition, of fulfilled potential, of appreciating a teammate's virtues while understanding his anxieties. But even the best have yet to produce a prefabricated, textbook version of the job applicable to football.

Former England cricket captain Mike Brearley was once described by Australian fast bowler and Ashes rival Rodney Hogg as having 'a degree in people' because he was blessed with a gift for drawing the best from his foot soldiers, notably Ian Botham.

But it is almost reassuring to discover that even celebrated leaders of men were not an immediate success in the officers' mess.

In his book *The Art of Captaincy*, a definitive read on the subject, Brearley tells how his first experience of being a captain, in an under-12s schools football match, was an excruciating ordeal. When his team, drawing 0-0 against rivals considered 'hot stuff' in the district, were awarded a penalty, he panicked and dashed around trying to find a teammate willing to take on the fearful responsibility. When none stepped forward, and Brearley was left to confront his nerves from the spot, his shot hit the bar.

Knowing full well the law which states that, after a penalty kick, another player other than the taker must be the next to touch the ball, Brearley gambled on the schoolmaster referee not knowing it, and tucked the rebound into the net. He was wrong about the referee, the goal was correctly disallowed and Brearley's team collapsed to a 5-0 defeat. Even now, he says, he trembles and sweats when reliving 'the anxiety of the awful moment, as well as from embarrassment at my absolute lack of coolness. Captaincy material, was I? It is hard to believe.'

On the basis that captains are as fallible as the next human being, down the years Watford have been blessed with some articulate skippers. These are the stories of their contribution to the Hornets' chronicle, or passages from their careers as Golden Boys.

Thanks to Richard Walker and Jon Marks at Watford Football Club for their help, to Paul Levene for solving assorted nit-pickery in the research department and, most of all, to the subjects themselves.

Your correspondent has had the privilege of seeing them all play – from Keith Eddy scoring from the spot against Reading in the FA Cup third round in 1971 to Troy Deeney in the class of 2018 – and the goodwill they exude towards Watford, without exception, speaks volumes for them and for the club.

And after working with Luther Blissett, Ross Jenkins, Steve Sherwood and Ian Bolton on *Rocket Men*, the previous volume in this series, followed by another select group of Watford legends for *Captains*, it is time to close all investigations into that old adage which says you should never meet your heroes – because it's a load of cobblers.

1

KEITH EDDY

THE MILKMAN DELIVERS

The summer of 1966 was a momentous time for everyone connected with English football. Keith Eddy signed for Watford.

Of course, the good times included a notable footnote at Wembley on the last weekend in July, when we thought it was all over against West Germany as Geoff Hurst broke clear, with the hourglass down to the last grains of sand, to seal England's World Cup triumph on home soil.

Sir Alf Ramsey's squad enjoyed a slap-up celebration banquet at the Royal Garden Hotel in Kensington, with their wives and partners confined to sandwiches in a side room, and his players were given the princely sum of £1,000 each – or £647 after tax – as a bonus by the Football Association. In a rare moment of largesse, Ramsey also negotiated a free raincoat for each of his heroes, but the swinging sixties did not make footballers rich. Before the final, England captain Bobby Moore had addressed his teammates with a bulletin closer to austerity than extravagance, announcing, 'Lads, they are giving us a £22,000 bonus if we win it . . . between all of us.'

If rejoicing at the FA's *faux* generosity was confined to a few weary glances and shrugs of resignation at England's Hendon Hall hotel retreat, Sir Alf's national treasures were not the only players who felt undervalued that summer. On the Furness peninsula, the southern heel of the Lake District where they still build submarines in the shipyards, 21-year-old Eddy had a sinking feeling of his own.

Fourth Division Barrow were never one of English football's big hitters, and their wage structure was incompatible with a dynamic young player's ambitions.

'I can't remember what I was getting paid, but compared with a few of the older guys who were probably past their best, I was poorly remunerated,' says Eddy. 'You got paid more during the season, and the club kept you ticking over on a basic retainer during the summer months, but it wasn't a king's ransom, and in the summer of 1966 I had got myself a job as a milkman to top up my income.

'I had a young kid working with me on the round. I drove the float and he did nearly all the deliveries to doorsteps and fetching the empties. We weren't exactly Batman and Robin, but we were a useful double act and we liked to think we drove the fastest milk cart in Barrow.

'In those days I always used to get myself fixed up with a bit of extra work – a sort of summer holiday job, if you like – to pay the bills. One year I also worked as a bartender, pulling pints and emptying ashtrays – worlds apart from the age of £100 million players these days.

'Brighton had come in for me during the season and Barrow turned down their £15,000 offer, but I had already decided I wasn't going to sign a new contract. It was their loss – Watford signed me in the summer of 1966 for a fraction of the cost, and I like to think I gave them decent value for money.'

Decent? The Hornets' £1,500 outlay on a commanding defender who was equally at home as a midfield anchorman was almost an indecent proposal, but Barrow were grateful to ease the thrombosis in their close-season cash-flow and Watford manager Ken Furphy's new recruit was not just a bargain: to

land a player of manifest promise for peanuts was an absolute
steal, a highwayman's heist.

Compile a list of Watford's best value-for-money signings
of the last 60 years and Eddy has to feature prominently in any
eclectic top five. At £10,000 Cliff Holton's transfer fee from
Arsenal was steep, for a Fourth Division club of the Hornets'
pedigree, in October 1958 – but he was worth every penny,
many times over, after plundering a club record 48 goals in
the 1959–60 promotion season, including League hat-tricks
on consecutive days. (There was uproar over his preposterous
and premature sale to Northampton for £7,000 after just
three years.) Graham Taylor always rated £12,500 Ian Bolton
as his finest investment on Watford's meteoric rise between
1977–83, and one of Bolton's most treasured possessions is a
Christmas card from his old boss, long after their careers had
diverged along separate paths, with the message: 'Still £ for £
my best signing!'

Even now, the £95,000 transaction bringing Tommy
Mooney to the club in 1994 looks a snip for a force of
nature, and in years to come Malky Mackay's judgement after
ploughing the £550,000 proceeds of Sir Elton John's concert
at Vicarage Road on Troy Deeney – which, it must be said,
was not vindicated immediately – deserves to be bracketed
with the wisdom of Solomon.

But at £1,500, which would buy a two-bedroom terraced
cottage in the mid-1960s, Furphy's punt on Eddy was as safe
as houses.

Eddy had joined the payroll at Vicarage Road by the time
England captain Moore wiped his muddied hands on his
red no.6 shirt before accepting the Jules Rimet trophy from
the Queen at Wembley. He remembers watching the World
Cup final on TV as the Hornets cranked up their pre-season
preparations, but the significance of that extended Saturday

afternoon matinée has only grown on him, like the rest of the
nation, with the passing years.

'It was wonderful for the country at the time, but I never
thought that England would still be waiting to win another
World Cup more than half a century later,' says Eddy. 'And
we didn't have much time to wallow in the glory – three weeks
later the new season kicked off and, at club level, it was back
to work.'

And when reality kicked in, the glamour of Jules Rimet
was conspicuous by its absence for Watford and their eager
debutant in midfield on a thankless away day at Feethams.

The Hornets have lost only twice against Darlington, both
1-0 defeats early in the season. One was the nadir in August
1975, which briefly consigned Watford to 92nd in the Football
League, bottom of the pile, for the only time in the club's 137-
year history . . . and the other was Keith Eddy's debut. He roars
with laughter at the trivial notoriety now, but ultimately that
false start in the north-east would prove costly as Furphy's side
missed out on promotion by a single point, pipped to a maiden
voyage in English football's second tier by Middlesbrough's late
surge for the chequered flag.

Elsewhere on the first day of term, Tottenham's Dave
Mackay and Leeds firebrand Billy Bremner were getting up
close and personal at White Hart Lane. The photo of an
unimpressed Mackay accosting a fellow Scot with a fistful of
his shirt, and a youthful Terry Venables keeping a safe distance
in the background, became an iconic image. Watford's failure
to leave the blocks promptly on the starter's pistol was, sadly,
an early portent of their struggle to win away from home. In
Broken Arrow, a 20-minute drive out of Tulsa, where Eddy
has lived for 40 years, they were enduring a record-breaking
freeze as we rolled back the archives, and Watford's bipolar
form in his first season at Vicarage Road is still enough to make
his teeth chatter now. 'We were so strong at home,' he says.

'The big teams near the top of the table couldn't hurt us. In the end, we only hurt ourselves.'

Eddy's belief was underscored by the wasteful manner in which the Hornets squandered points. Their only three home defeats that season were against mid-table Mansfield, Scunthorpe and Leyton Orient. Even reigning champions Liverpool, riding the crest of Beatlemania and Bill Shankly's genius, were held to a goalless draw in the FA Cup fourth round in front of a record 33,553 crowd in Hertfordshire before the plucky underdogs went down 3-1 before a noisy 54,000-plus congregation at Anfield in the replay.

But for all the glamour of a commendable double-header against Shankly's household names, the three games Eddy remembers most from the gut-wrenching anguish of that season were all swathed in disappointment. Trailing 1-0 at promotion rivals Middlesbrough, but giving as good as they got, Watford were undone when goalkeeper Bert Slater – who had won promotion with Liverpool in the early days of Shankly's reign – was forced to retire hurt with injury.

In an era when substitute keepers were an unexplored phenomenon, Eddy volunteered to hold the fort in goal, but he was powerless to prevent Boro going on to win 3-0, another pivotal moment when Watford picketed the gates of triumph but never enjoyed the glow of consummation when the Second Division beckoned.

And the Hornets' last two games were portraits of pure anguish and frustration. Held to goalless stalemate at Vicarage Road by Colchester, they were runners-up in the clubhouse after a 1-1 draw at Oldham – but, crucially, Boro had a game in hand, from which they required only a point at home to Oxford to squeeze through the loft hatch at Watford's expense on goal average. They won 4-1, and Eddy's first season among the Golden Boys ended in colossal exasperation.

'We were so unfortunate not to win the game at Oldham,' he says. 'It was one of those games where we did everything but score the winner. We were throwing kitchen sinks at them, but it just wouldn't go in. That's the nature of football – someone's joy is somebody else's broken heart, and this time it was our turn to be disappointed.

'Although Middlesbrough still had to get over the line, the dressing room was very hushed, very subdued afterwards. Ken was player-manager in those days, and normally he would come in after his shift at right-back and say whatever he felt needed to be said. But this time I don't recall him saying a word. We were so close to promotion, but in the end we only had ourselves to blame for missing out.'

***

The only goal Eddy contributed to that dangerous liaison with promotion in his first season at Watford came against Grimsby Town, whose ranks included a full-back of infinite promise called Graham Taylor.

It would be another decade before GT became a familiar messiah at Vicarage Road, but for his predecessor Furphy, who turned 36 in the summer of 1967, the demands of sustaining his dual role as player-manager were becoming increasingly trying. In another campaign of unfulfilled potential, punctuated by injuries to Furphy, Eddy was already earmarked for captaincy.

Forthright in the dressing room, and equally assertive on the pitch, Furphy trusted the bargain signing who was fast emerging as the beating heart of Watford, but the pair crossed swords briefly when the Hornets rushed to cash in on a prodigious talent with indecent haste.

Tony Currie, a teenage midfielder of exotic gifts, had slipped through the net at Queens Park Rangers and Chelsea at schoolboy and youth level, but his impact on the 1967–68 season transcended artistic licence and maverick skills at Vicarage Road. Currie had scored two League hat-tricks before his 18th birthday, against Peterborough and in the record 7-1 drubbing of Graham Taylor's Grimsby, before Furphy sanctioned his £26,500 sale to Sheffield United – a decision with which Eddy disagreed vociferously.

'I had a terrific rapport with Ken, and we didn't fall out very often, but I told him exactly what I thought about selling Tony,' says Eddy. 'It was a huge mistake. I felt we were cutting off our nose to spite our face. This boy was the most gifted young lad I had ever worked with. If he had stayed I thought he would help us to win promotion, and his market value would have gone up even higher. Watford would have been sitting pretty on a talent the big clubs would be climbing over each other to sign. I told Ken, "If you let him go, you'll regret it" – but he wouldn't listen. I liked Ken, and he did a great job as Watford manager, but he could be a moody devil when he dug his heels in. With Tony Currie I felt we had a player who could produce those bits of magic that turn games.'

Eddy's fears were realised by another infuriating near-miss with promotion. Turning inconsistency into an art form, Watford finished sixth – just six points off the top two – and their season was undermined again by impoverished away form, finishing as the division's lowest scorers on the road.

Later, Eddy and Currie would join forces again at Bramall Lane, where the teenage prodigy had continued to flourish and express himself, scoring on his debut against Tottenham but missing the next game because it was his wedding day. In 2014, as part of the club's 125th anniversary celebrations, Tony Currie was named Sheffield United's greatest ever player. Eddy's reservations that Watford had sold a tremendous player on the cheap were ultimately proved correct. When Furphy's managerial career took him to the Steel City, he appeared to acknowledge as much by making Currie his captain.

'I used to tell the players to give him the ball and he'd destroy the opposition,' says Eddy. 'Off the field he was a quiet kid, but when he pulled on a pair of boots and crossed that white line the transformation was dramatic. It was like Clark Kent diving into a telephone kiosk and coming out seconds later as a great showman.

'He was so comfortable with the ball on either foot, and when he invited opposition players to come and get the ball off him he could pick a pass or find a teammate when it didn't seem possible. He was probably the best English player I ever played with in my life. It's all conjecture now, of course, but you do wonder how it might have worked out differently for Watford if we had kept him for longer, but in the end he disappeared like a firework: he burst into flame, he was fantastic to watch . . . and then he was gone.'

Happily for Furphy, newly installed skipper Eddy and everyone connected with Watford, the disappointments of losing a box-office talent and another flirtation with promotion would be blown away the following season.

In the last half-century few campaigns have been as convincing, or as satisfying, as the Hornets storming to the Third Division championship in 1968–69. From back to front there were notable contributions across the board: goalkeeper Mike Walker's record 26 clean sheets, striker Barry Endean's 20 goals, Stewart Scullion's mesmerising skills, and the discovery of the club's original 'supersub' – Bernard Lewis sprang from the bench to score with his first touch in the 2-1 win at Plymouth on the run-in to the title – were all essential ingredients.

The captain contributed nine goals, four of them from the penalty spot, where Eddy had the enviable sang-froid of a spaghetti western gunslinger in a shootout with the bad-guy bandit. He relished the responsibility, saying, 'I had captained the team a few times the year before, but I was now established in the role.

'I don't think it was worth anything extra to me in terms of wages, and you didn't even get an armband in those days. But from schoolboy level upwards I had captained every team I played for, and I enjoyed doing it. I always said my biggest asset as a footballer was my mouth, talking to other players, bossing them around and trying to keep us organised as a team. I felt leadership suited me. I trusted myself more than I trusted anyone else, which is why I took the penalties.

'That's not blowing my own trumpet – either you're cut out to be a leader on the pitch or you're not. At eight years old I was captain of the under-11 team at my junior school in South Walney, an island off the coast of Barrow-in-Furness, because I was big for my age and quicker than a lot of boys who were older than me. I used to run past people and think, "It can't be that difficult to make it as a footballer." But when I moved up to secondary education most of the schools in our area played rugby rather than football.

'Fortunately, one of my junior-school coaches, a guy called Len Wilson, encouraged me to keep playing football. It's funny how you meet people who can shape your life, even at an early age, and I will always be grateful that he believed in me. Years later, after I had chiselled out a decent career as a professional, I bumped into him and he told me, "I always knew you would make it."

'But without people like him, it makes you wonder how many gifted young players are lost to the game. They are the unsung heroes.'

Eddy enjoyed the satisfaction of going back to Barrow and scoring in a 4-1 win as Watford, who had scored only two goals in their first four home games, gathered irresistible momentum before Christmas – a run which included a tense 1-0 win against the neighbours from over the border in Bedfordshire at Vicarage Road.

In all there would be four derbies with the infidel in the 1968–69 campaign, culminating in the notorious Battle of Kenilworth Road at the end of the season which set a regrettable benchmark for violence on and off the pitch. Following an early-season defeat up the road in the League Cup, the return Third Division fixture was abandoned after 62 minutes in a blizzard. It was 1-1, with Endean on target for the Hornets, when the snow became impenetrable.

By the time the game was rearranged, in the final week of the season, Watford were already up and their desperate rivals – unbeaten at home – were heading for a near-miss with promotion. This time Endean and Tom Walley were both sent off in a game where the ball often appeared to be an optional accessory to the main event and the visitors went down 2-1, not that it mattered when the final table was assembled. Somehow, 25,523 fans – including a huge following, in celebratory mood, from Hertfordshire – managed to squeeze into a cramped ground which has been treated to only limited refurbishment in the last half-century. Play was held up three times as fans encroached on the pitch and the St John Ambulance volunteers estimated nearly 100 people needed first-aid treatment for cuts and bruises. Later that night in St Albans, a marginal constituency where both clubs enjoyed a substantial fan base, there was unprecedented trouble.

'I don't recall much about the games themselves, because derbies are invariably tight and the football is usually too scrappy to be memorable,' says Eddy. 'But there was definitely no love lost. Watford fans loved it when we won promotion at the expense of our local rivals, and to be honest the players enjoyed it, too.'

Promotion and the title aside, an obvious highlight of
Watford's season was drawing 1-1 with Manchester United, the
reigning European Cup holders, in the FA Cup fourth round
at Old Trafford – and a record 34,099 packed Vicarage Road
for the replay. The Hornets were only four minutes from a
stupendous upset in the original tie when Walker, favourite to
collect an optimistic cross into his box at the Stretford end,
collided with Brian Garvey, and Denis Law pounced from close
range to force a replay.

Eddy's recollections of a thunderous Cup tie include his
unlikely running battle with a national treasure.

This was the era in which United's holy trinity of Bobby
Charlton, George Best and Law were at the peak of their powers.
But they were frustrated by Watford's tenacious roadblock, as
the Hornets skipper recalls, 'Scully had put us ahead with a
scorcher from 30 yards. If he ever hit another shot as cleanly as
that one at Old Trafford I would love to have seen it. Then we
defended for our lives, and it was a bad goal to give away at the
end when we had worked so hard.

'I was surprised that Charlton, of all people, was always
moaning. We didn't give them any room to play, and he didn't
seem to like it when we closed down United's supply lines.
Look, I don't want to say anything that goes against the grain
because his standing in the game worldwide is untouchable. He
is one of the true greats and that's the way I will remember him.

'But on this occasion he was getting very uptight, and
for 90 minutes I'm afraid I fell out with him. He wasn't the
unflappable guy the whole world admired, and at one point I
called him an "arsehole" – which wasn't very gentlemanly of
me – because I thought his attitude towards us was a bit aloof
and, on this particular day, he was an arrogant sod. Of course,
I would never be so dismissive of him now, because the man is
a sporting icon, but we must have got under his skin because

he was very frustrated. They were the European Cup holders, losing to a piddling little team from the Third Division.

'It was a real sickener when Mike came for that cross and Brian couldn't get out of the way. The boss had warned us that Law came alive when the ball was loose around the six-yard box, and the only time we gave him half a chance he punished us.'

United were less yielding in the replay, although Watford gave another good account of themselves on a tricky pitch. The game had already been postponed once when Sir Matt Busby's giants came to town, and fortune deserted the Hornets at the second time of asking as Rodney Green had a goal disallowed for a foul on United keeper Alex Stepney, and Duncan Welbourne rattled the bar.

'It was very difficult to play – even George Best couldn't keep his feet,' remembers the Hornets captain. 'But he still produced a bit of magic for their first goal. It looked for all the world as if the ball was going out for a goal-kick, but somehow he got there when the frozen ground looked favourite, and Law did the rest at the far post.'

Watford lost 2-0, Law's second goal on the night finally putting the tie to bed, but they won 10 and drew two of their next 15 games in the League to leave them at the gateway of Division Two, and the Football League's upper slopes for the first time in the club's history. They took the chequered flag on an electrifying night in April, Roy Sinclair's winner against Plymouth punctuating a memorably restless game. Argyle's gripe that Sinclair's shot, which bounced down off the bar, had not crossed the line cut no ice in the Hornets' champagne bucket.

For Eddy it was glorious vindication of his migration from the Furness peninsula three years earlier – but his celebrations were nearer quietly contemplative than uninhibited.

'I loved every minute of that season. There is no better feeling than being captain of a winning team when you can feel the whole town getting behind you, but when we achieved what we had set out to do, my overriding emotion at the end of that Plymouth game was only relief.

When you have invested so much hope, so much energy, in winning promotion; when the moment arrives you feel elated but also exhausted. After the game I went down to my local pub, the Castle, and sat quietly in a corner, literally drinking in the moment. We had been on edge, on the brink of something special, and I didn't want to waste the memory of it in a blur of nightclub excess. I just sat there in my corner watching people come and go, in my own little world. A few regulars came over and congratulated me, others offered to buy me a pint . . . it was just a lovely way to go up.'

***

Better late than never, Keith Eddy had the privilege of scoring Watford's first-ever goal in English football's second tier.

Sadly for the Hornets, they had to wait nearly 500 minutes – yielding a single point, in a prophetic goalless draw with fellow strugglers Charlton Athletic – to break their duck, in a 2-1 home defeat by Sheffield United. The hesitant start included a narrow home defeat by Queens Park Rangers, and half a century later the 27,968 attendance who witnessed the Hoops' 1-0 win at Vicarage Road in August 1969 remains Watford's highest for a home League game.

In a passable re-enactment of the proverb about London buses, after ending the drought Eddy scored again four days later against Liverpool in a 2-1 League Cup second-round defeat at Vicarage Road. He was to miss out on a momentous reunion with the Kop almost six months later, when Watford atoned for the drudgery of their maiden season in Division Two with a marvellous run to the FA Cup semi-finals.

Ken Furphy would not be the last Hornets manager to discover that the step up from the third tier to the second arguably required the most adjustment of all when climbing through the divisions, and much of Watford's League campaign was beset by a form of altitude sickness.

Eddy was ever-present, though, and probably the team's most consistent performer – until he suffered a knee-ligament injury at Carlisle just 10 days before the FA Cup quarter-final, which became a red-letter date in the club's history. And it was cruel on the captain that he should be a frustrated spectator for a game which catapulted the Hornets into the national spotlight.

Watford had chiselled out a 2-1 win at Bolton Wanderers in the third round; Colin Franks' 25-yard shot had upset First Division Stoke City, with England World Cup winner Gordon Banks in goal; and they edged past Gillingham in the last 16. But few outside Hertfordshire gave them a chance of toppling the Liver bird from its perch, even with home advantage on a lunar landscape pitch.

'When people ask me about the biggest differences between football today and the game I played professionally, the two most obvious aspects are the sums of money involved and the pitches,' says Eddy. 'I watch Premier League matches on TV now and they are all played on carpets, like crown green bowls, but we had to adapt to all kinds of surface: grass in August, mud in winter, sand in the New Year, and all three if the weather was changeable. Some weeks it seemed like you needed studs, snowboots, sand shoes and dancing shoes in your kitbag.'

In Cup football they used to say the pitch was a great leveller when the aristocrats tiptoed into the giantkillers' back yards. It was probably true, to an extent, when Liverpool came unstuck at Vicarage Road in February 1970. The surface cut up like a municipal golf course fairway when hackers without a handicap certificate take divots the size of manhole covers with each swing.

It suited Watford down to the ground, although Endean's winner – a flying header smuggled through Tommy Lawrence's grasp – owed much to Ray Lugg's delicious, see-you-later nutmeg of Liverpool left-back Peter Wall and perfectly weighted cross.

Eddy was off his feet as Endean claimed his place in Cup folklore. 'As much as I was gutted – absolutely gutted – to be missing out, I was there, rooting for the lads, kicking every ball. I wasn't just the captain or an employee – I had become a Watford supporter. I loved my time at the club, and one of my biggest regrets is that I wasn't on the pitch when that final whistle sounded against Liverpool. But it was a marvellous performance. For 90 minutes I didn't think for one second about my injury. I was completely immersed in the game.'

Watford's reward for their seismic contribution to the quarter-finals was a date with Chelsea in the last four at White Hart Lane. Again, Eddy was an invalid in the crowd, and the abysmal pitch looked like Southend beach when the tide was out, as the Hornets were dealt a rough hand.

Although they were ultimately outclassed, going down 5-1 to the eventual winners of the trophy, Terry Garbett's first-half equaliser sustained Furphy's dreams of a Wembley appearance – at least until the quicksands sapped Watford's resistance in the second period. Eddy, however, remembers the game for a bone-shuddering collision he still rates as the heaviest tackle he's ever seen.

'We were in the hat with Manchester United, Leeds and Chelsea, and they were all praying for the same thing – they all wanted to draw Watford in the semi-finals,' he says. 'As it happened, Chelsea got the best of the deal, and although we were holding them 1-1 at half-time, on the day they were too strong for us. But there was one incident which made my eyes water.

'Duncan Welbourne was a tough customer, and I always enjoyed playing with him, but he never shirked a tackle. He went into one challenge with Eddie McCreadie where neither man was going to back down – and it left him a zombie, reduced to walking wounded, afterwards. If you watch games from 1970 and apply the laws in the way they are applied today, you would end up with five-a-side every week. That Chelsea team could play, but they didn't take any prisoners.

'Players now are fitter and faster than ever before, and they have nutritionists, masseurs, dieticians, sports scientists, phsyios and doctors to squeeze every last drop out of them physically. But I do worry that we are heading towards football as a non-contact sport.

'I'm all in favour of outlawing tackles where people are chopped down from behind, and I don't like to see any challenge which endangers the welfare of an opponent. But it makes me sad when I turn on the TV and players fall over if they feel a gust of wind. Football is a contact sport, and there has to be an element of blood and thunder – when I was at Watford robust challenges were part of life. I don't like seeing players trying to get their fellow professionals sent off by rolling around and then jumping to their feet as soon as the referee has shown a red card.

'Speed, skill and fitness levels may have improved in the last 50 years, but it seems to have been at the expense of honesty.'

A week after the semi-final anti-climax, Eddy rushed back from his knee injury to help the Hornets gather vital points in a 2-1 win against Cardiff to maintain a safe distance from the drop zone. They limped across the line – literally, in the case of their struggling captain – by taking only three points from their last seven League games.

It was a hollow achievement – just as the FA Cup third-place playoff against Manchester United at Highbury was a charade for which they had little enthusiasm, and even less gas left in the tank. The 2-0 defeat by United, Watford's sixth game in 15 days, attracted a sparse crowd of 15,105 on a Friday night and was the first fixture of its type. (It lasted only four more years before the Football Association abolished the meaningless chore.)

Eddy, still well short of optimum fitness, was patched up to face United, but a soporific defeat and the legacy of his injury has always made him regret it.

'It wasn't right, and looking back I shouldn't have tried to play again so soon,' he admits. 'Every time I kicked the ball with my right foot I grimaced and needed a sharp intake of breath. I was trying to get through every game without hurting my knee, but I only made it worse. It was a relief when we stayed up, with only two points to spare, but I didn't do myself any favours there.

'At least we will always be the answer to a pub quiz question about being the first side to lose two FA Cup ties in the same season.'

***

Fog. Thick, swirling, asphyxiating fog. There was never a chance of the game going ahead, even if we'd all turned up with industrial-strength turbines to blow the pea-souper away.

This is where a wide-eyed seven-year-old from Rickmansworth joined the party: a New Year pall of impenetrable haze forced the postponement of Watford's home FA Cup third-round tie with Reading in January 1971, but when he took his seat in the wooden Shrodells stand for the rearranged fixture four days later, at least it was worth the wait.

Barry Endean's hat-trick, Stewart Scullion's opportunism and Keith Eddy's near-infallible nerve from the penalty spot gave the Hornets an emphatic 5-0 win. Not a bad way to catch the bug. You always remember your first football match, especially when the Golden Boys are on top form and the visiting goalkeeper is called Steve Death. (In fairness, Death served Reading with distinction for 13 years before he became a golf-course greenkeeper.)

It was easily Watford's biggest win of the 1970–71 season, but in truth it was another campaign suffocated by fear of relegation and missed opportunities. There were narrow 1-0 defeats, home and away, against the rascals from up the road – which would become an all-too-familiar phenomenon during the Graham Taylor era at the back end of the decade – and the Hornets scored only 18 goals in 21 home League games. 'I remember the Reading game, mainly because there wasn't much else to get excited about that year,' says Eddy. As if to underscore the captain's point, Watford wasted the hard graft of a 1-1 draw at Oxford in the fourth round by losing the replay 2-1 at Vicarage Road.

For trainspotters and stats anoraks, there was a notable absentee at the 1-1 draw with Orient on 21 November 1970 – a fixture that ended Duncan Welbourne's club record 280 consecutive League appearances spanning 2,248 days. But since winning promotion in 1969 the Hornets' progress had given way to stagnation, and two seasons of dicing with relegation finally caught up with them.

In the final game of the season, on May Day at Bramall Lane, Watford proved exemplary guests at Sheffield United's promotion party, slipping to a 3-0 defeat which was the first instalment of a morale-sapping 18 months without an away League win. After tap-dancing on the trapdoor to Division Three for a couple of years the Hornets made no mistake in 1971–72. Weighed down by an appalling record on the road – they managed just a single point away from home, at Norwich, until March – they wore lead boots this time. It would prove to be Eddy's last season at Vicarage Road, and it was by far the most demoralising.

Eddy puffs out his cheeks and exhales wearily at the thought of it. 'I'm not going to lie. It was a miserable time,' he admits. 'Every week I would go home after the game and moan to my wife Jackie that the attitude was terrible and we'd played like a team who expected to lose.

'Confidence is a huge part of football: if you believe you are going to win, quite often you will; but if you just pitch up hoping for the best, without that built-in belief which is such an important part of a player's mentality, you won't stand a chance. On the coach to away games, you could sense the mood was defeatist, as if people were thinking, "How many are we going to lose by today, then?" I'm not saying we stopped trying, but it cheesed me off that other people could think like that. By Christmas we needed snookers to stay up – but we didn't even have a cue. We went down by something like 15 points, it wasn't even close. We were so poor that I was the club's leading scorer that season! Having said that, I didn't want to leave Watford that summer. As captain I took the view that I had helped to get the club into this mess, and I was going to help them get out of it again. So when Sheffield United came in for me that summer, I didn't want to go. When I went up to Sheffield to talk terms, it was raining, I didn't feel particularly inspired by what I saw and, when I met the manager, John Harris, for the first time, to be honest I was less than impressed. I didn't sign anything on the day. I told him I wanted to think about it, which was the truth.'

Watford chairman Jim Bonser's response to relegation had been bullish, blustering that the Hornets were 'in the business of keeping our good players' – but when the Blades came calling with a £50,000 bid for Eddy, which was a record for both buying and selling club, inevitably balance sheets won the day. Bonser had already rubber-stamped the sale of winger Stewart Scullion to Sheffield United 12 months earlier for £25,000, to help pay for the main stand extension at Vicarage Road. For some fans, cashing in on the inspirational captain was a sale too far.

But Eddy's first instincts – to stay put – were overturned by a heart-to-heart with his wife: 'When I got home, I sat down with Jackie and told her I wasn't sure about the move. She was the one who hit the nail on the head. She told me, "If you turn down this opportunity, and you never get another chance to play in the First Division, you'll regret it." Of course, she was right.'

It would take only six months for Watford's former captain to come back and haunt them as Eddy scored the Blades' winner in the FA Cup third round at Vicarage Road.

'On the day, we were very fortunate to go through, and I suppose it was written in the stars [that it had to be at Watford's expense],' says Eddy. 'It was a pretty shabby goal – I just poked at it and somehow it went in – and it was my first game back after two months out with an Achilles tendon problem. I wasn't 100 per cent fit because I had a small lump in my foot, which they later discovered was gout – but I was desperate to play because I didn't get the chance to say goodbye to the Watford supporters when I was sold.

'Nearly all my memories of the place are fond ones, and when Premier League games are on TV now in Oklahoma, I always make an effort to watch if Watford are playing. The ground has changed a bit, hasn't it?'

For Eddy, whose Cumbrian accent has survived four decades living in mid-America, there would be a gratifying postscript in the final chapter of his playing career when he crossed the big pond in the mid-1970s to join New York Cosmos, where he was captain of a side including highly rated forward Edson Arantes do Nascimento - better known as Pele.

Superstar and captain would attend media conferences, with all the questions directed at Pelé, unless diplomacy was required, in which case he would defer to Eddy for ambassadorial answers to curved balls, and the former Watford skipper would marvel at his unlikely role, in a parallel universe, as consular aide to the greatest player in the history of the game.

'There were times when I would sit there and think, "This guy has won the World Cup with Brazil so often they got to keep the trophy, and here I am, sat next to him, the winner of a Third Division championship medal,' says Eddy. 'It was incredible to be part of the same team as a man who was untouchable in terms of what he had achieved in the game.

'Although he was double-marked everywhere he went on the pitch, and he wasn't quite as fast as he once was, he could still perform tricks that took your breath away. I often played as sweeper, so I just stood at the back and enjoyed the view.'

Reunited with Ken Furphy in the Big Apple, Eddy was even afforded the privilege of being the Cosmos' penalty-taker in exalted company. There had been gasps of astonishment when Pelé had failed to score from the spot on one occasion. A few weeks later they were awarded another penalty, and under manager Furphy's explicit instruction Eddy stepped forward to take care of the formalities. When Pelé remonstrated with the bench, so the story goes, Furphy waved away his protest with the priceless line, 'Sorry, son – but Keith's here now.'

Eddy's playing days in the States, living in a swish rented villa on Long Island and playing with an all-time legend, were ended by a torn groin muscle. Such was his standing in the game, on both sides of the Atlantic, that coaching offers soon came his way. 'That was a surprise,' he admits. 'I had never coached anyone in my life.'

Almost out of curiosity Eddy agreed to become head coach of Toronto Blizzard, taking Scottish-born Charlie Mitchell – a fringe player at the Cosmos – as his assistant but, worn down by two and a half years of long-distance air travel to every away game, he resigned and took up Mitchell's invitation to explore the potential of Tulsa, Oklahoma.

'He kept telling me what a wonderful place it was, so I took the family down to have a look. I thought we would only be staying there for a few months, because we intended to go back and live in New Jersey, but we opened a couple of nightclubs and sports bars, I founded the Tulsa Soccer Club – and we've lived here ever since.

'It was a great place to bring up the kids, and usually the climate's not as harsh as the north-eastern states in winter – although we've had an exceptionally cold one this year which has broken records. But it's the place I've called home for half my life.'

Keith Eddy missed only one penalty for Watford – in the promotion shootout against Swindon at the County Ground in 1969 – although he remains convinced it should have been retaken because goalkeeper Peter Downsborough was 'in the air' before his kick had left the spot. Ultimately, it didn't matter because Barry Endean settled a pulsating duel and Watford pipped Swindon to the title anyway.

If there was a shootout to determine the Hornets' finest penalty-taker of all time, Eddy would be right up there.

And if there was an inflation-proof index to measure Watford's greatest value-for-money signing in the transfer market, the part-time milkman from Barrow who cost just £1,500 would surely be in the very top bracket, too.

Yes, 1966 was a vintage year for English football.

2

DENNIS BOOTH

TIDDLYWINKS

On a warm Monday evening in the early summer of 1979, Dennis Booth set off for work from his unpretentious home in Chesham Way, just off Tolpits Lane on the Holywell estate, two hours before kick-off. Like a condemned man allowed one last smoke, he lit up a cigarette to channel the nervous energy through a haze of nicotine on the 15-minute walk to Vicarage Road through the untidy maze of west Watford's unsymmetrical streets.

In mid-season, on the same journey, he would encounter random familiar faces, the odd well-wisher and sporadic blank looks from passers-by who recognised the face but could not put a name to it. But for the last game of the 1978–79 season the stakes were high and there was a palpable sense of occasion in the air. For Watford, a marathon 58-game campaign boiled down to win or bust. A win against Hull City, who had thrashed the Hornets 4-0 on Humberside six months earlier, would take Graham Taylor's side into the Second Division for only their fourth season outside the lower divisions in the club's history. Anything less, and they would have nothing to show for nine months of goals, famous Cup shocks and the nation's most prolific double act up front.

By the time Booth was on his final approach to the shop floor he was the pied piper of Holywell. An entourage of supporters clad in scarves – this was an age before the era of blubbing into your replica shirt – pursued him like the crowds

of disciples pursuing false messiah Graham Chapman in Monty
Python's *Life of Brian,* which would be released later that year
amid some controversy.

'Graham Taylor insisted on his players living within a
15-minute drive of the club so we were fully integrated into
the community and enjoyed being part of it,' says Booth. 'I
was happy to go along with that rule, and we lived 15 minutes
away on foot. It was also handy for going to Watford General
Hospital on Christmas Day to hand out presents to people
who were spending the festive season on the wards, which
was something Graham liked us to do every year. One year, as
captain, I had to wear a Father Christmas outfit and I remember
moving between the beds, giving it "ho, ho, ho" and trying to
spread a little happiness. I went over to this young chap, shook
his hand and said, "Hello there, what brings you in here?" He
replied, "Oh, I got stabbed last night." That was a bit of a
shock. Not quite Joseph, Mary and no room at the inn. But
usually I enjoyed my walk to work. Those times at Watford
were among the happiest of my life.'

For Booth and his eager retinue heading for a big night out
with Hull, it was a glorious sunset in every sense. Watford's 4-0 win
carried them through the skylight in a blur of heady celebration.
The captain arrived at the players' entrance on Occupation Road
to find fans ripping up entire volumes of *Yellow Pages* – fuel for
the awesome tickertape welcome which greeted the team before
kick-off. It was way past the enchanted hour by the time Watford
had drained the directors' lounge of champagne and chairman
Elton John had sent out for 50 portions of fish and chips to
distribute among his triumphant staff.

But it had been a nervous wait for the game to come round
and, in truth, it was a fretful first hour on the pitch. Roger
Joslyn's early breakthrough had settled the butterflies in a
colossal 26,347 crowd, but it was not until Ian Bolton's penalty,

Ross Jenkins' 37th goal of the season and Luther Blissett's header in the last 20 minutes that the party was in full swing.

Booth recalls, 'There were nine days between our penultimate game at Sheffield Wednesday and the decider against Hull. I had missed the game up at Hillsborough because I had flu. The gaffer told me to stay in bed on the Friday, not to travel with the team the night before, and Bertie Mee [Watford's avuncular assistant manager], who was driving up on the Saturday morning, would pick me up and bring me straight to the ground if I felt better.

'But on the day of the game I could barely stand up straight when I got out of bed. My head was swimming, and although I was desperate to play, the team could not afford a passenger who was staggering around like he was seasick. As it happens, we won 3-2 and took it down to the wire, but there was a long gap before the Hull game and the boss took us off for a friendly against Sochaux. I know they are a French team, but for some reason we might have flown to an airport in Germany.

'Either way, we played this friendly on the Friday night and we were a bit late getting back on the Saturday – we got home just in time to watch the Arsenal–Manchester United FA Cup final where Alan Sunderland got the winner in the last minute. To be honest, it wasn't the best preparation for a game on the Monday night, and it felt as though we'd cut it a bit fine, but it turned out grand.

'I remember giving Wilf McGuinness, who was a player and manager at Manchester United, a bit of stick that night. He was Hull's first-team coach at the time and I may have been asking him how fast he could still run when the referee, Tony Glasson, blew the final whistle. When it said 90 minutes on the scoreboard I asked Terry, "How long to go?" He said, "Next time the ball goes out of play in the corner, start heading towards the tunnel – I'll be right behind you."

'It would have been a travesty if we hadn't gone up that year. At a time when gates were falling all over the country, the crowds were flocking to Watford. Graham Taylor gave the people what they wanted to see – goals, entertainment and attacking play. I watch teams play keep-ball today and they don't have any purpose. Twenty passes in your own half of the pitch looks nice, but possession doesn't win football matches unless you do something with it. Drives you mad.'

Booth had joined Watford 18 months earlier from Lincoln City, renewing an acquaintance with Taylor which had been forged when he arrived at the Imps on loan from Southend in 1974. The arrangement soon morphed into a permanent transfer and Booth was an ever-present in his three full seasons at Sincil Bank, where he recorded a remarkable, and almost certainly unique, feat.

Never a player of serious repute for aerial power, he scored a hat-trick in seven minutes in a 4-3 win against Bury, each of his goals a header. There have certainly been quicker hat-tricks – this observer happened to witness Sadio Mane's treble in two minutes 50 seconds for Southampton against Aston Villa in 2015 – but none is evident in the record books of three headed goals by the same player in fewer than seven minutes.

'Graham spotted me playing for Southend reserves at Cambridge,' says Booth. 'He scouted a lot of signings personally and stood on the terraces among the punters, because when he spent his chairman's money he used to treat it as if he was spending his own.

'He was a very serious man, and you had to know when the time was right to break the ice with humour. But he was the biggest influence on my career – including how far I could run. During my time at Lincoln and Watford I trained harder than under any other manager. Although his playing career was ended by a chronic hip injury Graham was still a great runner himself. He could still beat nearly all the lads on cross-country training runs. If you had been out the night before, and you were blowing, he would tell you, "I can smell it on your breath."

'At Lincoln he used to organise runs across the common over the back of Sincil Bank, and the Canwick Park golf course next to it. He would stand at the furthest point away from the ground and, to make sure nobody cut any corners, you would have to loop round him like swimmers turning past the marker buoy in a triathlon race. And his runs across Cassiobury Park at Watford were almost legendary in terms of endurance. He would hide up trees and bark at anyone who was taking it easy at the back.

'Graham was ahead of his time in so many aspects of management – from compiling stats to making his teams the fittest in their divisions – and his record speaks for itself: seven promotions, five of them with Watford, and it took him to the biggest job in the game. I remember coming home one night in 1976, when he was still at Lincoln, and saying to my wife, "I think he's going to manage England one day." And I was proved right.'

Approaching his 70th birthday in 2019, Booth has just about caught his breath again after Taylor's lung-bursting demands of cardiovascular hardiness, which included five-hour sessions without a drink. Before Watford settled into regular practice accommodation in Stanmore, and later at the University College sports grounds at London Colney, training sessions were often nomadic feats, with Shendish Manor, on the slopes above Apsley and the former John Dickinson paper mills, a preferred hideaway.

'In five hours we would get one 20-minute break when he split us into three groups for practice games – two would play against each other and the other would get a breather,' says Booth. 'He didn't believe in drinking water during training, only after the session was finished. One of his favourite sayings was, "Don't look for outside help." And that included water bottles.

In fairness, he was trying to build our mental strength and resistance to pain and, of course, the science of rehydration has moved on in the last 40 years. But in those double sessions from 10 a.m. to 3 p.m. we weren't allowed a drink.

'During one of Graham's five-hour specials, Pat Molloy – Watford's old physio and trainer, a wonderful character – saw I was struggling and slipped me a fruit pastille. It was only one little sweet but it tasted like a five-course banquet. I couldn't have cared less how many calories or how much sugar was in that fruit pastille: it was heaven.

'Sometimes, just when we thought our work was done, instead of piling into a minibus Graham would tell us to run back to the ground from Shendish, which was about five miles. Once, when we were running through Langleybury, sprinklers were watering the cricket pitch and quite a few of the lads veered off the main road to enjoy the splash of cold water across their faces, only for this voice to yell, out of nowhere, "Get away! Don't look for outside help!" There was no escape.

'When you were finally allowed a bottle of pop, you held this orange and lemonade in your hand and you didn't know whether to sip it, swig it, knock it back in one go or tip it over your head to cool off. When John Ward followed me and Sam Ellis from Lincoln to Watford in 1979, he drove back up to Lincoln one teatime – before he had moved the family down – and drank about 15 cans of coke on the way because he couldn't quench his thirst fast enough.'

As well as being a strict drill sergeant on the training pitch, Taylor had an occasional volcanic temper, which came to the fore if he was unhappy that events were not unfolding to his satisfaction. Once, when Elton John paid him a visit at home, and ganged up with GT's wife Rita to cheat over a game of cards, he overturned the coffee table in a monumental strop – only to realise he had been set up, and fallen for their ruse hook, line and sinker, when the chairman and Mrs Taylor burst out laughing. He had been turned over once before, by the mischievous Booth, over a game of 'tiddlywinks' as he attempted to illustrate a modified team shape in the classroom at Lincoln.

On a Subbuteo pitch – the flick-to-kick table-top game, played on a tablecloth of green baize with football-pitch markings – Taylor used plastic counters to demonstrate an adjusted formation he wanted the Imps to adopt, before taking them outside to put it into practice. Unhappy that his players had not absorbed his instructions, or exercised his new tactic satisfactorily, the squad returned indoors, where the taskmaster admonished his group. Frustrated to the point of exasperation, Taylor slammed his fist on the table so hard that some of the counters fell on the floor, spluttering, 'Can we not grasp it?' Patience exhausted, he ordered the players to reconvene in the classroom first thing the following morning in the hope they would 'grasp' the new shape accordingly.

But when the players reassembled around the Subbuteo pitch the next day as instructed, and Taylor poured his 1970s prototype Prozone counters on to the baize from the small tin in which he kept them, he was astonished to discover several were decorated with tiny strips of sticking plaster. 'What is going on here?' blustered Taylor. 'What has happened? What is the meaning of this?'

Booth, struggling to maintain a deadpan expression beneath his Mexican bandit moustache and plentiful, seventies rock guitarist hair, had administered the Elastoplast with surgical precision and piped up, 'Well, boss, some of them were injured last night after you knocked them on the floor.'

As Booth's teammates, who were all in on the prank, dissolved into laughter, Taylor didn't know whether to join in or to hit the roof. 'The gaffer didn't laugh out loud, but I think he just about saw the funny side of his tiddlywinks being patched up to play after intensive treatment,' says Booth. 'He didn't like giving me the satisfaction of delivering the punchline and he was saying, "Don't encourage him, lads. Don't let him have the last word or we'll never keep him quiet." I wasn't the naughtiest boy in class, but I could be a chirpy little beggar. Deep down I think the boss enjoyed dealing with strong characters in his dressing room. It tested him, it kept him on his toes. I'm sure I've still got that canister of tiddlywinks somewhere as a souvenir. I don't think the sticking plasters survived, though.'

Such is the warmth and good humour generated by the tiddlywinks anecdote that *Watford Observer* doyen Oliver Phillips revealed it even raised a laugh at Graham Taylor's funeral in 2017. The wake at Vicarage Road was winding down when GT's widow, Rita, spotted a cluster of his former Lincoln players chortling through a nostalgic trawl of the good times and wandered over to ask, 'What about the tiddlywinks story?'

***

Dennis Booth dropped down a division when he signed for Watford from Lincoln in the autumn of 1977. His debut for the Hornets was away at Hartlepool, where his roommate was 19-year-old striker Luther Blissett.

'We came back with a win, but I'm not sure what Luther made of his new roomie,' he says. 'He was a clean-living young lad, trying to force his way into the first team, and I was the senior pro who liked a drink and a smoke. When I first played with him Luther was often on the right wing – he was a great athlete, and he could run like a gazelle – but that role wasn't quite right for him. We went out and bought Brian Pollard from York soon after, but there was something about this young boy that gave him a bit of star quality.

'We used to train indoors on a Monday and go to a dance class called Popmobility to improve our aerobic fitness. Luther could bust some moves, and I always felt there would come a time when he would break through as a striker, but he had to be patient because Watford had Ross Jenkins, Keith Mercer and Alan Mayes, who all scored goals for fun in the Fourth Division.

'It was early the following season when Keith was struggling – I think he had pneumonia – and Luther came off the bench to score twice against Newcastle in the League Cup. The rest is history. Keith was one of the bravest forwards I ever came across, because he went in horizontal. Bravery doesn't come cheap; he would have been worth a few bob in today's market.

'But you could never have enough forwards in a Graham Taylor team. Although he was a full-back in his playing days, we hardly ever worked on the defensive side of the game. I think it bored him. Everything was geared to attack – at Lincoln he had experienced centre-backs in Sam Ellis and Terry Cooper, who knew how to organise a back four in their sleep, and it was the same story at Watford. First it was Big Sam and Alan Garner, then Steve Sims and Ian Bolton – they were all terrific partnerships, but everything was geared to attacking, scoring goals and playing the game in the opposition half of the pitch, which is what the punters want to see, isn't it?'

Booth settled impeccably at Watford, making 34 consecutive appearances as they ran away with the Division Four championship, ferreting unselfishly in midfield and organising the team with secretarial efficiency. Late in 1978 he took over the captaincy from Ellis, whose priorities had started to lean more towards coaching, culminating in that glorious promotion party against Hull.

Another major highlight was the League Cup win at Manchester United, where Blissett's pair of soaring headers took the headlines but Booth's relentless scuffling – and inch-perfect cross for the winner – was a man-of-the-match contribution.

New signing Steve Harrison, Booth's former teammate at Blackpool, had only joined Watford three weeks earlier – on the recommendation of his old Tangerines chum – and he was frequently invited to relive the drama. 'He had recorded it on a Betamax tape or something,' Harrison told author Lionel Birnie for his book *Enjoy the Game*. 'I was in Croxley Green, he lived [close by] in Tolpits Lane, so after training we'd go for a few jars in the Irish club round the corner and he'd say, "Let's go home and watch me video." I'd say, "No, not again Boothy" and he'd say, "Go on – just the good bits." There wasn't a lot of time to get bored or homesick.'

The arrival of Ray Train midway through the campaign added depth to the squad but also cost the Hornets continuity of selection, which was reflected to an extent in their results as they stumbled towards the winning post. 'We ended up with a League Cup team who went all the way to the semi-finals, and a team for Division Three, which probably cost us a little consistency, but those days at Watford were magic,' says Booth. 'I came home one night after we had beaten someone quite early in the season and said to my wife, "Something special is happening here." I knew I wouldn't be at Watford by the end of it, but I realised there was something going on which I would treasure later. It wasn't just because of Elton John's influence – the gaffer didn't go out and throw millions at it – but you can't put a price on the success we had.

'I had started out in professional football on £15 a week with a £4 win bonus, £2 for a draw and £5 for every point above 45 – which meant you were in the top half of the table because it was only two points for a win in those days. And Watford had a crowd bonus, which meant the players were effectively on a percentage of gates above a certain level. When we got to Division Two, one game against Chelsea paid for our summer holiday with the kids in Bournemouth. There were nearly

25,000 people there. [Before that] I remember running round the dog track in our yellow "Puffa" jackets with the Fourth Division championship trophy and showing it off to 18,000 fans. The crowds Watford used to get back then were incredible – attendances all over the country might have been falling away, but the punters kept coming to Vicarage Road. There was no mystery to it: we were giving fans what they wanted to see.

'All those Cup shocks we used to produce were not by accident. When we beat Stoke in the League Cup quarter-final their manager Alan Durban was saying to us afterwards, "What did Graham Taylor say to you lot?" He couldn't believe how we played with so much energy, deep into extra time. Garth Crooks was sitting in the players' bar looking like he wanted to cry.

'But that was the time when I had a deep-seated pelvic injury and I couldn't get rid of it. I had to wear swimming trunks really tight to get through games, and I can tell you it's not easy trying to win promotion, or turn over Nottingham Forest one step from Wembley, when your budgie-smugglers are clamped around your undercarriage like a shark's jaws. They were a bit too streetwise for us, those Forest lads. Some of their defenders – Frank Clark, Kenny Burns, Larry Lloyd – were not the quickest, and we thought we could hurt them if we managed to turn them round, but they had too much experience, and they had been round the block too many times, to fall short.'

The same could be said for Booth himself when the Hornets lived dangerously during their first season in the Second Division after back-to-back promotions. Although they were never stranded on the bottom rungs of the ladder in the 1979–80 campaign, nor did Watford ever manage to build up a head of steam in the League, where their best results were sporadic. They went 104 days without an away goal, an unwanted phenomenon the Hornets revisited in the Premier

League era under Walter Mazzarri and, remarkably, for 229 days on Javier Gracia's watch. One of the barren excursions was a sterile 0-0 draw at Fulham, where the 10,126 spectators included Britain's first successful heart transplant patient, Keith Castle.

In the *Watford Observer* cartoonist Terry Challis depicted the scene as Mr Castle attended his next check-up with cardiologists at Harefield Hospital. 'Have you been avoiding too much excitement?' asked a white-coated caricature with a stethoscope. 'Most definitely,' replied the cartoon image of Castle, who lived another six years beyond his life-saving surgery.

But the bright interludes were all too intermittent. Taylor felt his team were overawed when they went down 2-0 at Chelsea, and was disappointed to hear one of his players observe in the changing room afterwards, 'They weren't as good as I expected.' Even an early-season home win against West Ham, where Blissett scored both goals, was overshadowed by the violent infiltration of East End pond life in the Vicarage Road end. And renewed acquaintance, for the first time in seven years, with the rival tribe over the border was a joyless reunion, Kirk Stephens' winner in added time providing the cold turkey on Boxing Day at Vicarage Road.

But another fine Cup run sustained morale and proved an adequate distraction from the proximity of the dotted line at the wrong end of the table, and it turned Booth into an unlikely star of prime-time light entertainment on the BBC.

A vibrant third-round win at Queens Park Rangers, a seven-goal rollercoaster against non-League Harlow Town – which was not quite as close as the 4-3 margin suggests – and a huge upset of Wolverhampton Wanderers at a heaving Molineux earned the Hornets a home quarter-final against Arsenal. Blissett, for whom the goals had reduced from a torrent to a modest stream, completed the 3-0 rout of Wolves, who had just reached the League Cup final and fancied their chances of a second trip to Wembley.

Booth was thrilled for his old roommate, who became an occasional lunchtime guest at the captain's table on matchdays. 'No airs or graces about Luther – that was the beauty about the fella,' he says. 'Every now and then he used to come round to our house for a bite to eat before a home game. We used to train on Saturday mornings for an hour, just a few set-pieces and warm-up, and there was no point in Luther going all the way back to his mum's house in Willesden before jumping in his car and coming back to Watford again, so he would come round to ours for a pre-match meal.

'He loved his cars, Luther. He could have been a garage mechanic. If one of the lads had a problem with their motor, he would offer to have a look under the bonnet and fix it. Although I had left the club by the time he got called up by England, that was a special time for us all – the first Watford player to win an England cap. He also brought me an AC Milan top from his spell in Italy, black and red stripes with a lone star above the crest, a lovely cotton shirt, not the acrylic material which makes you sweat like a horse. Fantastic lad, Luther – what a great career he had.'

Watford's FA Cup run came to an end against the Gunners, Malcolm Poskett's late reply not quite enough to earn the Hornets a deserved replay in a 2-1 defeat, but their quarter-final exit later earned Booth nationwide fame as a comic stooge.

Popular sketch show *Not the Nine O' Clock News* – starring Rowan Atkinson, Griff Rhys Jones, Mel Smith and Pamela Stephenson – could have chosen any number of expectorating footballers for their 30-second skit 'Gob of the Month', an irreverent take on *Match of the Day*'s goal of the month competition, where one lucky viewer who agreed with the pundits could win up to £1,000 of Premium Bonds. Arbitrarily, two of the candidates featured were 'Peter Lloyd of Watford' (Booth) and 'Rob Hughes of Ayr United' (Ian Bolton), both caught on film in the Arsenal Cup tie.

'I didn't know it was still on tape,' laughs Booth. 'I feel a bit sorry for "Webby" [Bolton's nickname in the Hornets dressing room] because his was actually a piece of chewing gum. Mine was the real thing. I don't know why they picked us out, or why they studied footage of that game. If anything, we should have been on *Spitting Image!* Probably not one to show your grandchildren, but there you go.

'We gave Arsenal a good run for their money that day. I was up against Liam Brady in midfield, and we both got stuck in, but he was class. And Pat Jennings, who started out at Watford, was in goal for them. I always had the feeling that Pat liked to dominate his box by coming off his line very early, and I tried to catch him out, but he got back to make the save. Arsenal went on to lose the final against West Ham. It didn't register at the time, but we beat West Ham at home and drew with them away that season, so it makes you wonder . . .'

Booth was too long in the tooth, and too indebted to Taylor, to hold any grudges against his mentor when they parted company at Vicarage Road. Following the arrival of England under-21 international midfielder Martin Patching, Taylor warned his captain that first-team opportunities would be restricted at Watford, and Booth – still only 31 – did not feel he was ready to wind down his playing career among the supporting cast, even on an adventure as exciting as the Hornets' climb.

Although his grafting style was not always on the glamorous side of football's sweet science, Booth's character and comic repertoire were vital ingredients as Watford established themselves in the old Second Division. If some of the voices among his impersonations were familiar – Brian Clough, Norman Wisdom,

Tommy Cooper, Graham Taylor – his humour was infectious, and Taylor afforded him licence to keep the dressing-room mood upbeat and bright.

At half-time, during an undistinguished performance at Brentford, Taylor had refrained from distributing teacups or administering home truths in the dressing room by staying outside in the corridor. In the manager's absence, Booth and Harrison took it upon themselves to convey advice by mimicking Taylor, who happened to be listening outside and could hear every word of their imitation. When the double act had run out of lines, Taylor came into the changing room and observed, 'Well, those two have told you what you need to do, so get out there and do it.'

Taylor's ability to get his message across in a single sentence, especially in a half-time team talk, was one of his most enviable skills. At Aston Villa he would deliver a famously succinct pep talk when they trailed lowly Crewe Alexandra 2-0 at the break and faced an ignominious exit from the FA Cup as victims of a third-round upset. He strode into the away dressing room at Gresty Road and announced, 'Gentlemen, you got yourselves into this f****** mess – now you get us out of it.' Villa came back to win 3-2 in a game which had kicked off at lunchtime, but Taylor's anger at their slovenly display for 45 minutes did not subside immediately. On the coach journey home he was annoyed when players cheered at the news that top-flight Coventry had been knocked out by non-League Sutton United in a famous giantkilling. Taylor ordered the coach driver to pull over on the hard shoulder of the M6, stood up at the front of the bus and bellowed, 'That could have been you today – and don't you ever forget it.'

Booth recalls, 'Graham always knew where to draw the line – when it was time to be serious, and when you could let your hair down. That was a hallmark of his time at Watford.

He always got the tone right. If you were messing around in training, he would just say, "Right, that's enough." The end-of-season awards at Baileys nightclub was always an occasion where you knew it was safe to cross the line.

'I don't remember too much about them, except one night Steve Harrison and I dressed up as two women – Harriet and Henrietta or something – and we slaughtered Graham. It might have got a bit vulgar, to be honest, not the sort of caper you'd put on for the family enclosure or a Junior Hornets tea party. But those nights went down well with the supporters and we had a bit of fun.'

Booth's last game for Watford was a 5-0 defeat at promoted Sunderland in April 1980. For the last half-hour at Roker Park he was replaced by a fellow resident on the Holywell estate, an 18-year-old called Kenny Jackett, whose father Frank had played for the Hornets in the 1950s, and who grew up with the Vicarage Road floodlights visible from his bedroom window.

He joined Hull City, where his career soon ran along reassuringly parallel lines with Watford's fortunes. In 1982–83, the season when the Hornets finished runners-up to Liverpool as the second-best team in the land, the Tigers won promotion by finishing second in Division Four behind Wimbledon, who were beginning their climb from basement to roof garden. Any comparisons between the rise of the Crazy Gang and Taylor's similar achievement at Watford should be annotated with the observation that the Hornets' style, while undeniably direct, was much nearer sophistication than its crude imitations.

In his kindergarten year as a cub reporter – learning the joys of Teeline shorthand outlines, newspaper law and the trail of democracy from parish council to Whitehall – on a block release course for trainee journalists in Newcastle, out of curiosity yours truly ventured 25 minutes down the line to

Darlington with an old school chum one night to watch Booth play for the Tigers.

Remarkably, 36 years later, he could still recall being accosted by a pair of inquisitive Watford supporters outside the players' bar at Feethams, and shooting the breeze for an hour in the car park about the good times at Vicarage Road – which were still gathering momentum, and would add promotion to the First Division to the slate six weeks later – after Hull's 2-1 defeat.

'David Speedie and Alan Walsh were playing up front for Darlington that night,' Booth recalls. 'Speedie signed for Chelsea not long after, and Walsh was no slouch.' (Booth's memory serves him well – Walsh went on to win two league titles with Besiktas in Turkey).

After winding down his playing days on Humberside, and serving as assistant manager to Brian Horton with Hull, Booth's coaching career led to a reunion with Taylor at Villa Park, where he contributed a valuable supporting role behind one of English football's most celebrated goals.

'David Platt was the best player I ever worked with and I was very honoured when he asked me to become his assistant at Nottingham Forest,' Booth told Carlisle's *News & Star* in 2010. 'He worked so hard at his game. He was so dedicated and would regularly stay behind after training. His goal against Belgium [at the World Cup finals in 1990, a last-minute winner in extra time taking England into the quarter-finals] wasn't a fluke because he practised it often on the training ground – and it was me who crossed the balls for him. He'd want them knocked into a certain place where he could practise his scissor-kicks.'

Wise head on the pitch and trusted lieutenant on the training ground, Booth's connections with Taylor spanned three decades – and he also worked with another faithful GT acolyte, John Ward, at Bristol Rovers and Carlisle either side of the millennium.

But at Vicarage Road he is remembered fondly as the shop steward who presided over some mighty Cup shocks and held the fort stoically as Watford gained a foothold in Division Two while Taylor's breathless revolution paused briefly for consolidation.

As captain he was not afraid to put an uppity apprentice in his place with a withering one-liner, but nor was Booth under any illusions about his limitations as a player. If he was a water carrier, as modern-day football parlance calls hard-working and competent midfielders who cover the hard yards with neither complaint nor recognition, Booth did not run on tap water: he was Perrier or Evian.

'I enjoyed being Graham Taylor's captain because he wanted you to have an influence on the dressing room,' he says. 'And if things didn't go right, he would clamp down on me harder than other players because he expected me to set the right tone. The job wasn't just about leading the team out at five to three, tossing a coin and shaking hands with the ref before kick-off. It came with added responsibility, like organising ticket allocations for the lads and their families. When we went on those Cup runs, and the requests for tickets ran into dozens for the big games, the gaffer expected his captain to sort the dressing room out. That side of the game never bothered me. As far as I was concerned we were all in it together. They were good times working for a great man.'

3

PAT RICE

THE MISSING LINK

It's just gone 4.45 p.m. on a May Day bank holiday, and the season is over. Watford have beaten Wrexham 1-0 at the Racecourse Ground, Luther Blissett's late goal – drilled into the far corner after a trademark run down the inside-right channel – taking the spoils back to Hertfordshire. Some of us should have been at home, revising for a history mock A-level paper about the Crusades the following day, but had persuaded our parents that four-hour coach journeys to and from North Wales would provide ample time for some last-minute cramming. Regrettably, the textbooks and revision notes remained in the luggage rack and the resulting grade was, inevitably, several rungs lower down the alphabet than expected. (In fairness, the real thing six weeks later went a bit better.)

The Hornets had finished a season of consolidation in the old Second Division with three consecutive wins, Blissett supplying late winners in each of them. When the music stopped, and Watford had finished ninth, their enlightened captain appeared to orchestrate a brilliant public relations manoeuvre which is a rite of passage now – but it was a brand-new concept in 1981, certainly in a so-called dead rubber with nothing at stake but League points.

On the final whistle Pat Rice ushered the players towards the away end, where several hundred Watford supporters had travelled in decent numbers and good voice for what was, in essence, an end-of-term chore. The fans roared their approval

at the gesture, which fortified the bond manager Graham
Taylor had already forged between his squad and what he often
called 'the man on the terraces'.

Rice recalls the mutual admiration society, but admits, 'If
I know anything about the man, I would think the input for
that gesture would have come from Graham on the touchline.
These days, players going over to acknowledge the supporters
– even when they have lost and the fans aren't always in a
receptive mood – is all part of the game. Everybody does it. But
Graham was always on the same wavelength as the fans; that
was one of his gifts. Much as I would love to claim the credit
for "inventing" that ritual, in reality it was probably the boss
telling me, "Get the players over there to thank the supporters
for turning out to back us." And, in fairness, it was an inspired
move. It was already an established tradition to take a lap of
honour after Cup finals, but back then I guess it was not such
a common gesture.

'Graham was always top class when it came to looking at
things through the eyes of the supporters. I'll always remember
the day we beat Sunderland 8-0 at Vicarage Road, and when
we were leading 4-0 at half-time he wouldn't let us sit down in
the dressing room because he wanted to keep the momentum
going. He had us running on the spot to keep the muscles
active, and when we were coasting, 15 minutes into the second
half, without any further goals, he gave me half a bollocking
from the bench. He told me to fire up the lads and make sure
the game didn't peter out into an anti-climax. I can remember
him shouting, "Hey, do you want these people to come back
and watch you next week?"

'That was a measure of the man. He didn't just want to win
football matches – he wanted to do it in a style that made the
punters want more.'

Checking the dressing-room temperature in the summer of 1981, Taylor announced: 'It's time we made another move.' And after back-to-back promotions, followed by two seasons of restocking the fridge, he was proved right. Rice, parachuted in from Arsenal six months earlier and immediately installed as captain, would be a vital missing link. In football, 'experience' is often a synonym for old age. But when it is applied in the right area, at the right time, and added to the right mix of players, it is gold dust – and Pat Rice's influence at Vicarage Road was pure bullion.

At 31, moving from Highbury to Vicarage Road was not an obvious career move for a battle-hardened right-back who had played in the FA Cup final and Cup Winners' Cup final for the Gunners six months earlier. Both those excursions had ended in defeat, West Ham prevailing by the only goal at Wembley and Valencia edging a penalty shootout 5-4 at the Heysel stadium in Brussels, where unspeakable tragedy would unfold five years later.

Rice was by no means washed-up, but he was a man in demand. In November 1980 Millwall (then in the Third Division) had offered him the player-manager's job, and the 49-cap Northern Ireland international had asked for 24 hours to consider it. 'To be truthful, I wanted to carry on playing, because you are a long time retired and I felt I had at least another two or three years left in the tank,' says Rice. 'When I got home from speaking to Millwall – out of courtesy, I had asked to consider their offer overnight – my wife said Bertie Mee had been on the phone to ask if I had signed anything. Bertie was the Arsenal manager when we won the League and Cup Double in 1971, and he was so well-connected in football that he probably knew I had got an interview for the Millwall job before I did.

'I knew he had been Graham's assistant manager at Watford for a couple of years, and they had been making a few waves by winning promotions and going on a few Cup runs, so I was intrigued enough to call him back. Bertie told me, "Don't sign anything until you have spoken to Graham Taylor." Thankfully, I took him at his word.'

Taylor had despatched Sam Ellis, his first signing at Vicarage Road in 1977 and now on the coaching staff, to scout a reserve-team game between Queens Park Rangers and Arsenal, possibly with a view to keeping tabs on young striker Raphael Meade, but his attention soon alighted on a robust defender keeping his standards resolutely high. When Ellis reported back to the manager, Taylor asked him, 'So, have you found me a player?' Ellis, who knew the value of sound leadership on the pitch, replied, 'No – but I have found you a captain.'

Taylor, rushing to head off Millwall's interest, offered the Gunners skipper a five-year contract, of which the first two and a half years would focus on playing and the second half offered a pathway into coaching. 'Watford were offering me everything I wanted,' says Rice. 'Security, extending my playing career, and a potential route into management and coaching. I thought dropping down a division would be a doddle, but the next four years were the hardest I ever worked on a football pitch. Boy, did we work hard. We trained so hard you were on first-name terms with exhaustion. But do I regret Bertie's intervention? Not for a minute, not for one second.'

Mee, a physiotherapist by trade and a surprise appointment at Arsenal when Billy Wright was sacked as manager in 1966, was not an acclaimed tactician – but he was famously well organised and as military in his approach as his previous career with the Royal Army Medical Corps. One scribe who turned up ten minutes late for an appointed interview with him at Highbury because of sketchy service on the Piccadilly line was informed he had missed his slot and sent packing empty handed.

When Taylor was hospitalised by appendicitis in October 1978, and Mee held the fort for three games, the Hornets took maximum points off Brentford, Carlisle and Chesterfield with regimental efficiency. He was, in every respect, a safe pair of hands and the ideal sounding board for an ambitious young manager.

'Bertie's organisational skills were second to none,' says Rice. 'He was a tough taskmaster, hard but fair. There was a purpose behind everything he said – he never raised his voice just for the sake of it, and you never felt he was whistling in the dark. He was the perfect foil for Graham, a wise old head who brought credibility through everything he had achieved at the Arsenal. He had that military background and, after working with him for ten years, I had a tremendous respect for him. I had never come across Graham before, but if Bertie rated him I knew he must be worth a listen because, trust me, Bertie didn't suffer fools gladly or dish out praise lightly.'

Such was Rice's unshakeable trust in Mee's judgement that he did not even check the League table when he signed for Watford, arriving almost simultaneously with striker Gerry Armstrong from Tottenham and midfielder Les Taylor from Oxford. 'I didn't even realise they were in the bottom eight of the Second Division at the time,' he admits. 'I got a bit of a shock after I joined and saw where they were. But they had produced some unbelievable Cup upsets, so I was pretty certain they would be looking up the table and not over their shoulders. A few months before I arrived at Watford, Arsenal had won at Vicarage Road in the FA Cup quarter-finals, and it was a very, very tough game. I knew, after my first training session with the lads, that the squad belonged higher up the table. There was too much ability in that group to worry about us sliding into trouble.

'Graham introduced me to the other players by saying, "This is Pat Rice, he will be our captain, because of his age he might get the odd day off – and he will be me on the pitch."

Let me tell you straight away, I never got a day off when the other players were in for training. Not a single one. Don't get the wrong impression that I was shown any favouritism. There was many a time when he called me into his office and tore me off a strip. And occasionally, when he saw fit, he would give me a bollocking in front of the other lads. The gaffer didn't stand on ceremony.'

Is it true that he once gave the squad a public dressing-down at Watford Junction? 'Yes, he did - he called a team meeting on the platform, on our return from an away game, and went through us like a dose of salts. I can't remember where we had just played, but we must have lost, and he'd obviously spent the train journey stewing over whether to give us a public flogging. There we were, stood under the platform lights with the kit skips and medical baggage around us, getting the sharp end of the gaffer's tongue. Chelsea must have been playing up north that day as well because there were loads of their fans on the same train. They were leaning out of the window shouting, "Go on, Graham, get stuck in! You tell 'em." I wouldn't say we were a cocky bunch, but that experience brought us back down to earth.'

Rice took no prisoners at right-back, where his positional sense never deserted him in 137 appearances for the Hornets, even if his legs were wading through treacle towards the very end of his career. In *Rocket Men*, the previous volume of *Tales from the Vicarage*, goalkeeper Steve Sherwood revealed he never felt more secure than playing behind a settled back four where Rice was calling the tune, with Steve Sims, Ian Bolton and Wilf Rostron providing the rest of the human shield in front of him. And when opponents tried to intimidate some of the Hornets' younger players – notably wingers Nigel Callaghan and John Barnes – they found themselves answering to a voluble captain who was prepared to stand up for his teammates. One synthetic hard man at Notts County, whose verbals strayed into the realm of violent threats, was advised to steer clear of Rice's flank unless he could take the flak as well as dishing it out, and Watford never got another peep out of him.

Rice was resourceful, resolute and his methods were rustic where necessary. But above all he was a great communicator, demanding information from teammates and processing it like the ingredients of a recipe. Rarely, if ever, was he isolated or left twisting in the wind. 'Communication is something I more or less took on board when I first got into the Arsenal side,' he says. 'There were some very strong characters in that team who would hammer you if they couldn't hear you – people like Frank McLintock, Peter Storey, Bob McNab, George Graham – and it was a great environment for learning your trade. Frank once gave me an almighty bollocking on the pitch because I wasn't talking to him. He really laid into me, yelling, "Talk to me. I need to know where you are and what you can see." It's no fun being torn off a strip by your captain in front of 40,000 people, but it was a valuable lesson.

'When you are playing right-back and the ball is coming down the opposite flank, that's where you have to find your voice. A centre-back might be in position, but if there's a guy breaking from midfield behind him you've got to cover his run or give your mate a shout to let him know of the danger. I took that advice on board throughout my career. At Watford I was one of the biggest voices in the dressing room – but as captain, that's the way it should be. When you're up against it, and you're looking for leadership, you don't want your captain to be sat in the corner as quiet as a church mouse. You need him to set the example and tell a few home truths if needed. When you have captained the Arsenal and played in 500-odd games, you've seen most things on a football pitch – good things and bad, skills and mistakes – so I was able to put that experience to good use at Watford.

'Was I harsh on them? You would have to ask the other players but, yeah, I was prepared to be blunt. If I had something to say, I would always say it to their faces, never behind their backs, so even if they didn't like what you were saying, at least they knew you were being honest.'

Rice was not the quickest defender, but in those 137 appearances for the Hornets you could count the chasings he was given by opponents on one hand – with fingers to spare. Aston Villa's Tony Morley once gave him a hard time, in an FA Cup tie where Watford missed a glut of chances at the other end, but wingers who had him 'on toast' were a rare breed.

Modestly, he attributes his contribution to the quality of players around him at Vicarage Road, saying, 'I don't think Steve Sims and Ian Bolton got enough praise, to be fair. You don't finish runners-up in the entire Football League if your centre-backs can't play, and those two were really, really good players. For you to do your own job well, you need decent players around you, people who can spot the danger and who've got your back if you make a mistake. Sims and Bolton made a great partnership. I enjoyed playing with those two lads because they did a lot of unsung work. In football, ordinary players become good players when they have class acts around them, and in some cases good players become great players. That's what Simsy and Ian Bolton did for us. Ross Jenkins and Luther Blissett, quite rightly, got a lot of praise for the goals they scored, but how many of those goals started from Sims winning a header or Bolton picking them out with one of those raking passes?'

Occasionally, Rice's accent on communication would put him at odds with Watford's brand as market leaders for safe, inclusive, family clubs in an age littered with tribal hooliganism and primitive standards of behaviour on the terraces elsewhere. Like all the players, he subscribed to manager Taylor's ethics and he genuinely admired the club's status as standard-bearers for family enclosures with no adults admitted unless accompanied by a responsible child. 'Everybody has a family stand now, but at the time Watford's initiative was the best by miles,' says Rice. 'For one reason or another, a lot of football supporters in the late 1970s and early 1980s had to watch games from inside cages. I am so lucky that I played for two clubs where the fences never went up. But Watford set standards for decent behaviour, and Graham was the driving force behind that. Ann Swanson, who ran the Junior Hornets and family enclosure on matchdays, was a big part of that culture. Our kids were mascots at one home game and the way she looked after them, and my wife, was amazing. Other players whose children became mascots all said the same thing – she was fantastic. Graham was very passionate about cultivating future generations of support through family enclosures, and Ann was the perfect lady to put his wishes into action.

'But it's amazing what comes out of your mouth when you're angry, and on one occasion Ann came up to me and told me, very respectfully, there had been complaints about my language in front of the kids. At first, I didn't realise what she meant, and I was like, "Bad language? Me? When?" I would never walk into a room where there were seven-, eight- or nine-year-olds and start effing and blinding, but then I twigged that she was talking about my language on the pitch. When we were kicking towards the Vicarage Road end – and the family enclosure was on my near touchline behind the benches – amid the general noise of the crowd I didn't realise they could hear me telling Nigel Callaghan to track back, stop drifting inside or ignoring my runs. Evidently I resorted to industrial language, the language of the shop floor, and I didn't realise the fans down that side could hear me. Sometimes I would make a 40-yard run to overlap Nigel and he would use me as a decoy, but at my age I didn't always appreciate making long runs for nothing!

'What a great player Cally was, by the way – or, perhaps, what a great talent he was, and what an even greater player he could have been. He played in front of me, and I guess he often bore the brunt of my basic vernacular, but he was a fantastic crosser of the ball. People talk about John Barnes, and what he went on to achieve, but Nigel was a great lad as well. You might be able to double-mark one of them, but you couldn't double-mark both. As a pair of wingers they were unbelievable. Every day in training, I used to think, "Thank God I don't have to mark you on Saturday." I used to say Cally had feet like golf clubs, because he could drive crosses like a four iron or float them in like a pitching wedge. He was so talented he could hit them first time, on the run, and he usually chose the right club.'

Approaching his 70th birthday in March 2019 Rice can reflect on a phenomenal career in which he won the Double three times with Arsenal – as a player in 1970–71, and twice more as a coach in Arsène Wenger's backroom staff (in 1997–98 and 2001–02), a distinction he shares with Bob Wilson.

Only once, in November 1982, did he go back to Highbury as an opponent and come away with the points, in a memorable month when Watford did their own 'double' in north London – by winning at Tottenham and Arsenal in the space of 21 days.

Rice had decorated the Hornets' first-ever game in the top flight with his only goal for the club, on the opening day of the season, in a 2-0 win against Everton. Much as he would love to assure us it was a worthy forerunner to David Beckham's famous goal for Manchester United against Wimbledon 14 years later, it was, by his own admission, a fluke: 'What I was trying to do was drive the ball in at head-height towards Gerry [Armstrong], who was still on cloud nine after enjoying a fantastic World Cup campaign for Northern Ireland in the summer, but I sliced it and turned away in disgust. Neville Southall [the Everton goalkeeper] must have misjudged the flight for the first few yards, or the ball must have swerved as a result of me slicing it, but the officials decided he carried it over the line. I'm not even looking at the ball when the crowd at the Vicarage Road end get a bit excited, and next thing I know, the ref has signalled a goal. I could go around claiming I set the template for Beckham, but I simply haven't got the brass neck to do that. If it had been a tee shot, it would have ended up miles off the fairway in thick rough. I'm not complaining about the result, though.'

For Watford, Rice's slice of luck ushered in the first of 22 wins and 74 goals in their first taste of the penthouse, signalled a powerful statement of Graham Taylor's attacking principles and, conversely, provided a spectacular rebuke for those who underestimated them.

In the summer of 1982 Sir Bobby Charlton had wept after Brazil were knocked out of the World Cup quarter-finals because he felt they were the finest team never to win it – and, in fairness, Zico, Sócrates, Falcão, Éder and friends could play a bit. But while imitation is the sincerest form of flattery, Watford felt some of the more gilded rivals in their new orbit tried to pass the ball out from the back with Brazilian flair; in reality, few First Division sides had the personnel capable of playing that way, and few were equipped to withstand the Hornets' relentless artillery.

Although the eight-goal romp against Sunderland was lovely annihilation, and going top of the table in September completed the journey from wooden spoonists – 92nd in the League – to number 1 in the space of seven years and 12 days, in many respects the north London double was a high watermark, not least for Watford's adopted warhorse wearing the number 2 shirt.

Rice had enjoyed the ultimate satisfaction of clinching the title for Arsenal on enemy territory at White Hart Lane in 1971, but the feeling of going back 11 years later and upsetting the applecart was no less rewarding when Watford beat Tottenham 1-0. The ramifications of that result, and the tidal waves of uneducated criticism it brought the Hornets, is covered elsewhere in this volume, but Rice's anecdotal snapshot from the game underlines how much Taylor's side were taken for granted: 'I remember Glenn Hoddle was coming back from an injury, and when we kept Tottenham penned in their own half he was shouting to some of the Spurs players, "Don't worry, they'll blow up, they'll blow up." But we didn't blow up, did we? I was thinking, "You'll be here a long time waiting for us to blow up, Glenn" because we had lads like Les Taylor, who could run all day. There were people who felt we were not knowledgeable enough to take on First Division sides in terms of skill or experience, and a few times our results might have reflected that, but we were a very fit team and we were full of running.'

Three weeks later Rice made a nostalgic return to Arsenal, where he'd made 528 appearances, and the occasion did not escape the attention of Fleet Street's London-based scribes. It was, by any yardstick, an eventful afternoon.

'Reporters were ringing me up to ask how I felt about going back to the Arsenal, and whether I had anything to prove,' Rice says. 'Yes, I was looking forward to going back to Highbury. No problem on that score. Did I want Watford to take all three points? You'd better believe it – they were paying my wages, they had appointed me captain – of course I was desperate to win the game, same as any other. But what did I have to prove to anyone at Arsenal? Absolutely nothing – I had won the Double, I had played in five FA Cup finals, a European final, and I had risen through the ranks to become captain at one of the finest clubs in the world. I didn't have anything to prove, and I wasn't going to try harder than in any other game. I just wanted to walk off the pitch knowing I had made an honest contribution to the side, and hopefully we would get a result.'

In a tale of two keepers, Arsenal's George Wood endured a torrid afternoon while Steve Sherwood had an outstanding second half as the Hornets won 4-2. The Gunners, like Tottenham before them, were surprised by Watford's firepower and tenacity. Sherwood's defiance was arguably the zenith of his decade at Vicarage Road, as Rice observes, 'Steve was a terrific keeper, and especially a fantastic shot-stopper, but he needed people around him to gee him up a bit. He was a top lad, a really nice guy, but sometimes you wished he would get angry, bawl his defenders out, or come off his line more. But what a good career he had.'

Manager Taylor, conscious of the growing controversy around Watford's up-and-at-'em style, banned his players from speaking to the media after storming the marble halls and becoming the first side to hit four past Arsenal that season. (Only Tottenham, who trounced the Gunners 5-0 at White Hart Lane the following April, would enjoy a more productive 90 minutes against them.) Taylor was happy for the result, and Watford's buccaneering approach, to speak for itself, as Rice says, 'Everyone knew John Barnes was coming through and proving a force at that level; Cally was a force; Luther was a force . . . there was so much power in that side. When we were on-song, opponents struggled to contain it. Maybe we caught Arsenal on an off day, but the scoreline didn't flatter us. In general, I would say we caught the First Division napping. The following season they were more ready for us.'

Whatever the purists might say about Watford's direct football, it was an astonishing feat to go from Fourth Division makeweights to runners-up behind Liverpool within six years. Nobody has come close to repeating the feat, and the colossal sums of money swilling around at the top end of the English game mean it is almost impossible to countenance such insubordination now.

Rice initially found the discipline of pushing up to the halfway line, penning opponents in their own half as Sherwood's enormous clearances fell out of the sky, hard graft. It was also a culture shock when he was required to hit the centre-forwards, dragging their markers out of position, down the channels, where he had been used to shorter-range, safety-first passes at Arsenal. But he was mightily impressed by Taylor's set-piece repertoire, notably the famous 'Watford wall', where three or four yellow shirts would line up directly in front of the ball at free-kicks within shooting range, denying the keeper valuable time to read the likely outcome.

And he was a reliable conduit for Taylor's messages from the bench, often hearing a familiar voice piping up: 'Hey, Pat, remind them what I said.' Rice was, to all intents, GT's spokesman on the pitch – and when the captain spoke, the rank and file paid attention. It was an interesting dynamic, not least because Taylor was only four years older than Rice. While he had won major honours in the game at Arsenal, and commanded respect in his own right, the Hornets skipper never challenged the manager's methods or decisions in front of the other players. The mutual respect, and observation of protocols, was never fudged. Taylor could, as Rice concedes, 'lay down the law' if he was dissatisfied, but his authority was never compromised.

Rice was among the mourners at Taylor's funeral after the Hornets messiah's sudden death in January 2017, and when asked how he would remember GT, his tribute, like so many others', transcended football.

'Graham Taylor's achievements as a manager speak for themselves,' he says. 'But I will remember Graham Taylor the man. He was always straight with you. He always told you exactly how he felt. You might think you were playing OK, and he would tell you to your face, "You were crap." In that regard he was the same as Bertie Mee – he didn't stand on ceremony. If you didn't do as he wanted, he could have a ruck with you and, boy, he could take the paint off the walls if he wasn't happy. He didn't always do it in front of the whole squad – if you had to be told off for something, often he would be courteous and bring you into his office . . . and tear you off a strip in there instead.

'But he was always scrupulously fair – that's probably what I liked most about him. He was a fabulous manager, as his record shows, but he was also a fabulous man because he was honest and fair.

'And, of course, his work in the community was second to none. At a time when a lot of people were turning their backs on football, Graham asked us to go out and meet the public – and the public responded by turning out to watch us play. That wasn't just good public relations, it was genius. Simple, but genius.'

Rice laid bare his surprise at the sheer scale of Watford's community involvement in an interview with *Enjoy the Game* author Lionel Birnie, saying, 'I'll be honest – at the start, it was all a complete surprise to me. I went along with it because it was what the gaffer wanted, but I'd not done that sort of thing before. We went up to the town one day before Easter and joined in the egg-and-spoon and three-legged races, and the players were getting prizes! It felt like being with your family, coming into work. You knew the groundsman, the people who worked in the kitchens, the tea lady. They were only too willing to help you, with encouragement or whatever. If I needed to do a bit of work in my garden, [groundsman] Les Simmons would lend me a fork or a pair of shears.'

Taylor's accent on interaction between his players and the fans they were representing on the pitch helped to foster solidarity in the dressing room. At every level, from laundry to boardroom, there was a unique sense of communal belonging at Watford, which was hard to define yet easy to detect. Rice quickly tuned into the family-club wavelength. He says, 'Although the training was hard – my god, it was hard – there was a great camaraderie running through the squad, and the players were respectful of each other. I guess it's called "team spirit" these days, but in many cases we weren't just teammates, we were friends who socialised away from football. We used to organise a day at the races together, go out for a meal with our wives or girlfriends, and some of the lads would even meet up in Spain on their summer holidays.

'And one of the best things we did was the end-of-season awards night at Baileys nightclub, which was an absolute scream. In my experience, or to the best of my knowledge, no other club ever did anything like that. You would never get that at Manchester United, Tottenham or Arsenal, with the players performing impersonations of the manager or chairman in front of the supporters, but we had some gifted comedians in that dressing room. Steve Harrison could bring the house down with a one-liner. There was a warmth about Watford which made me feel a part of the club very quickly – and after 16 years at Arsenal as apprentice and professional, I never thought I would feel the same way towards another club. I consider myself incredibly fortunate that I found another home from home. I was made to feel I belonged at Watford right away. I was never made to feel like an outsider.'

That mutual respect endured right through to Rice's farewell appearance in Watford colours – appropriately, it was against

Arsenal, in the last League game of the 1983–84 season – a week before the FA Cup final. Taylor went on the pitch before kick-off to thank the fans for their support and for buying 35,000 tickets to Wembley, for which some of us queued seven hours or more, and gave the visiting Gooners a wave, chortling, 'We're even rolling out old Ricey for you.'

Being the consummate professional, Rice had no intention of winding down his career by trotting along the touchline like a show pony in a dressage arena, and the Hornets signed off with a 2-1 win, sending them to their appointment with 'Abide With Me' in good heart. He remembers being so late with one lumbering, lunging challenge on Paul Davis that it was almost early, like a delayed train that could be mistaken for one conforming with the published timetable, even though it was ludicrously behind schedule. And just when he thought his work as a player at Vicarage Road was done, Rice found himself at the centre of Taylor's only major selection dilemma for the Cup final.

Wilf Rostron's unjust suspension left youngster Neil Price – who had coped admirably in Europe and the semi-final against Plymouth – in the frame to face Everton at Wembley, but Taylor was sorely tempted to hand Rice a curtain call on the grandest stage of all. Although David Bardsley had been passed fit after a knee injury, and Rice had been standing by to fill in if the flying right-back had not made it, there was still an option to go for experience ahead of youth on the left. But one of Rice's outstanding attributes, as well as being a top-class communicator and organiser, was his unselfishness. He was not a full-kit narcissist determined to seek glory until the last shafts of limelight had faded into the dusk, nor an office politician promoting his own virtues at the expense of worthy colleagues. Rice was, however, aware of his limitations and the potential long-term damage of denying young players a once-in-a-lifetime privilege of playing in a prestigious final watched by hundreds of millions on TV all over the world. Taylor always considered himself fortunate to find the right leader, at the right time, to delegate his instructions on the pitch; now, a week before the biggest game in Watford Football Club's history, he was blessed that Rice declined to pull rank.

'Graham always wondered if he made a mistake by not playing me in the final,' confides Rice. 'But, in all honesty, I was never going to make that decision for him. He called me into his office and asked me what I thought about playing at Wembley, because I was such an influence on the team. Of course it's nice to be held in such a high regard, but I told him, "If you think I'm going to say I should play in the FA Cup final, I'm not going to do it. I've played in five of them, I've been lucky enough to finish on the winning side twice and I've lifted the Cup as winning captain. I've gone through just about every emotion it's possible to experience in Wembley finals – but some of these lads may never get the chance to play in another one. Sorry, gaffer, I ain't going to make that decision. It's your call."

'As manager, Graham was the one who had to live with it – and, quite rightly, he didn't play me. If I had been in his position, I would have come to the same conclusion.

'I played my part on the day, and took my place on the bench, but would the result against Everton have been any different if I had played? I would be flattering myself if I thought so – I was knackered. I never played another competitive game in my career. Of course, it would have been nice for Watford to win, and I still hope they will go back to Wembley and lift a trophy one day. But at least I could sign off with a clean conscience, knowing I hadn't denied a young lad one of the biggest days of his life. I can live with that.'

It is no surprise to Watford supporters who lived through the early 1980s that Rice went on to become an integral part of

Arsenal's plentiful success under Arsène Wenger. Leadership is not measured by air temperature, water depth or the number on a shirt. In so many respects, it is unquantifiable. Yet when Rice supplied that missing link in the Hornets squad, his influence was reflected in results, performances and discipline. When Rice was calling the shots from right-back, Watford had only one player sent off in three years – Luther Blissett's retribution for a series of roughshod tackles at Newcastle on the opening day of the season in August 1981. He may not have been the quickest defender to wear the shirt. His skill-set may not have been the most exotic to grace Vicarage Road. And his only goal for Watford may have been unintentional.

But for all we know, history might have turned out very different without the wise old head badgering Nigel Callaghan to stay wide, his communication, his hotline to Taylor and, yes, the gravitas that comes with being a Double winner from Arsenal.

What is undeniable about Pat Rice's legacy is this: if he was the captain who set the template for mutual admiration societies between players and supporters when he led his troops over to say thank you to the travelling contingent on a May Day bank holiday at Wrexham, he should consider this appreciation of his contribution to a golden age in Watford's history as a compliment returned.

4

LES TAYLOR

MEDAL OF HONOUR

Behind the glass in operating theatres at the John Radcliffe Hospital in Oxford, medical students and aspiring surgeons would gather to watch the doctors at work. Privileged hospital staff with access-all-areas passes were allowed to join audiences in the viewing galleries as specialists went through their procedures with infinite care and microscopic accuracy. Little did many of the consultants (and even fewer students) bearing witness to the real-life medical dramas realise that the licensed onlookers included a hospital porter who was also the captain of Watford's beaten 1984 FA Cup final side – by his own admission their captain 'by default'.

As of 2018, just 16 men have ever led their teams out for the only FA Cup final appearance in their clubs' history without lifting the trophy. Among them was former Watford manager Glenn Roeder and Hornets prodigy Tony Currie, who shared the armband for Queens Park Rangers in 1982 (Roeder was suspended for the replay) - and two years later the honour fell to Les Taylor.

Towards the end of his playing career Taylor had signed for Colchester United on a two-year contract, with an option to join the coaching staff, but walked away midway through the deal, without being paid up, because he was not doing himself justice on the pitch. A knee operation six years earlier, when he was in his prime at Vicarage Road, was taking its inexorable toll, and Taylor was honourable enough to resign from his beat instead of continuing to draw a wage as a tribute act to the all-action, ubiquitous midfielder who had been such an important cog in the machine at Watford.

At 34, and wondering what he was going to do with the rest of his life, he was happy to take a job at his local hospital, sterilising the instruments and cutlery between operations and organising the right sets of utensils for each theatre. Between shifts, or in a spare half-hour, Taylor would join the medical students in the viewing bays because he was fascinated by the surgical precision that had been required to sustain his own playing career and to satisfy an innate curiosity to 'see what it was all about'.

In a parallel universe, a porter's fetching and carrying – not always appreciated, although you wouldn't half miss it if it wasn't there – was a logical extension of his working life. At the peak of his powers, Taylor was one of the best box-to-box workhorses in the business. He was diligent, relentless, ubiquitous.

Les Taylor only captained Watford three times, and one of those games happened to be the highest-profile game in the club's history. When he led the team out at Wembley to face Everton he was Watford's fifth captain in the 1983-84 season alone – yet he was no novice in the role. By the time he signed for the Hornets in November 1980, he had played 219 League games for Oxford United and had been their captain for two years when Graham Taylor came calling with a player-plus-cash deal that involved striker Keith Cassells going in the opposite direction.

Among Taylor's most engaging traits was an ability not to take himself too seriously, especially when his shots from outside the box landed in a different postcode. Oliver Phillips, doyen of the *Watford Observer* coverage of all things yellow for 40 years, once told Taylor he used to fear for the clock above the old Rookery terrace whenever Sir Les was inclined to put his laces through an attempt at goal. All horologists' leave in Hertfordshire was cancelled when Taylor or his worthy predecessor in midfield, Roger Joslyn, took aim speculatively, although somehow the timepiece survived.

But we remember Taylor fondly for his exceptional energy and exemplary application during the peak years of Watford's golden era. It required a hideous conspiracy of circumstance, injury and suspension for the captaincy to fall in his lap on FA Cup final day, but as a foot soldier in the ranks he was a jewel of the regiment.

***

After banking five wins out of seven for starters in Division Three, with 20 goals into the bargain – plus a League Cup upset of Newcastle United after Luther Blissett's two-goal cameo from the bench – Watford had started the 1978–79 season with the air of a side who were not going to hang around for a replacement bus if their train was cancelled. As it happens, on the opening day in the League, Hornets supporters travelling on a football 'special' to Walsall were delayed, in time-honoured British Rail fashion, and arrived at the Saddlers' old Fellows Park ground to find their team two goals down before a spirited fightback and a 4-2 win validated their fashionably late entrance.

Six weeks into the campaign we got our first glimpse of Les Taylor, albeit in the opposition's shirt, at Vicarage Road in another 4-2 win, at home to Oxford. Before kick-off manager Graham Taylor was handing over the keys to a 12-year-old bright yellow, red-and-black striped Austin 1100 car on the pitch. It had the turning circle of a Sunday league central defender and, it transpired, it was a light-hearted birthday present to the Watford boss from his chairman Elton John. In the late 1970s, especially if you drove a Ford Capri, it was fashionable to adorn your motor with a sun strip bearing the names of the devoted couple in the front seats. Elton mischievously had the windscreen of his gift from the second-hand car lot garnished with one reading 'George and Rita' – referencing a rival chairman who, for some reason, had called Graham Taylor 'George' all night at an earlier evening fixture, and the Hornets messiah's wife.

Watford manager Taylor had woken up, on his 34th birthday, to find the vehicle – the bonnet signed by club staff – parked on his front lawn. A cursory inspection of his unsolicited gift's bodywork soon revealed the prankster's identity, and GT won a personal wager with his rock star chairman by driving the distinctive car around town for a couple of days before presenting it to a local charity, for their future use, at the Oxford game.

Les Taylor only has a vague recollection of a car in the centre-circle before kick-off – but he remembers what happened next. 'Aye, I remember that game at Watford – it was a hot day, and Ross Jenkins was on fire. Right foot, left foot, headers . . . everything he touched turned to gold. [Jenkins scored all four Hornets goals that afternoon.] I remember thinking that Graham was going places with that side, but little did I know I would be joining them within a couple of years. And when it happened, my move to Watford came out of the blue. I learned sometime later that Oxford were in financial trouble and they had to sell to survive. There were two clubs interested – Chesterfield, who were in the same division as Oxford, and Watford, who were about sixth from bottom at the time but in a higher league. I was going to speak to both of them, but as it happened I went to see Watford first and I didn't need to go anywhere else. Graham Taylor was a fantastic salesman. He sold the club to me like double glazing for my front windows. I'm not sure I got a word in edgeways, but I didn't need to say anything. Once the boss had finished talking, I knew there was no point in speaking to Chesterfield because there was no way they were going to top what Watford had to offer.

'Just after I signed, they brought in Pat Rice – who had played in the FA Cup final and in a European final for Arsenal the season before – and Gerry Armstrong, who had played about 100 games for Tottenham, so it was clear Watford meant business. As soon as Graham Taylor paused for breath it was like, "Where do I sign? Can I borrow a pen?" It was that simple.'

At £250 a week, plus win bonuses and a crowd bonus [a share of the gate from attendances in excess of 15,000], Taylor knew he wasn't going to become a millionaire overnight, but moving up a division was worth a tidy pay rise. He jumped straight off the top board with alacrity.

It cannot be easy to make your Watford debut amid the mild hysteria of a derby against the infidel. In 1996 home-grown legend Paul Robinson stepped off the bench and into the fire and brimstone at the age of 17 for his first-team baptism after Dominic Ludden was forced to retire hurt in the early stages of a frantic 1-1 draw (Darren Bazeley's deflected, 94th-minute equaliser was particularly sweet). Two years earlier another 17-year-old, central defender Gary Fitzgerald, had been thrown in the deep end in the same fixture and was hooked at half-time after sinking without trace in a 4-2 defeat. It was his only appearance for the club at senior level.

Taylor's entrance – like Robinson, as a substitute – came during the groundhog day cycle of 1-0 losses, in various shades of angst or injustice, whenever the neighbours locked horns in the so-called M1 derby. From Kirk Stephens' last-gasp header on Boxing Day in 1979 to Malcolm Poskett's disallowed goal in the fruitless siege of Kenilworth Road the following year, it is fair to say Watford's luck had been in short supply when bragging rights over the Hertfordshire–Bedfordshire frontier were at stake.

And fortune was keeping a low profile again when Taylor, never the quickest player on the pitch but often one of the canniest, sprang the Hatters' tedious offside trap on another frustrating night at Vicarage Road.

'I can't remember who played the ball over the top, but I timed my run well and it was just me and the keeper, Jake Findlay,' he recalls. 'He came miles out of his area to meet me and I headed the ball over him, but I was probably 30 yards out and I couldn't get enough purchase on the header to score. By the time the ball came down, there were covering defenders to avert the danger, but I could still have been the hero. Malcolm Poskett got to the byline and drilled his cross through a crowded six-yard box. I was almost standing on the line – I can only have been a yard out, if that – but it came so fast the ball went through my legs. Instead of becoming an instant hit with the fans – as the man who scored on his Watford debut against Luton – I was nutmegged right on the line and missed a sitter. It still bugs me when I think back to it now – it wasn't until we were both in the First Division that we spanked them.'

Taylor was not an immediate fixture in the Hornets' first XI, partly because of swashbuckling Cup exploits for which he was ineligible. That was the season, 1980–81, where Watford had produced the most miraculous turnaround in the history of two-legged ties, overturning a 4-0 deficit against Southampton to win the return 7-1, and the new recruit in midfield had joined the payroll after another eye-watering result.

He says, 'A week or so before I arrived, Watford had just beaten Nottingham Forest 4-1 [to reach the League Cup quarter-finals], which was another good reason for me to sign. I remember thinking, "If this lot can beat the European Cup holders, they must be onto a good thing." But it meant there was a Cup team and a League team for a few weeks, so it wasn't until Christmas that I got a run in the side and began to establish myself there.

'But I must stress that Graham made me feel welcome from the moment I set foot in the club, and outlined how I was an important part of his plan. He made it plain that I was a cog in the machine, if you like, and I would play an important role in keeping the machine ticking over.

'Little did I know what was going to happen over the next three or four years. When you are a young kid you have your dreams about the things you want to achieve as a footballer – reaching the top flight, going to Anfield and Old Trafford, playing at Wembley – and I was lucky enough to fulfil nearly all of them at Watford. The only one that got away was an international cap, but I will always be grateful for those years. I developed a real affinity with the club, an unbreakable bond. It's more than 30 years since I left Vicarage Road now, but the association still runs deep. It never leaves you. It's deep in my heart.'

Taylor's true worth to his namesake's 'machine' manifested itself in the promotion season of 1981–82, when the discovery of John Barnes, and restoring the Jenkins–Blissett axis as warhead of a formidable front line, gave the Hornets a new licence to plunder. Equally vital, in terms of supplying ammunition, was Taylor's midfield partnership with Kenny Jackett, which would be suspended by the latter's knee injury midway through the campaign, although Jan Lohman proved a willing alternative.

The season began with a trip to Taylor's Geordie homeland, with a contingent of his family making the short trip from North Shields to St James's Park for Watford's 1-0 win over Newcastle. A feisty contest, which included the only red card of Blissett's career, was settled by Nigel Callaghan's stupendous volley. 'I've looked everywhere for it on the internet,' says Taylor.

'I wish I could see it again, but it seems there weren't any cameras there. What a hit that was. Deserved to win any game of football.'

And for Taylor, a memorable year culminating in promotion and plentiful Cup scalps was crowned by recognition from supporters as their player of the season. To uneducated outsiders it was surprising that a midfielder should win the fans' blue riband award because the word had spread that Watford apparently didn't have a midfield. Jealous chaff – mainly at clubs whose defenders had been unable to cope with the Hornets' supreme fitness, directness and unrelenting waves of attack – were spreading the word that Watford's style was allegedly kick-and-rush.

More often than not, Barnes' limbo-dancer elasticity, Callaghan's sublime delivery and Jenkins' and Blissett's methodical mayhem in the box would disabuse the cynics of their prejudice – and even if opponents managed to clear their lines, a dynamic minesweeper with a shock of, er, strawberry blond hair and Groucho Marx moustache would be lurking to mop up any half-baked clearances and recycle the danger.

Cards on the table: we had a ball, and at the heartbeat of all the merry-making was our bargain Geordie ferret. Gilded internationals or journeymen plodders, Taylor never gave his rivals a moment's peace. For a young scribe taking his first steps in the newspaper business, the 1981–82 season was full of good cheer. For five months, as the Hornets closed in on the promised land, I learned the joys of council minutes, court reporting and newspaper law in Newcastle-upon-Tyne, in between frequent pilgrimages home and away to watch history unfold in a golden haze. When Taylor won his player of the season award, I made sure his achievement was celebrated on Tyneside among the pages of the *Evening Chronicle* 'Pink', one of the marvellous teatime editions which rolled off the presses at 5 p.m. on a Saturday with all the football results and tables. 'Geordies Fill the Watford Gap' ran the headline, with Taylor's gong as the focal point of an article which noted the proliferation of north-eastern accents in Watford's dressing room, Eric Steele, Wilf Rostron, Mick Henderson and Teessider Malcolm Poskett among them. Taylor was chuffed to receive a call from his mum in North Shields saying he was big news in his home town.

'I've got to say it was a nice surprise when the fans voted for me as their player of the year,' he says. 'In that team, there were so many players who deserved it that I never gave it a moment's thought [beforehand]. But in football, supporters are usually the best judges! When all the nonsense about kick and rush started flying, I wondered if teammates, the manager and backroom staff were the only ones who appreciated the work Kenny and I did in midfield. It was extra special that the fans noticed it as well, because nobody else outside Watford did.

'To be effective in that role, you need to read the game well, and fortunately I was good at doing that. When the high ball went up to Ross – or George Reilly a couple of years down the line – my job was to anticipate where it was coming down and pick up the second ball. When we did it well opponents were pinned in their own half, and they had to soak up the pressure. Some of them stood up to it well, others cracked. The key was to hit them early, let them know they were in for a hard 90 minutes. Sometimes we would be in the corridor, banging on their dressing-room door, shouting, "Are you lot ready? Come on, we're waiting for you!" There were days when we knew we were going to be 2-0 up in 20 minutes because they wouldn't be able to cope with us. It was such a good feeling to be part of it.'

Taylor sensed his popularity among Watford's core support was flourishing when the Hornets went to Wrexham, half a dozen games into the League season, and his looping header from the edge of the 18-yard box was the only goal of a hard-earned win. A special train for travelling supporters – in the good old days when a British Rail charter was the best way to reach distant away games in midweek – had a carriage reserved for the team on the homeward journey. When the players appeared on the platform at Wrexham station, a few hundred yards from the Racecourse Ground, to board the late-night express calling at Hemel Hempstead and Watford Junction, Taylor was serenaded by a Hornets choral society chanting his name. He acknowledged the tribute with a theatrical bow.

'Coming back on the train with the supporters was down to Graham Taylor,' says the Watford match-winner. 'It made us feel like we were all in it together, which was the general idea. Sometimes players would go and mingle with the fans in the supporters' club after games, and there was a clever sponsorship deal with the Benskins brewery. If we won, fans would get a free pint on a Thursday night and the players would take it in turns to go down the pub and socialise with them. Of course, we didn't drink alcohol less than 48 hours before a match, but it was a great way of bringing the supporters closer to the players.'

Chipping in with six goals during the 1981–82 season – half of them against Queens Park Rangers – Taylor, like many of his teammates, was reaching the best form of his life. If Watford's peak years were the two or three seasons leading up to the 1984 FA Cup final, as many would attest, it is no coincidence that so many of the club's first-choice players all produced their finest football in that period.

There was a delicious paradox that QPR should be on the receiving end of Taylor's sharpest finishing, because Rangers' manager Terry Venables, who would succeed Graham Taylor as England coach 12 years later, was a conspicuous critic of Watford's high-octane approach. Where Venables' acolytes saw possession – technical refinery and composure – as nine-tenths of the law, many of us saw a tedious offside trap choreographed

on a plastic pitch. It must have hurt Venables that his team was
twice breached by Taylor's drilled finishes, having burst through
the inside-right channel, as QPR were demolished 4-1 in the
League Cup, and the Hornets' Geordie hustler was on target
again as the Hoops crashed 4-0 in a rearranged Second Division
fixture three months later. By now El Tel (as he became known
when he coached Barcelona) had his excuses rehearsed –
Rangers, he revealed, were unable to cope with the unfamiliar
'slope' at Vicarage Road, which he managed to portray as the
north face of the Eiger. There is, undeniably, a gentle contour
which runs from the north-western corner of the ground down
towards the Rookery, perhaps comparable with the slope at
Lord's cricket ground, but to use it as an excuse for conceding
eight goals in two games was risible.

'Graham said I was going through a purple patch,' says
Taylor. 'To be fair, it did feel as if everything I tried was coming
off for a while – whether corners were being half-cleared and
falling to me on the edge of the box, or I was simply in the
right place at the right time to pick up the bits and pieces, I was
having a great time.'

Probably Taylor's most memorable goal of all, though not
necessarily the tidiest finish, was his winner at Tottenham when
the Hornets took the First Division by storm in their first
season among English football's landed gentry.

This was allegedly the game where Watford's style would be
rumbled, where their shortcomings would be exposed, where
they would be found out. Although the Hornets' first dozen
games had not been a cakewalk, in a five-week period after
the clocks went back they would be tested by Spurs, Arsenal,
Manchester United and Liverpool.

First up was a trip to White Hart Lane, and they arrived
with a raging sense of injustice after an undeserved 3-2 defeat
at Notts County the previous week. Leading 2-0 at Meadow

Lane, and bossing the game convincingly, the Hornets were undone by a preposterous refereeing decision on the stroke of half-time which changed the course of the match irrevocably. Goalkeeper Steve Sherwood, collecting a cross, raised his knee as a token of self-preservation as County striker Trevor Christie bore down on him, apparently with collision in mind. Referee Peter Willis, a County Durham police officer, somehow interpreted Sherwood's action as dangerous play and awarded the home side an indirect free-kick, barely six yards out. With all 11 Watford players camped on the line, Brian Kilcline bulldozed his free-kick through the yellow wall to begin an unlikely fightback that was completed nine minutes from time. It was a nonsense decision which made Watford feel as if providence had already decreed the points would be taken from them, and Christie later admitted he thought the free-kick would be awarded against him. In high dudgeon, the Hornets headed to north London with just three points from a possible 15 to show for their travails since the 8-0 demolition of Sunderland 42 days earlier.

With Glenn Hoddle returning from his latest injury, and home supporters in the bumper 42,215 crowd expecting him to give Watford a guided tour of his passing range, the Hornets produced a monumental performance. Forcing Tottenham back repeatedly under a barrage of 19 corners, they didn't allow Hoddle a meaningful kick.

'Our game-plan was to stop them playing completely, and not let them have the ball,' says Taylor. 'We defended from the front and never gave them a second to dwell on it. Hoddle and Ricky Villa could kill you with their passing if you let them, so we spent the entire game on the front foot.'

For all their admirable endeavours, it looked as if Watford would have to settle for deadlock. Then, with three minutes left, Blissett launched a long throw from their left flank into the

Spurs box, testing the resilience of a tiring defence who had been forced to absorb an unexpected avalanche of pressure. Taylor, making an unauthorised run into the area like an airport sniffer dog on the trail of a smuggler's contraband, for once disobeyed his manager's orders: 'Graham wasn't too happy,' he recalls. 'He wanted me to stay back, in the event of a counter-attack, and I could hear him shouting from the bench at the top of his voice: "Les, no! Get back, Les!" But I got lucky with a rebound and poked the loose ball under Ray Clemence for the winner. There wasn't long enough left for Tottenham to respond but, as a team, our performance was a fantastic statement. Afterwards Graham asked, "Did you not hear me calling you to hang back?" I didn't usually answer him back, but I was full of it after winning at White Hart Lane so I replied with something like, "Don't worry, boss – I had everything under control. Just leave the football to me!" It was a bit cheeky, but he let it go because it was such an outstanding result and he knew how hard we'd worked for it.'

Fleet Street's assembled dukes were not impressed, however. Watford's perverse reward for raining on Hoddle's parade was ferocious criticism. This observer was so taken aback by the one-eyed verdict of the Fourth Estate's scribes as he scanned the back pages on the following Monday morning, he fell off a wall waiting for his bus outside Watford Junction. Taylor was also shaken by the reaction. 'I can remember we got hammered in the London Press,' he recalls. 'One writer called us a pack of mad dogs beating our heads against a wall to try to force a crack. There had been rumblings about our playing style before, but that was like a storm breaking overhead. It wasn't right. They just didn't get it. The way we played wasn't perfect, but when you went to a Watford game in those days you were guaranteed goalmouth action. Shots, crosses, corners, set-pieces – things to get you out of your seat, things to excite the crowds behind the goal. A couple of weeks later we went to Arsenal and won 4-2. It didn't make our critics change their tune, but in the dressing room there was an air of satisfaction, along the lines of, "What are you going to write about now, then?"

'When I watch Premier League games these days, too many of them are based around defenders exchanging 18 to 20 passes with each other and none of them is in the opposition half. Where's the excitement in that? When the punters part with their hard-earned money, they want to be entertained – and the way Watford played in the 1980s was all about entertaining the fans. That's probably why our attendances were going up while they were falling nearly everywhere else. Graham Taylor was disappointed if we didn't have 20 goal attempts in 90 minutes. That's how committed to attack he was.

'Instead of GPS tracking and all the modern technology available to compile stats today, the boss would have observers sat in the stands compiling facts and figures about individual performances. People talk about stats as a breakdown of games as if they were a new invention, but the boss was ahead of his time in that regard. We would come in on a Monday morning and he would have whole files telling him everything about each player's game: shots on target, crosses, tackles won, how many times we'd given the ball away in our own half . . . everything relevant to the way he wanted to play. And if the stats didn't measure up to his standards, he would get into us. Even if you thought you'd played well, he would say, "You didn't get enough crosses into the box, or goal attempts, or forward passes inside the final third" – and he would have it all on a chart to back it up. There was no comeback, no room for argument, if he was armed with those facts. It sounds dead boring, all that number-crunching, but it meant all the players knew what they had to do, and we took it all on board.'

Taylor's industry, and compliance with every imaginable statistic his manager challenged him to meet, took Watford to the brink of Europe – until he broke his toe in a 2-2 draw at Sunderland just 12 days before the credits rolled.

'On the final day, when we beat Liverpool and the news came through that we had qualified for Europe, it's a shame I wasn't on the pitch at that moment, but I knew I had played my part,' he says. 'And Martin Patching – whose knee injury was one of the reasons Watford went out and bought me in the first place – scored on his comeback after two years out, so you could only feel happy for him when he had been through so much. My broken toe recovered well enough over the summer, but then I got injured again in a pre-season friendly at Oxford, of all places.'

Little did he suspect it at the time, but this setback would have longer-term consequences. Surging beyond his old teammate Gary Briggs at the Manor Ground, an abrupt challenge stopped Taylor in his tracks. In the impact of the tackle, he felt a sudden tugging sensation in his knee – never a good sign. But in the age of magic sponges and running off knocks – a euphemism for pretending it didn't hurt when a bruising collision was bloody painful – Taylor resolved to carry on. After all, crunching tackles were no match for his inherent grit. Taylor's supreme fitness had rewarded him with thigh muscles like rugby balls and calf muscles like fillet steaks, but for all the impeccable physiology of his quads and lower leg muscles, it was the bit in between that was damaged. Taylor played on, but he was off the boil in the first two games of the season, a wasteful home defeat by Coventry and a defensively-fragile 2-2 draw with Ipswich. Surgery, which would become the backdrop to the day job when he stopped playing, was the only option, and he underwent a cartilage operation just before Watford embarked on their European tour in the UEFA Cup.

'I was gutted, to be honest,' he reflects. 'We had worked so hard to get into Europe the previous season, and when the time came I was on crutches. In the week I had mine done, Ian Rush had a knee operation after picking up a similar injury. But Liverpool's medical budget was way beyond ours, and where I had my knee opened up, he had keyhole surgery, which was a revolutionary surgical technique in those days. The operation mended my cartilage, but I was out for four months – Rush was only out for six weeks. And, if I'm honest, I never felt quite the same afterwards. I had to put ice on it between games and I didn't feel as sharp.'

Taylor missed the monumental UEFA Cup wins against Kaiserslautern and Levski-Spartak of Sofia, and he attempted a comeback in time for the home leg against Sparta Prague in the third round, but rushing back did him few favours. A further month on physio Billy Hails' treatment table was required before another return to the fray, looking more like his old self, on Boxing Day. Although Europe had largely passed him by, at least he was back in time for Watford to join the party in the FA Cup third round.

**

It had to be *them,* didn't it? And why did it have to be away from home at *that* architectural relic?

When the FA Cup third-round draw was made, a fortnight before Christmas in 1983, Watford fans knew who put the 'grot' into Santa's grotto. Kenilworth Road had brought the Hornets no joy, and even less justice, for 20 years. A Cup tie in bandit country was not what we had in mind for a New Year detox in the first week of 1984. And when the Hornets were 2-0 down inside 20 minutes – to two deflected goals, which was absolutely typical of their luck at the 'Kennel' in recent years – it looked like curtains for Watford's hopes of a Cup run. Curtains in horrid permutations of orange, navy and white.

But for those of limited or negligible religious convictions, perhaps there was a God, after all. By the interval, John Barnes' free-kick and Mo Johnston's penalty had restored parity and a classic, seven-goal replay was settled by Mo Jo's header in extra time. Lovely jubbly.

Better still, some of the big guns likeliest to barricade the road to Wembley began to fall by the wayside. Manchester United came unstuck at Bournemouth, Liverpool were shocked by Brighton, and Taylor reflects, 'All of a sudden, it dawned on us – this could be our year. That's still the beauty of the FA Cup, and we let it slide at our peril. It's always full of surprises. You never know when you might get an opportunity to go to Wembley.

'You wouldn't say we got the luck of the draw, because out of Luton, Charlton, Brighton and Birmingham, only one of those draws up until the semi-final was a home tie. But our forward line was clicking into gear, and with a front four of Barnes, Reilly, Johnston and Callaghan we knew we could hurt anyone.'

The quarter-final at Birmingham, where Watford had never won before, was a memorable test of sphincter and rectum in a bear pit atmosphere, with Taylor striking the critical blow 12 minutes from time. He recalls, 'We heard they were expecting a full house [40,220 turned up, easily Birmingham's largest gate of the season] and we left our pre-match hotel in lots of time, but we got stuck in traffic and didn't make it to the ground until 25 minutes before kick-off. Graham Taylor gave his team talk on the bus and one of the coaching staff had to run ahead to make sure the teamsheet was handed in on time because the traffic was going nowhere. By the time we made it to St Andrew's there was no time to warm up. It was a quick change and out onto the pitch. But I'll always remember that game because my goal put us 2-1 up after we had spent much of the second half under pressure.'

Taylor was hovering just outside the box when Kenny Jackett's short-range cross towards George Reilly was only half-cleared. Shifting the ball onto his left foot, not his favourite, Taylor unleashed a rising shot which arrowed under the angle of future Hornets keeper Tony Coton's crossbar and post. Barnes added Watford's third a couple of minutes later to settle the argument, and all that remained was to negotiate Small Heath's tribute to Dodge City on the homeward journey.

'I never hit a better one with my left foot,' says Taylor. 'And whenever I bump into Tony Coton now I still remind him it was a great pleasure to beat him at his near post.'

The semi-final draw took Watford back to the Second City, across town at Villa Park, to face Third Division long shots Plymouth Argyle. Whether it was the pressure of being favourites, for a club who had so often relished being Cup underdogs previously, or whether the Hornets' confidence had been dented by a 6-1 hammering at Norwich seven days earlier, Taylor endured a 'scary' afternoon, where his reserves of energy for once deserted him. And amid the tension Watford – whose fitness was based on their manager's famous exhortation, 'Hey! You don't get cramp at this club!' – found themselves cramping and running through treacle.

'We were one step from Wembley and I think the nerves and emotion got to us,' Taylor admits. 'I had never played in a Cup semi-final before, and apart from Steve Sherwood I don't think any of the other lads had experienced one, either. I started developing cramp after only 20 minutes and I couldn't understand it. By the end, we were hanging on. I was struggling for the last half-hour. I could barely run because it hurt so much. For someone like me, whose game was based on getting around the pitch, it was awful. The harder I tried to run, the more it hurt. I wasn't injured, but I spent most of the second half wondering how I was going to get through it. In the end, one fantastic run and cross [from Barnes] and one flying header at the near post from George is all we needed, but Plymouth nearly equalised late on and I wouldn't have fancied our chances in extra time.'

What happened on the countdown to Wembley tainted Watford's enjoyment of their achievement and the big day itself.

Established captain Wilf Rostron's red card over the border, three weeks before the Cup Final, completely devalued the Hornets' satisfaction of a first win at *that* place in two decades, and it thrust Taylor centre stage when he least expected it.

Whenever history knocked at the Hornets' door, referee Roger Milford seemed to be playing trick or treat. Of course, that's an exaggeration – Milford took charge of some Watford games with no major controversy – but at least twice, at the moment of truth, he saved his treats for their opponents and his egging for the team in yellow. The FA Cup quarter-final replay against Liverpool in 1986 remains a sore point for all those who saw through Ian Rush's desperate fall in the box when the Hornets led 1-0 with four minutes to go. Forget all else that came before or after: that was the moment when Liverpool effectively won the Double that season. But Rostron's sending off up the road was a personal catastrophe because his red card was a poor decision and the consequences were sickening. It cost him the only chance he would ever get to play at Wembley.

'Wilf didn't deserve to be sent off,' says Taylor, who had a decent view of Rostron's clash with Paul Elliott which led to both players being dismissed by Milford – although the Watford captain was more sinned-against than sinner. 'Another referee might have seen it differently, but once he had made his decision there was no going back. He's not going to change his mind. Sadly for Wilf, and for us as a team, there was no right of appeal in 1984. He was devastated, absolutely devastated, and it was a massive blow for us. He was one of our outstanding players that season. It wasn't long before the penny dropped that he would be suspended for the final. I can't remember if it was one of the players or the staff who mentioned it first, but we all felt terrible for him. At the time, I didn't give it a moment's thought that it might be me who would captain Watford at Wembley. Nobody said anything until we knew Wilf had no chance of playing, that there was no way of skirting around his ban. Then Graham Taylor asked to see me, a couple of weeks before the Cup final, and when he told me I would be our captain on the day my jaw hit the floor.

'To be fair, earlier in my career I had been the youngest captain in Oxford's history. I was always a talker on the pitch and I thought of myself as a decent motivator of people around me, but when Graham asked me to stand in for Wilf, I must admit I let my mind wander. What would I do if we won it? All sorts of things went through my head. Plan A was to push Wilf up the steps to lift the Cup because he deserved it. He was our captain, and even if he couldn't play in the final itself, I wanted him to have the honour. But in the build-up to the game, we weren't even sure if Wilf was going to be there. I think the boss gave him the option of coming with us on the team coach and being part of the day or steering clear of the whole thing. Wilf was a fantastic teammate, but in the nicest way he could be quite a stubborn man, so I couldn't take it for granted that he would lead us up the steps to the Royal Box. And there would probably have been somebody from the FA trying to stop him anyway because he was banned, so we needed an alternative.

'Plan B was to let Elton lift the Cup, which would have been easy to fix because he was already in the Royal Box. Along with Graham he did so much for the club, and in many ways our success on the pitch was his dream coming true, so in my mind that was settled: if Wilf wasn't allowed up those steps, we thought it would be the perfect gesture if Elton – or maybe Elton and Graham Taylor together – did the honours.

'Either way, as far as I was concerned, I was captain by default. Wilf was suspended, Steve Sims was injured and Pat Rice, who was club captain but had barely played all season, was coming to the end of his playing days. I was one of the oldest ones left.'

The Watford manager had, in fact, toyed with giving Rice a sentimental farewell appearance at Wembley, where he had played in five FA Cup finals for Arsenal between 1971 and 1980. A week before the Hornets swayed up English football's most celebrated promenade, on the last day of the League season, Rice made a nostalgic encore against the Gunners in a 2-1 win at Vicarage Road, the final instalment of a career spanning 665 games for Arsenal and Watford.

But right-back David Bardsley had recovered from a slight knee-ligament injury in good time to declare himself fit, and GT took the unusual step of announcing his Wembley side a week in advance to the players, hoping it would settle them and enable them to focus on the final without wasting nervous energy on speculation about selection – and Les Taylor would be the skipper.

Most of the narrative surrounding Watford's contribution to 19 May 1984 has been well-chronicled over the years: Elton's tears during 'Abide with Me'; AC Milan striker Luther Blissett reduced to envious bystander and ITV pundit less than a year after he had left Watford in a then-record £1 million transfer; Michael Barrymore's unfunny cabaret at breakfast, at the behest of television companies with hours of airtime to fill in the build-up; and, of course, Andy Gray's controversial goal which did for the spectacle what a pin does for an inflated balloon.

Less well known is that Watford's captain by default forgot to execute one of the big day's token but symbolic deeds. Look closely at photographs of Taylor shaking hands with Everton skipper Kevin Ratcliffe in the centre-circle before kick-off and he has no pennant to exchange with his opposite number.

'Either I left it on the bench during the warm-up or in the dressing room before the teams came out of the tunnel,' he reveals. 'But I forgot all about it and I've no idea what happened to it. Whoever picked up the pennant probably didn't realise they'd got a little piece of Watford's history. I felt a bit sheepish later, but at least it wasn't as if I forgot the ribbons to tie around the Cup.'

After a promising start, Watford's back four – the youngest in a major Wembley final, comprising Bardsley (19), Steve Terry (21), Lee Sinnott (18) and Neil Price (20) – were squeezed by Everton's experienced forwards. The occasion itself was dubbed the 'friendly final' because the fans' sporting behaviour bucked the trend of English football's descent into hooliganism, but the game was an anti-climax.

Taylor could take only finite satisfaction in his personal performance and his contribution standing up well under the additional burden of captaincy. 'The best chances on the day probably fell to me,' he says. 'One skimmed the post, and another was going in until the slightest deflection off [Everton left-back] John Bailey took it just wide, and we didn't even get a corner for it. Even now, I close my eyes and one of those shots goes in . . . and then I snap out of my daydream and reality kicks in again. Once Everton went ahead, the belief seemed to drain from us. In the whole of our Cup run, that was the worst we played. We probably got to Wembley because of our front four, but when it mattered most we couldn't get them in the game. I remember going to a party afterwards at [Watford director] John Reid's house, with a big marquee in the garden, but it felt a bit odd celebrating after you've lost a final. What I'll always remember is how many fans turned out on the Sunday morning when we did a bus tour around the town. Incredible.'

The following season, when he made 48 appearances in all competitions, was effectively Taylor's last as the heartbeat of Watford's midfield. Although the campaign finished with three memorable games in seven days – consecutive 5-1 wins against Tottenham and Manchester United, followed by a narrow 4-3 defeat at Liverpool – the Hornets manager felt his 'machine' was in need of new spark plugs. Brian Talbot, an FA Cup specialist who became the first player to win the trophy in successive seasons with different clubs (in 1978 and 1979), was signed from Arsenal to replace Taylor in the first team. It is fair to say Watford's jilted Wembley captain took it badly.

'Graham felt I had lost something since my knee operation,' he concedes. 'He was very honest with me and, looking back now with 20–20 hindsight, he was probably right. But it still hurt to hear your manager basically say your best days were behind you. For five years I had put my heart and soul into playing for Watford, and did nearly everything I had ever set out to achieve in the game. It wasn't the end of my career, but it was the end of a chapter.

'In all my time I never got sent off and never got suspended. I played hard but fair, and I'm proud of that record – although I don't think I would have lasted a season in the modern game. But after 200-odd games I could see the writing on the wall. I knew the day was coming where it was time for me to leave. For the first time in my career I felt neglected. No, not neglected – rejected. I can remember we had a social gathering, a Christmas "do" with alcohol involved, and I said a couple of things to Graham Taylor which I later regretted. I can't remember exactly what I said, and it's probably just as well, but I was a bit outspoken where I should have bit my tongue. The day I left Watford, and signed for Reading, I went to see the boss and apologised because I knew, deep down, what he had done for me. Hands down, he was the best manager I ever worked with. He was a great man.

'He gave me the platform to play in the First Division, an FA Cup final and in Europe, but the club was changing and I felt I was getting left behind. I didn't go running to the papers, but I hated the thought of leaving Watford because they gave me my happiest times as a footballer.

'At least I went back to Wembley with Reading in the Simod Cup final [a short-lived knockout competition for clubs in the top two divisions] and we beat Luton 4-1 in the final. I thought Watford fans would approve of that, although in fairness Luton did go back there a fortnight later and beat Arsenal to win the League Cup.'

When his playing career ground to a halt at Colchester and, for one game, at Baldock Town – where Watford would pick up striker Kevin Phillips five years later – Taylor switched vocations and began his intermission as a hospital porter. But he was invited back to Oxford to help with coaching sessions at their centre of excellence, and 24 years later he is still the club's youth development manager.

'In a sense my working life has come full circle,' he says. 'I left home at 16 and came down from the north-east to join Oxford. They gave me that opportunity to forge a career in the game, and they have always been good to me. In return I have been their captain, in charge of youth development and I even coached the women's team part-time for a while, which I really enjoyed.

'You get a real buzz from seeing young players step up – in my early days doing this job, we had a lad called Dexter Blackstock who grew up locally in Blackbird Leys and Cowley, and he went to Southampton for good money, on to Nottingham Forest for big money and eventually played international football for Antigua and Barbuda. We have produced a few international-class players here, but they don't always get pushed at that level because Oxford are not in the Premier League.

'But there are also too many youngsters now who get an opportunity, blessed with all the talent you could ask, and they just don't take it. If you knuckle down and work hard, you never know where your career might take you. I'm still the only captain to lead Watford out in an FA Cup final – hopefully someone else will get the privilege soon – but for sentimental reasons that day will always mean a lot to me, and the medal did as well.'

The runners-up medal presented to Taylor by HRH the Duchess of Kent at Wembley in 1984 sold at auction in Chester for £3,960 in June 2010. The last time he saw it was when he gave it to his ex-wife, for their daughter to inherit, 14 years earlier.

5

WILF ROSTRON

ROGER AND OUT

Classy club, the Arsenal. Marble halls, bronze busts and all that.

Once, on the retreat from a successful night in Europe, the chartered plane taking the Gunners home had just levelled off at cruising altitude after take-off when chairman Denis Hill-Wood suggested champagne to toast a job well done. Moments later, the cabin steward sheepishly approached Hill-Wood to offer his profuse apologies. 'I'm terribly sorry, sir,' he fawned. 'We seem to have left our crate of champagne on the runway.'

Deeply troubled by this catering malfunction, Hill-Wood briefly contemplated triumph at 33,000 feet without bubbles before reaching his splendid conclusion. 'Oh dear,' he mused. 'Well, we'd better go back and fetch it, hadn't we?'

Air traffic control records do not reveal whether the Gunners chairman's pitch for an aeronautical u-turn was successful, but the club remained under the control of three generations in the Hill-Wood dynasty for 84 years. His son, Peter, a personable, forthright, cigar-chomping Old Etonian, took over in the boardroom and maintained the family tradition for uninhibited candour by sacking manager Terry Neill after a poor sequence of results, which included losing to Watford, home and away, during the Hornets' first-ever season in the top flight. When Neill rushed into print with his memoirs, he was astonished to find his old chairman at the book's launch, asking for a signed copy.

Wilf Rostron began his professional career at Arsenal and loved it. Originally scouted by the Gunners on Wearside, where he was already on the talent-spotters' radar as an England schoolboy international, he would be given every Friday afternoon off school at St Thomas Aquinas in Sunderland, catch the train down to London, stay overnight in digs then turn out every Saturday for Arsenal's youth team or reserves.

'It was the high life,' he laughs. 'I was allowed to bunk off school early on a Friday because it was only games lessons, so I was missing football at school to play football for Arsenal, and they knew where I was going. I would nip across town, pick up my ticket and jump on the train down to London. Those old Inter City trains went at a fair old lick. It used to take all day to get down there by road, but on the train it was only three hours. I felt very grown-up.'

Arsenal's manager, at the time Rostron first set foot in Highbury, was Bertie Mee, who had guided the club to the League and Cup double in 1971. The pair would cross paths again at Vicarage Road before the decade was out, but the teenager's first impressions of him were favourable.

'Very straight-laced, he was. Very proper. He was the first manager I worked under in the game, and players all said the same thing: you always knew exactly where you stood with him,' says Rostron. 'The great thing about Bertie was that he came and watched games at all levels if Arsenal's first team were playing at home, and if he liked what he saw, you got a game at the next level. I was still only 16 when I first played for the reserves there. Pat Rice was already well established in the first team at Arsenal when I walked in the door. He became another familiar face later in my career.'

Three weeks after turning 17 and graduating from apprentice to professional terms, Rostron was thrilled to be included in the Arsenal squad who travelled to Barcelona for a prestige friendly in the Nou Camp in October 1973. The incomparable Johan Cruyff had finally completed a world record £920,000 transfer from Ajax (after the move had been held up by three months of red tape and squabbling over the schedule of instalments), and Barcelona had lined up a series of exhibition friendlies to help bring the king of Total Football's fitness up to speed. In a smart move Arsenal had consented to the mid-season trip if Barcelona agreed to a reciprocal visit to north London five months later, with an explicit guarantee that superstar Cruyff would play, to provide the opposition for long-serving winger George Armstrong's testimonial.

'For a kid of 17 who had just left home, to be facing the world's greatest player being unveiled in front of 100,000 people was a fantastic opportunity,' says Rostron. 'If we were not the first team to play Barcelona after Cruyff had signed for them, there was a lot of attention on it. I thought I was only going on the trip for experience, but a few hours before kick-off Bertie Mee pulled me to one side and said, "You are playing tonight." I was only a young lad, and I hadn't even played for the first team at that stage, but I was getting a chance to show what I could do against the man everyone was talking about. At that time, Cruyff was undisputed as the best footballer on the planet. Maybe the plan was to give me 45 minutes and see how I got on, but it felt like it was the best thing that had ever happened to me. I was so excited.

'And then I got injured in the warm-up. I felt my calf go. Apart from the odd bruise, I'd never been injured before in my life. When I realised I couldn't play I was absolutely gutted. To come out of the tunnel, with 100,000 people there, or however many it was – the ground was full – and sit on the bench was so frustrating. I can't tell you how disappointed I was that night.'

Arsenal lost 1-0, and there was a sinister symmetry – prestigious occasion, once-in-a-lifetime opportunity, 100,000 crowd, worldwide audience tuning in, and defeat – when Rostron suffered the other big regret of his career.

'I got over that one – missing out on playing against Cruyff in the Nou Camp,' he muses. 'It took a while, but ten years later, I had just about got it out of my system.' Rostron breaks into a rueful chuckle, and his enduring good humour serves him well, but the rest of us can't bring ourselves to laugh when an honest-to-goodness professional is robbed of the biggest day in his career.

***

Wilf Rostron was, by common consent, the best left-back ever to pull on a Watford shirt. Compile a hybrid XI of the Hornets' greatest-ever team, and the majority of those who saw him play would include Rostron in their line-ups. It speaks volumes for his industry, application and popularity that he was twice voted as the club's player of the season in consecutive years when Luther Blissett scored 30 goals and played for England in one of them, John Barnes floated like a butterfly and stung like a Hornet on the wing, and Mo Johnston could make 24 goals in 35 appearances look easier than chat-up lines on nocturnal assignments.

Part in jest and partly, you suspect, out of acknowledging the truth, dear old Wilf reckons he picked up the award in 1983–84 after winning the sympathy vote by a landslide. But he was such a good player that when Graham Taylor was asked to pick his optimum Watford–Aston Villa combined XI from the two clubs he managed highest up the League ladder, he chose Rostron – and not just because he had the foresight to convert him from left-sided forward to full-back.

Rostron was easy-going by nature, never too full of his own importance, and he made the conversion from winger to left-back - in the space of a single tutorial on the training ground – without a murmur. But while he never kicked up a fuss, Watford supporters feel he was dealt an unfair hand, that his crowning glory was taken away from him unjustly, that the proudest moment any footballer could covet was vandalised by an unspeakable conspiracy of circumstances. And how appropriate that the stars should form such a dastardly alignment at Kenilworth Road, of all places.

If he is bitter about the only missing jigsaw piece in a career spanning 404 appearances in all competitions for Watford, he camouflages the resentment well. But the great pity of Wilf Rostron's contribution to one of English football's feelgood stories is that a Wembley final appearance somehow eluded him, in varying shades of cruelty, five seasons in a row.

What endeared him to the fans was his downright honesty. Rostron never shirked a tackle, and if he was required to man-mark an opponent he would do it with the diligence of a Jack Russell refusing to let go of a burglar's trouser leg. But he never set out to kick a fellow professional. When Taylor pinned the teamsheet on the training-ground noticeboard ahead of the following day's fixture, Rostron accepted it as gospel. If he had been asked to report to the ground at 4 a.m. in his pyjamas, or drive the team bus to an away game, he would have absorbed the instruction with an ambivalent shrug and no dissent.

When Watford's resources at centre-half were not just skeletal but down to the last bare bones, three days after they had reached the FA Cup final, Rostron played at centre-half against Manchester United without complaint. And the Hornets kept a clean sheet.

In short – and there was only about 5 feet 7 inches of him – Rostron was a manager's dream. He was a nugget of gold. He may have been denied his finest hour by a narcissist with a whistle and a highwayman's deck of cards, but scroll through Watford's best moments between 1979 and 1988 and he was involved in nearly all of them: the seven-goal miracle against Southampton, the demolition of European Cup holders Nottingham Forest, promotion to the promised land, the eight-goal romp against his hometown club, runners-up behind

Liverpool, making waves in Europe . . . Rostron wore the badge proudly in them all, and he did the badge proud.

If his form, shortly after arriving at Watford from Sunderland for £150,000 in 1979, was initially fitful, it could be attributed in part to the strain of living in a hotel for five months with a young child while his wife, Jill, was expecting their second baby.

Rostron had resorted to kidology when signing for the Hornets, revealing in Geoff Sweet and Graham Burton's book *A Tale of the Unexpected* how he travelled to discuss terms with Taylor and asked to sleep on it overnight so he could discuss the deal with his missus. That night Rostron told his wife he had already signed on the dotted line – and when her reaction was supportive, he knew it was the right move. 'Jill was a Sunderland girl, and had never moved away from the north-east before,' he says. 'But once I had seen how she reacted, and she was absolutely fine about it, I went back to Watford and signed the next day.'

On his exploratory drive south Rostron had fallen into the trap, like many other long-distance travellers, of thinking Watford Gap services signalled journey's end, little realising he had another 60 miles to go. Happily, he was not deterred by an extra hour behind the wheel, although property prices in Hertfordshire were a sobering prospect. 'We drove all that way, and when we finally got there it felt like the estate agents were having a laugh,' he says.

First impressions count for a lot in football, and Rostron's Watford debut was sprinkled with promise in a 2-0 win against Newcastle at Vicarage Road – a satisfying result for a 'Mackem' against his old rivals from across the Tyne–Wear divide. But just as the Hornets needed time to consolidate in more gilded company, after successive promotions, their new winger blew hot and cold as he adjusted to his new surroundings.

Taylor had embarked on an overhaul of his squad, and in truth Watford ended the 1970s as they had begun the decade – happy to keep their heads above water in the rapids of the Second Division. But as his family coped admirably with one of the longest stays in hotel accommodation until chat-show clot Alan Partridge plundered the all-you-can-eat breakfast buffet with his 12-inch plate, at least there were familiar accents at the bar.

Among the other new recruits checking in under Taylor's reshuffle were defender Mick Henderson, who had been Rostron's teammate at Sunderland, and goalkeeper Eric Steele, a Geordie whose days at Brighton had been numbered after an out-of-character but conspicuous punch-up with teammate Gary Williams in front of 52,000 fans at Old Trafford.

The colony of north-east expats would convene at the refuelling station, and Rostron was grateful to the players' wives who virtually formed a rota to make sure his pregnant other half was not left to struggle alone in the hotel, but he found those early months at Watford difficult. Occasionally, the light that flickered on the left wing would burst into flame, notably in a dazzling first half in the FA Cup third round at Queens Park Rangers, the first of seven Cup runs where he played in the quarter-finals or beyond for the Hornets.

When you reel off all seven on the scroll of honour, Rostron sounds surprised. 'I didn't realise we played in so many,' he says. 'But our game was probably suited to Cup football. We were always prepared to risk losing games in order to win them.'

By the end of the 1980–81 season Rostron was in and out of the side, and he had started only two League games in the promotion campaign the following year when Taylor made an inspired call as his solution to a defensive quandary.

Keith Pritchett and Kenny Jackett, the Hornets' two qualified left-backs, were both injured and, on the evidence of

Watford's fortuitous 2-1 win at Rotherham – decorated by Ian Bolton's freakish, wind-assisted equaliser from inside his own half – they were not going to sustain the last 20 games of the run-in with two right-backs, Pat Rice and Henderson, holding the fort in a lop-sided back line.

The following week Taylor pulled Rostron aside and told him, 'I'm not saying you are a left-back, but I think you can play there.' The pair left the main group and GT, a full-back himself in his playing days, indulged the willing understudy in a one-on-one tutorial.

'I'd love to tell you it was a masterstroke,' says Rostron. 'But there weren't many of us still standing who could kick with their left foot. I was just about the last one he'd got left. But he set up a private session for me and it began with him trying to take me on. No disrespect to the boss, but it wasn't too difficult to get the better of him, which was probably part of the plan, as it gave me confidence.

'Then he "borrowed" one of the youth-team wingers, followed by one of the reserves, and he kept raising the bar. I had to learn very quickly, because each time he brought in a new player to run at me, the power and pace increased, but somehow I coped and managed to handle it until the boss said, "Right, that's it – you're playing left-back tomorrow." I was happy to be back in the side, because I'd been sub a few times and on the fringes. Then I realised we were playing Chelsea, whose winger Clive Walker had given us a few chasings in the previous couple of seasons. But it worked out well, we won 1-0, I stayed in the team as left-back for the rest of the season and we won promotion – happy days. How did I slip into that new role so quickly? I couldn't tell you – but maybe it helped that, as a full-back, the whole game is unfolding in front of you. And we were such an attacking side that I didn't feel it stopped me from getting forward. It's funny how these things work out sometimes. Watford bought me as a left-winger, but I played the vast majority of my games for them as a full-back.'

There was soon tangible evidence that Rostron's conversion would not diminish his contribution in the final third of the pitch. He found the top corner, from outside the box, in a top-of-the-table draw with the heretics, and the Hornets were over the line, their place at the top table secure, after losing only two out of 18 League games with their rookie left-back.

And when Watford ruffled more feathers than a fox let loose in a chicken run, finishing second in the League, Rostron was ever-present, a reassuring blur of enterprise and bustle down that flank. His goals tended to be memorable, like the skimming-stone winner in added time against Aston Villa and a thunderous shot at Ipswich, but the most impressive aspect of his contribution to a marvellous season was his consistency.

Goalkeeper Steve Sherwood, who was no slouch himself that year, says, 'You always knew what you were going to get from Wilf, which was 90 minutes of total application. When he made that switch to left-back, you wondered how it might affect us as a defensive unit, but his concentration was top drawer. If he ever had a bad game, I can't remember it.'

Rostron was still mildly stunned to win the *Watford Observer* player of the season gong in a strong field where the front four created such merry mayhem.

'I was very, very proud of that award because it's the supporters who decide it and they are the people who pay their money at the gate,' he says. 'I would have voted for Luther, myself, and I probably did. I might even have cut the voting coupon out of the paper and sent it in. He was fantastic that season, a lad who had never played in the top division before and he scored 30 goals.'

Rostron is even more staggered when he learns of the stellar cast who never won the award: in the class of 1983, Blissett,

Barnes, Nigel Callaghan and Kenny Jackett were among those
never to wear the crown. 'None of them ever won it, but I
won it twice? That's incredible. Goals win games, and our front
four were difficult to stop when they played well, but we had
a fabulous camaraderie at Watford and that wasn't just limited
to the starting XI at first-team level. It ran through the whole
club. Everyone knew what their job was, and what they were
required to do if they wanted to stay in the team. We were fit
and, yes, we were direct, but we didn't just lump it up the field
and hope for the best. Each player understood his job, and it
was drilled into us until it became second nature.'

As time went by, one of Rostron's regular beats was as
an unlikely predator at the far post from Watford's near-post
corner routine. Taylor argued that opposing defenders were
inclined to ignore the diminutive full-back lurking in the box.
More fool them – for a wee Mackem, our Wilf was more than
decent in the air. In the 1983–84 season alone his seven goals
from full-back – none of them from the penalty spot – included
three headers.

'For some reason, I used to have to attack the far post at
corners,' says Rostron. 'If I wasn't the smallest player on the
pitch, I wasn't usually in the top 20 of the tallest. But it was my
job to try to get on the end of chances if we got a flick-on at
the near post, which was always difficult to defend. We used to
pack the box with yellow shirts, and it was a productive routine
because the delivery [from Nigel Callaghan] was nearly always
so good. As someone who started out further up the pitch, I
enjoyed being in the thick of it at set-pieces. I preferred to be
in the box.'

Never was Rostron's expertise as a secret weapon in the
final third better demonstrated than on Watford's wonderful
adventures in Europe. Passport control was effectively where he
took over the captain's armband from Pat Rice as the Hornets

embarked on a memorable tour of the continent, confounding the odds as they reached the UEFA Cup's last 16 before bowing out on a rutted ice rink in Prague.

It was Rostron who shook hands, exchanged pennants with German international Hans-Peter Briegel - a Dolph Lundgren lookalike built like a brick tenement block - and led the Hornets' wonderful blitz to overturn Kaiserslautern's two-goal cushion at Vicarage Road. Steve Sims had been skipper for the first leg in Germany, where around 2,000 cultural attachés from Hertfordshire joined the crusade against a club who had twice won the German Bundesliga (and have twice won it since).

One of the Hornets' summer signings, George Reilly, was ineligible because he joined the club beyond the deadline for UEFA competitions, while another, midfielder Paul Atkinson, had broken his leg in a pre-season friendly at Reading. To all intents, the side Watford put out in the futuristic stadium atop the Betzenberg hill overlooking the city, should not have stood a chance in such experienced company.

They were entitled to feel short-changed by a 3-1 defeat, where Rostron would have enjoyed a place in the record books as Watford's first-ever goalscorer in Europe with the equaliser if 19-year-old striker Jimmy Gilligan had not reached Callaghan's left-wing cross first.

'We were gutted to concede the third one quite late on,' says Rostron. 'But the away goal gave us an outside chance, and the way we took the fight to them in the second leg was absolutely incredible. That was a team of kids – we shouldn't have stood a chance, but they took us for granted.'

In Lionel Birnie's chronicle of a golden age, *Enjoy the Game*, and the story of Watford's miraculous win in Sofia against Levski Spartak in *Tales from the Vicarage* Volume 2, Graham Taylor revealed how he sneaked in to watch Kaiserslautern train before the return leg at Vicarage Road after groundsman Les Simmons had 'accidentally' left a gate open at the top of Occupation Road.

The purpose of Taylor's espionage was not to gain any tactical knowledge, but to ascertain the Germans' attitude. They pitched up in an assortment of casual clutter, which smacked of arrogance and an assumption that the tie was already done and dusted. It took just 10 minutes for Watford to wipe out Kaiserslautern's advantage in a breathless siege which defied logic.

Barely 12 months earlier, on the opening day of the season, I had reluctantly caught the 321 bus over the border into Bedfordshire, to cover Watford winning the reserves' Football Combination derby for the now-defunct *Evening Post–Echo,* while the first team were launching their maiden First Division campaign against Everton. Gilligan and Ian Richardson formed the Hornets' little-and-large double act up front that afternoon in the neighbours' corrugated dungeon. Now here they were, carrying the fight to good-quality opposition in Europe, in a fervid atmosphere cooking under the lights. Rising to the occasion, Taylor's boy scouts set about their task like fully qualified Marines. Two-goal Richardson, Gilligan, Richard Jobson, Charlie Palmer and John Barnes – all 20 or under – played with a maturity beyond their years; Steve Terry and Callaghan were almost seasoned campaigners at 21; and Rostron, who turned 27 the day after the game, was a confirmed veteran. The noise reverberating around the packed Vicarage Road end belied the absence of a roof, a phenomenon Rostron noted from the outset. 'Something seemed to happen at Watford whenever we played under the lights,' he says. 'We had a great relationship with the fans, which went beyond the actual games, but for night matches they seemed to find their voice. You couldn't just hear the difference – you could feel it.'

If Rostron slipped into captaincy as effortlessly as he pulled on a pair of socks, he did not feel any more or less qualified for the officers' mess than some of his teammates. He says, 'It wasn't difficult to be captain of those players. It goes back to what I said earlier about everyone knowing their jobs. You didn't need to be an arm-waver or finger-pointer. If someone was getting pulled out of position, a quiet word was usually enough, and one look at their face would tell you if they agreed. But those lads weren't hard to captain. Graham Taylor had us so well drilled, and so well organised, that the hardest part was calling "heads" or "tails" before kick-off. I honestly believe anyone in that team with a bit of experience, and who had played a certain number of games for Watford, could have done the job.'

The extra-time win in Sofia was, arguably, Rostron's finest hour. Despite their captain's thunderous first-time shot from the edge of the box to put them in front, Watford appeared to have missed the boat when they were held 1-1 at home by the Bulgarians, with a thankless trip behind the Iron Curtain still to come.

Their task looked even steeper, and the odds forbiddingly distant, when they fell behind from the penalty spot after just five minutes in the Vasil Levski stadium – and Rostron found himself a marked man. He says, 'I'd scored a real cracker at home, but the Levski players were after me in a big way out there when I caught one of their lads with my elbow. It was a total accident, honest. We both jumped, eyes on the ball, and I cut his head open, but there was no intent on my part. I didn't even know what had happened until the fella came running up to me, pointing to the damage above his eye. For the next 20 minutes he was chasing me all over the pitch, trying to kick lumps out of me. I was trying to apologise to him, and let him know I didn't mean it, but I don't think my sign language made it across the language barrier. His teammates all seemed to think it was deliberate, even though it wasn't. Some of the tackles in that game were a bit fiery and left nothing to the imagination. It could have got a bit nasty.'

Old stager Ian Bolton, like Rostron pressed into service as an auxiliary midfielder, ran himself into the uneven turf that night, warning 18-year-old Neil Price, making his first-team debut at left-back against speedy winger Bozhidar Iskrenov, to 'get stuck in as hard as you can' when the acrimony was at its most intense. Watford had already demonstrated a youthful exuberance by turning over Kaiserslautern in the previous round; in Bulgaria their performance was also a triumph of steel, backbone and rallying round their skipper when he was unfairly cast as a villain.

'They were a good side with five or six internationals,' says Rostron. 'To come through in such a hostile atmosphere said a lot about our young lads, but it also said a lot about the DNA of the club. The players who came in knew what they had to do.'

Rostron's crowning glory was his goal, deep into the second period of extra time, as Watford executed their near-post corner routine to perfection and their phantom poacher rose at the far post to put the Hornets 2-1 ahead on the night. It was a majestic header and a memorable celebration, Rostron's right-fisted upper-cut towards the bank of stunned Levski fans behind the goal a perfect euphemism for the knockout blow.

Seconds earlier, before his perfect dead-ball delivery had picked out Sims for the telling flick-on at the front post, Callaghan had been startled by smashing glass landing just behind him as bottles rained down from the heaving tribunes. As the referee trotted over to inspect the debris behind Callaghan, Levski's concentration wavered and Rostron called across to the Hornets' man-of-the-match: 'One bit of real quality, son, and we're there.'

For those of us who were there it was probably, in isolation, the greatest result in Watford's history. By the time Richardson had applied the proverbial cherry to the cake in the dying seconds Levski fans were lighting bonfires on the terraces as gestures of surrender, and manager Taylor, surveying the remnants of his decimated squad, was about to place a spoof advertisement in *The Times* as a call for reinforcements: 'Wanted: professional footballers. Many vacancies now available at First Division football club for men (or women) aged between 18 and 80 and prepared to work on a Saturday. Some playing experience desirable but preference will be given to those with two arms and two legs in good working order! Apply in writing, in the first instance, to G. Taylor, Vicarage Road stadium, Watford.'

***

As Watford's stand-in captain at the FA Cup final explains elsewhere in this volume, Les Taylor planned to send the suspended Wilf Rostron up the steps to collect the trophy if the Hornets had beaten Everton at Wembley.

'I wouldn't have let him do it,' says Rostron, even though his exclusion from the biggest day of his football life still rankles as much with Hornets supporters as Andy Gray's foul on Steve Sherwood and the defeat itself. 'For different reasons, I was just as gutted to miss out [three years later] when we lost the semi-final against Tottenham.'

There is no easy way to address the elephant in the room. In almost 50 years of watching Watford it remains the single greatest travesty that Rostron never played in a Wembley final. If Luther Blissett is our favourite son, Wilf is our favourite martyr.

In 1982, when Glenn Roeder was suspended from QPR's replay against Tottenham, at least he had the honour of leading Rangers out in the original FA Cup final. Twelve months later, Steve Foster was banned from Brighton's 2-2 draw with Manchester United but eligible for the replay. But fortune deserted Rostron the following year, a connivance of foul luck, self-important refereeing and a parody of justice bordering on blasphemy denying him a unique privilege among Watford captains.

More than three decades later he insists he feels no more torment, no more anger and no more resentment about missing out on the FA Cup final than he did in 1984. Somehow – and this is a tribute to his conspicuous lack of self-pity – Rostron regards his exile on the naughty step as simply 'one of those things and you have to deal with it'.

If that is the case, he is blessed with the equable temperament of a saint, but perhaps it is instructive that Wilf remembers the Hornets losing a Milk Cup quarter-final at home to Sunderland in 1985 (to a fluke goal on an icy pitch) more than the famous eight-goal annihilation of his hometown club. It suggests he was ideal captaincy material all along because he didn't get carried away by success or wallow in despair when setbacks came calling.

At least he has some happy memories of Watford's only FA Cup semi-final victory (in six attempts to date) after the narrow 1-0 win against Third Division underdogs Plymouth Argyle at Villa Park. He sounds surprised when I tell him that he looked nervous on the BBC footage as he led the Hornets out before kick-off. 'Did I? From my point of view, I wasn't any more nervous than normal,' he says. 'It's normal that you would have a few butterflies before such an important game, but nerves can actually help if you control them. Players who are nervous aren't usually complacent. That can't be a bad thing.

'We played crap on the day – or if not crap, nowhere near as well as we could – but we achieved what we set out to achieve, and that's all that matters in a semi-final.'

Little did Rostron suspect that a dastardly fate was heading his way a fortnight later. Although our conversation thus far had been the equivalent of dancing round handbags in a nightclub, eventually the time came to grasp the nettle and mention the name one dared not speak – Roger Milford. Or, as he is known to a generation of Watford fans, Roger bloody Milford.

Graham Taylor was convinced he contributed, unwittingly, to the wretchedness of 28 April 1984 at Kenilworth Road by telling referee Milford when the teamsheets were handed in, 'Don't worry, you won't get any trouble from my players today – they've got the Cup final in a couple of weeks.' The Hornets manager feared he may have planted a seed of controversy in the Bristol official's mind with that throwaway remark, although Rostron shrugs, 'He wasn't to blame. He didn't make the tackle that landed me in trouble. He wasn't the one who sent me off.'

Although he would prefer to erase the incident from his mind, as if wiping the contents of a memory stick, Rostron admits he has 'total' recall of it. 'I don't know what their lad [Paul Elliott] had eaten for breakfast, but some of his tackles were ridiculous,' says the Watford legend. 'He had already committed several fouls, and I'm pretty sure he had been booked, when we went in for a 50–50 tackle and I thought he was going to "do" me. I did raise my foot – only to protect myself – and although there was a collision of sorts, neither of us followed through to commit a foul. It was a funny type of tackle because we both ended up trying to protect ourselves and there was actually nothing malicious in it. When the ref blew, I thought the worst I could get was a booking because it wasn't even a foul, really. And when he reached for his pocket, if he was going to do anything I thought their lad was off because he was already on a yellow card. I had a word with the ref about the way he had been letting Elliott carry on and conducting himself because it must have been his fifth foul, and I said, "How many more is he going to commit and you let him off?" I don't know if my remark wound him up, but he brought out the red card and sent us both off. I couldn't believe it. I said, "You let him get away with all those fouls and you're sending me off for that?" I'm not even sure it was a foul, maybe a yellow card at worst, but a red? Come off it, man! Never in a million years.

'Looking back, I wonder if it might have turned out different if I hadn't said anything to the referee. Of course I regret the consequences, and maybe if I hadn't argued with him or discussed it with him he might have acted differently. But it was the only red card of my career, the only time I was ever suspended, and I couldn't have paid a much higher price.'

Did the penny drop straight away that he would miss the big day at Wembley?

Rostron hesitates momentarily. 'I did know, yes. The crowd were giving me all sorts when I followed Elliott up the tunnel and I shouted after him, "Hey, I'll miss the Cup final now – thanks a lot." A couple of weeks before, the lads had been warned that anyone banned for picking up ten bookings over the season was in danger of being suspended for Wembley, but everyone had made it safely beyond the cut-off point. The only way anyone was going to miss out was by being sent off.'

Graham Taylor took his wife Rita to watch a Shakespeare play in Stratford-upon-Avon that night, but he hated every minute of it – nothing to do with the Bard's script or the acting, but he knew the penalty for Rostron's red card would be monstrous. It ruined his night out and cast a shadow over the build-up to Watford's once-in-a-lifetime opportunity.

Rostron went home to Leverstock Green and warned his wife Jill the phone would probably be ringing off the hook. The only call he could remember answering, in the aftermath of Milford's caricature of fairness, was from Geoff Sweet, a journalist he knew from the *Evening Post–Echo*, where the presses had fallen silent fewer than six months earlier, missing out on huge sales of souvenir editions as the Hornets marched on Wembley.

'I stayed in that night and I got a few calls, but I didn't answer them,' says Rostron. 'I didn't see much point in going out and pretending to enjoy myself. I knew there was nothing I could do about it – in those days, there was no right of appeal. My ban wasn't going to get overturned. You just had to take your punishment and live with it. Although Jill used to come to matches, she wasn't really into her football that much – if that makes sense – but when I told her what had happened, she knew straight away what it meant. I just told her, "We will probably be getting a lot of phone calls tonight. Just leave them." When I think about it now, maybe I'm a bit surprised about how I dealt with it, but shouting and swearing wasn't going to make any difference. The damage was done.'

In the long term, Watford manager Taylor seemed more distressed by the outcome than his outlawed captain. Eighteen years later, writing in the *Daily Telegraph*, he said, 'For me, the build-up to Wembley started as soon as we beat Plymouth in the semi-final. Unfortunately, fate took a hand in the form of referee Roger Milford – he of the Shirley Temple curls and shortest of shorts. It was Wilf's only dismissal in his long professional career. He missed the final and never had another opportunity, while "Shirley" pranced away in a number of top games. They say forgive and forget. Perhaps I can the former, but not the latter.'

In *Tales from the Vicarage* Volume 2 Taylor admitted he was so angry with Milford's decision that he grabbed the Bristol official by the throat in the tunnel afterwards – and GT admitted he was lucky to escape disciplinary action by the Football Association for his red-card rage. When Milford later expressed his sorrow that Rostron would be excluded from the most glamorous works outing in Watford's 103-year history, he was shot down in flames again by Taylor, who was having none of his 'sanctimonious claptrap'.

Always a reluctant spectator when he wasn't playing, Rostron briefly contemplated giving Wembley a miss altogether because he felt 'a bit awkward' around teammates who were excited about the biggest occasion of their careers. Within a few days, however, he resolved to offer them moral support from the bench after Taylor gave him the option of travelling with the team and being part of the official entourage, or keeping a low profile.

'All the lads said how bad they felt for me, but I told them not to worry because there was nothing they could do about it,' says Rostron. 'I trained with them during the week, I was in the dressing room with them before the game, and I walked round the pitch with them afterwards, but in the end we all felt the same way – disappointed.

'That's my biggest regret about the Cup final: we didn't play anywhere near as well as we could. On the day, Everton were a bit too canny for us. Our back four was so young [David Bardsley, Neil Price, Steve Terry and Lee Sinnott were aged between 18 and 21] I just wished I could have been out there to help them. You kind of feel you could have given them a bit more confidence – not from shouting at them, but just settling them down.

'But the second goal shouldn't have stood, it absolutely killed us and we got beat. More than anything, I felt sorry for the lads who played more than myself.'

Milford, as supporters who lived through the mid-1980s will remember through gritted teeth, was not quite finished with inflicting his own brand of tyranny on Watford. Two years later, after holding Liverpool to a goalless draw in the FA Cup quarter-finals at Anfield, his late intervention in the replay at Vicarage Road was every bit as costly for the Hornets as Rostron's red card.

John Barnes' stunning free-kick, drilled into the bottom corner, looked like sending Taylor's side into their second semi-final in three seasons when Milford adjudged Ian Rush's fall in the box, which did not appear to be instigated by any contact from home keeper Tony Coton, to be a penalty. Jan Molby saved the day for Liverpool from the spot, Rush struck again in extra time, and another possible trip to Wembley disappeared from Rostron's horizon.

'Was it Milford? To be honest, I didn't twig that it was him,' admits Rostron. 'It looked harsh from where I was, but sometimes those are given and sometimes they aren't. But I always enjoyed playing against Liverpool – they were my favourite opponents because they were the real test of how good you were. I loved going to Anfield, even in the game where I gave away two penalties in front of the Kop, because Liverpool fans never gave us any stick. They clapped us off one night when we lost 4-3 after we had led 2-0 at half-time. Kenny Dalglish came off the bench and turned the game by playing out of his skin for 20 minutes. He was unplayable, and I think we got done by Rush in the last minute. But they were a great crowd. I know quite a few Liverpool fans and they stood up for Watford when others complained about our style.'

Rostron was more upset by the grotesque cruelty of the chain of events, 13 months later, which slammed the door shut on Watford's hopes of another Wembley final appearance.

The legend of the wine waiter – chief executive Eddie Plumley's son, Gary, signed as emergency goalkeeping cover from front of house at his Ebbw Vale wine bar – has long been enshrined in FA Cup folklore. In *Rocket Men* Steve Sherwood tells the story, in heart-wrenching detail, how the Hornets' preparations for the 1987 FA Cup semi-final against Tottenham were sabotaged by outrageous luck and, dare we venture it, a rare misjudgement by Graham Taylor.

First-choice keeper Tony Coton had already suffered a season-ending fractured thumb when Sherwood dislocated a finger in the week of the semi-final. Despite 'Shirley' passing a fitness test on the morning of the game, Taylor inexplicably gambled on throwing Plumley – who had played in Europe for Newport County – in at the deep end. Taylor's hunch backfired: Watford were 3-0 down by half-time, and two of the goals could be laid at their stand-in keeper's door. They lost 4-1 and, with that supine anti-climax, went Rostron's last chance of playing in a Wembley final.

True, Watford did reach the quarter-finals yet again, for the fourth time in five seasons, in 1988, and they led 1-0 before slipping to a feeble 2-1 defeat at Plough Lane against ten-man Wimbledon. But the Hornets were sliding towards relegation by then, and at the time we did not know if being bullied into submission by John Fashanu, Vinnie Jones and company was a blessing in disguise.

Sherwood never hid his despair at being left out against Spurs, but Rostron's testimony reveals the goalkeeping crisis had an unsettling effect on the players.

'It was incredibly difficult to take,' he says. 'I think it was the only time in my whole career, at any level, where we didn't have anyone left to play in goal – and it happened in the build-up to our biggest game of the season. To lose one senior goalkeeper in a training ground accident is bad luck, but when it happens twice . . . I couldn't believe it. We were looking at each other and saying, "What the hell are we going to do?" Our luck was so ridiculous that we could only laugh about it. We had gone past the transfer deadline, so we couldn't sign a keeper or bring one in on loan from another League club. It had to be a free agent.

'To be fair to the lad, he came in and performed fine in training, and that must have influenced the boss's thinking when he had to pick the semi-final team. But, obviously, he didn't have a great match, and it was all over by half-time.

I'm not blaming anyone, but when you make such a big change as a different goalkeeper it does affect the team. I don't think he was very tall, so in the back of our minds we were probably worrying about how he would deal with crosses, although that wasn't an issue on the day.

'I was asked to mark Glenn Hoddle – Kenny Jackett would normally have done it, but he was injured – so I moved into midfield to try and keep him quiet. Ninety-nine per cent of the time we would have played the game our way, but on this occasion we wanted to stop Tottenham channelling everything through Hoddle. Although the game was a bit of a disaster for us, pretty much from start to finish, I managed to get under his skin, because I wouldn't leave him alone. At half-time we discussed changing it, but there didn't seem much point in ripping up the game plan at 3-0 down, and Hoddle was unhappy when I still stuck to him. He was moaning, "Come on, Wilf – give us a break!" I think I annoyed him, which was quite funny, but the game was gone.'

Did it feel like the last chance of leading Watford out at Wembley may have disappeared with the ill-fated 'wine waiter' experiment?

'Not really – I honestly didn't think about it like that,' says Rostron. 'Some things are just not meant to be. What's the point in looking back and feeling bitter about individual moments when my nine-and-a-half years at Watford brought me so much enjoyment? I don't think the club ever changed in all the time I was there. Graham Taylor and Elton John ran it like a family firm from the day I walked in until we went our separate ways. And although there are people who were not OK with some of the things Dave Bassett wanted to do when he took over, I got on fine with "Harry" and I wish it had worked out better for him.'

Didn't Bassett drop you for the first time in about six years, though? 'Yes, but I obviously didn't mind that much because I joined him at Sheffield United later,' says Rostron, one of the last players to complete the notable Steel City double by playing for both Sheffield United and Wednesday.

'When I look back on my time at Watford it's not defined by any single thing, except mainly happiness. There was promotion, Europe and being voted player of the season twice, although I think the second one was a sympathy vote for missing the Cup final. I don't know what I'd say to Roger Milford if I met him now, because I don't think like that. I missed a football match that everyone would love to play in, but life goes on. Complaining about it now won't make any difference.'

When Rostron decided he did not fancy being chewed up, spat out and forced to move around the country like a pinball chasing jobs in coaching and management, he moved into the furniture business and settled back in his home town of Sunderland. It is 30 years since we last saw him in a Watford shirt, and a concerted ovation for his contribution to the club's history was long overdue by the time he appeared on stage at the Palace theatre in *Tales from the Vicarage Live* in September 2018.

And to fans who lived through the giddy excitement of that FA Cup run in 1984 – from the seven-goal thriller against *that* lot in the third round, to suppressing Birmingham's bullies and Plymouth's gallant underdogs in the semi-finals – Rostron will always be the man who led Watford's first-ever march on Wembley.

Suspension is temporary, class is permanent.

6

ANDY HESSENTHALER

RUNNING MAN

He had legs like tree trunks, upper arms like joints of ham and he ran all day long. He ran whether the playing surface was like the outfield at Lord's, the mudflats of the Thames estuary, the frozen wastes of Siberia or the swamps of Bengal. He liked running so much that you suspect he would complete the London Marathon and, after crossing the finish line on the Mall, realise he had left his tracksuit top at the start in Blackheath – and run all the way back to fetch it.

At first glance stockier than a stock cube, but fitter than a butcher's dog and blessed with the stamina of an elite long-distance runner, Andy Hessenthaler was a jewel of the fallow years at Watford between the two periods when Graham Taylor ruled our hearts and minds.

In an era before Prozone, GPS tracking technology and instant cardiovascular data, Hessenthaler was not just a captain of his industry – he was a phenomenal athlete. In an endurance test between four of the Hornets' greatest 'engines' of the last 40 years, it would be fascinating to discover who would have kept going longest or furthest in a footrace between Hessenthaler, Roger Joslyn, Les Taylor and Abdoulaye Doucouré.

During the 2017–18 season, Doucouré covered more distance than any player in the Premier League except Burnley's Jack Cork; in his prime, Hessenthaler would have given them both a run for their money.

Glenn Roeder was the manager who installed 'Hessy' as Watford captain in 1993. If you want to know how good he was, have a read of Roeder's testimony. It leaves little scope for doubt about Hessenthaler's energy, his desire and his quality. 'When I came back to the club as manager, I made Andy my captain because I could see very quickly he had the 100 per cent respect of all the players,' says Roeder, who was no stranger to the armband himself before he left Vicarage Road in 1991 for a short-lived mission as Paul Gascoigne's chaperone in Italy at Lazio. 'As captain, you have to wear many different hats, and he was very good at doing that. Wearing an armband doesn't give you any supernatural powers – it doesn't make you run faster, jump higher or get stuck in more than anyone else on the pitch. But in some cases it does identify you as a leader of men. Hessenthaler was a leader because people followed him. In my era, of the players I faced or managed, Paul Ince was probably the king of box-to-box midfielders in this country. Ince was a great athlete, no two ways about it, but if he had been able to outrun Hessenthaler over 90 minutes, he would only have outrun him by half a yard.

'Although he came into the professional game from non-League at a relatively late age, Hessy was probably equipped to play in the Premier League – in fact, to be truthful, I think he would have coped in a higher division. Whatever he may have lacked on a technical level, he had that ability to run non-stop, but he didn't just run around the pitch without a purpose. He channelled all that energy through a good football brain.

'It speaks volumes for his "engine" that he was among the few who carried on playing beyond his 44th birthday, and it must have been very tough when the time came for him to give it away.

'But if you want a single measurement of how important he was to Watford Football Club, he was a major contributor to us struggling in the season I left and we were later relegated from what is now the Championship. When I say he contributed to that outcome, I mean he burst a calf muscle during a warm-up in training and he was absent for half the season. I think we only won about three games out of the 20 he missed, which shows how important he was to the team. Hard as we tried to replace Hessy, there was nobody else like him – certainly not of the type where you could just go out and buy another one for the same price, or borrow one from another club on loan. It was a reminder of how the whole dynamic of a team, and the narrative of a season, can change when a serious injury occurs to one of your key players.

'When we had a fit Hessenthaler, you always felt we could compete. The other team might be better than us, but they wouldn't overrun us, or at least outrun us, in midfield. When he wasn't there, we didn't half miss him. That's why he was my captain.'

Roeder's punchline is the most sincere and flattering tribute of all to Hessenthaler's workaholic shuttles.

'One more thing about Hessy,' he adds. 'As a manager, I was lucky to deal with some terrific characters among the captains of my teams – real warriors, from Alan Shearer at Newcastle to Steve Lomas at West Ham. Of all the captains I worked with, Andy Hessenthaler was as good as any of them for setting the right example. As a footballer and, more importantly, as a human being, he was right up there with the best I've ever appointed.'

In an age when too many managers are seduced by 'boutique' signings from overseas instead of scouting the semi-professional leagues properly at home, the extraordinary value for money available in the game's tributaries is still there for those who can be bothered to look for it. And in the 1990s, when money was tight, two of Watford's best stories came from bookshelves where the cover jackets might have looked a bit dusty – but the pages of text in between were a rollicking good read.

Roeder was responsible for one of them: the tale of Kevin Phillips, the striker who stacked TVs in a Dixons warehouse for a day job, was featured in *Tales from the Vicarage* Volume 2. Phillips was plucked from obscurity at Baldock Town after Roeder stood behind the goal one freezing night, watched him warm up with purpose and intent, and left at half-time, satisfied he had already seen enough. To this day Roeder says it was the best £10,000 he ever spent as a manager.

In a similar vein, Hessenthaler was another bauble who turned out to be a gemstone; another rough diamond sustaining his dreams of becoming a professional footballer behind the façade of a mundane vocation.

'I was a plasterer by trade,' he says. 'After leaving school I did a four-year apprenticeship in a builders' yard and learned the ropes, so I knew my way around a cement mixer and piles of bricks. Once I had qualified, I was self-employed, out in the big wide world, but I built up a decent customer base, and plastering is like riding a bike: once you've learned how to do it, you never forget it. If you rang me up and asked me to plaster your walls tomorrow, I'd be straight round with a bucket and trowel. But as much as it gave me a decent living and paid the bills, I always wanted a crack at playing football professionally, if anyone was prepared to take a chance.

'My lucky break was down to Peter Taylor, who was Steve Perryman's assistant at Watford in the early 1990s, because I had played non-League for him at Dartford. We had a cracking team who scored 100 goals most seasons. When Pete moved on to Enfield, and I signed for Redbridge Forest – or Dagenham & Redbridge as they are now, after the clubs merged – I thought I was destined to spend my career outside the League, although Redbridge did win promotion to the Conference [English football's fifth tier on the pyramid] while I was there.

'But in 1991, about five or six games into the season, I got a phone call from Pete out of the blue, asking if I still wanted to test the water as a pro footballer – which was a rhetorical question, because he knew that's what I had always wanted to do. By now I was 26 years old and, to be honest, I thought it was never going to happen. I thought that ship had sailed. I had been linked with Ipswich, and one or two other clubs in and around what is now the Championship and League One, but none of them could make their minds up. Maybe they thought I had the fitness to cope with the physical demands at that level but were put off when the ball was at my feet! I wasn't the most articulate or expressive player in the world, but what you saw is what you got from me – sweat on the jersey and 100 per cent effort, skill to follow later.

'Watford were the first club to back their judgement with a firm offer, and I was never going to turn them down. It's what I had wanted all along, and it came with the added bonus of working with a bloke I knew and liked from Dartford. If full-time football didn't work out, I knew I could always fall back on the plastering and pick up where I left off.'

Hessenthaler would be serenaded by a minority of choral ignoramuses when he left Vicarage Road after five years of impeccable application. Little did they know the dynamo who never stopped running for the cause took a slight wage *cut* overall, if you aggregated his earnings from gypsum and part-time football, to join the Hornets for a bargain £65,000.

'Money wasn't the issue when I walked in the door, and it wasn't the only factor when I left, either,' reveals Hessenthaler. 'For me, it was all about finding out whether I could cut it at a decent level. There's always a bit of fortune involved in any transfer – sometimes it's about who you know rather than what you can do, and in my case Peter Taylor was the link – but ultimately it was Steve Perryman's call. He was the manager who was answerable to his chairman, and I believe he'd already had a look at me when he was in charge at Brentford before he went to Watford. Luckily he backed Pete's judgement. Forget about money – I had started on £40 a week at Dartford. I was chuffed to be joining a good club where I could live the dream.'

By September 1991 the Hornets' giddy success of the Taylor years from 1977–87 seemed a distant memory. Watford had been close to an instant return to the top flight on Steve Harrison's watch in 1989, and they were unlucky to lose a playoff semi-final against Blackburn under the now-defunct away-goals rule. But that frustrating night only reinforced Harrison's conviction that he was not cut out to be a manager, and when Elton John sold the club to formidable east London businessman Jack Petchey, the Hornets' fortunes settled into a tailspin of mediocrity.

Perryman's three years in charge are not remembered with misty-eyed affection by supporters brought up on the buccaneering feats of Taylor's teams, but let's get one thing straight: Perryman did a *fabulous* job to keep Watford in the second tier in 1990–91. He took over a dispirited, dysfunctional collection of old sweats and young players required to learn their trade in the throes of fighting relegation, shipwrecked and anchored to the seabed, and he led them to safety with a game to spare.

Such were the levels of despair and apathy which had set in under Perryman's predecessor Colin Lee that the Hornets did not even win a home game until December that season, and crowds had dwindled to around 6,000 when Paul Wilkinson's two goals saw off Plymouth Argyle on a wintry day when Watford somehow escaped the heavy snow which had forced the postponement of games as close as Wycombe and Tottenham on either side of Vicarage Road. (This was the day when former BBC commentator John Motson did his live report to camera for the popular *Football Focus* slot from Wycombe in a blizzard after their scheduled FA Cup tie had fallen victim to the Arctic plume.)

The celebrations at Oxford five months later, and the staying-up party of 4,000 fans gridlocked on the M40 afterwards, did not fool Perryman. It had been a close call with relegation –

too close for comfort – and his squad needed strengthening, notably in midfield, where the Hornets had been short of lung power to supplement Gary Porter's endeavour.

'Of all the chairmen I worked for as a manager, Jack Petchey was the most straightforward of the lot,' says Perryman. 'Maybe he wasn't the one who threw the most money around, but he didn't promise champagne and give you soda pop. I respected him for that. He wanted to run Watford as a sustainable concern, and in this day and age of Premier League clubs running up debts into hundreds of millions, I don't see too much wrong with trying to run a solvent business. Hessenthaler cost us £65,000 and it was money well spent – no arguments about that – but before we lodged our bid, I had to justify it to the chairman. He wanted to know why this lad was better than what we'd already got, why he would improve the team, and I had to convince him there wasn't another player in that position on the market who represented better value for money. Fortunately, I must have made a very persuasive case for signing Andy. He came in and made an impression right away.'

***

The events of Saturday 21 September 1991 will always chime with me as a reminder of how fickle sport, and life itself, can be.

It was the date of Chris Eubank's momentous super-middleweight world title sequel with Michael Watson at Tottenham's old White Hart Lane ground. Watson had lost the original contest three months earlier at Earls Court on a hotly disputed split decision, and those of us who followed Eubank's entourage back towards the dressing rooms had been required to duck the missiles and venom directed at the fortunate champion by disaffected patrons who did not share the judges' assessment.

In the rematch, Watson was comfortably ahead on all scorecards when he was poleaxed by a thunderous upper-cut in the closing seconds of the penultimate round, and saved by the bell, just moments after he had put Eubank on the canvas for the first time in 29 professional fights. Senses still scrambled, and barely able to reach the middle of the ring to touch gloves as the bell sounded for the last round, Watson was soon pummelled into submission by a fusillade of unanswered punches and, amid chaotic scenes with pockets of brawling punters, it seemed like an age before he was evacuated from the ring on a stretcher unconscious and clinging to life. Watson spent 40 days in a coma after emergency brain surgery, and doctors were astounded that his recovery eventually included the ability to walk and talk.

In a happier prelude to the harrowing events at White Hart Lane – at least for Watford supporters – hours earlier most of us had caught our first glimpse of Andy Hessenthaler in a Watford shirt. He marked his home debut with a goal, from reassuringly close range, in the 2-0 defeat of Charlton Athletic.

Beneath the satisfaction of scoring in his first appearance at Vicarage Road, however, Hessenthaler was concealing private grief from the outside world, and there was a hugely poignant dimension to his goal and celebration. Just days before he could fulfil his dream of playing League football in the professional ranks Hessenthaler's mother, June, had died suddenly in her sleep aged 54.

'Although she had been laid low by the flu, and she had lost a bit of weight through being a diabetic, everything seemed under control,' he says. 'It came out of the blue. Bronchial pneumonia. It was absolutely devastating for me at the time, and maybe football helped me to cope with the shock.

'One of my biggest regrets was that my mum never saw me play as a professional footballer, because she knew how much it meant to me. I like to think she would have been proud of what I went on to achieve as a late starter, because you don't see many players turning pro at that age. In a way, the fact I played into my forties was a tribute to her. I had promised her that if I got a chance to play at that level, I would squeeze every last drop from it.'

Watford, who had cheated the drop with little margin for error the previous season, had begun the new campaign with powerful evidence to suggest inconsistency would be their specialist subject again. Three consecutive home defeats against Wolves, Cambridge and Middlesbrough had dampened expectations by the time manager Steve Perryman turned to his new recruit, whose fitness needed only cursory assessment by Watford's medical staff to confirm he was oven-ready for the rigours of First Division combat.

'I guess my first challenge was to cope with the physical demands of full-time football from the outset,' says Hessenthaler. 'I wouldn't say I was more durable than some of the lads, but I didn't feel out of place. I had always done well at the long-distance stuff when I was at school, and I did quite a few runs for my local athletics club, Gravesend Road Runners, to top up my fitness in between training two nights a week in non-League. That was my way of showing extra desire, how much I really wanted to make the step up. I wasn't blessed with exceptional skill, so if I wanted to stand out from the crowd I needed to be different to everyone else. I loved running – in terms of stamina I was good at it – and I hoped it would get me noticed if it got me around the pitch.

'Going into Watford after I signed, and doing the fitness work, I loved it. Trevor Putney took me under his wing when I started out, because he was commuting to work round the M25 like me, and he was a great character to show you the ropes. Trevor is one of the funniest men I've ever come across in football, and his humour helped to make it enjoyable when I was a new kid on the block. He used to joke that I could run all day and it was only when you threw me a ball that you had a problem – on the other hand, Trevor said he couldn't run but he was top dog with a ball at his feet, so we made a right pair. To be fair, Trevor won player of the year at Ipswich in between Paul Mariner and Terry Butcher, who were established England internationals, so all joking aside – and there was plenty of it from him – I was keeping decent company.'

Although he could have been forgiven for thinking he was an investment for the future, and the Hornets would phase him into the first-team picture, Hessenthaler was gratified to be fast-tracked into the squad almost immediately. That was undoubtedly a tribute to the Running Man's energy and staying power, and within a week of signing he was invited to join Watford's excursion to the seaside.

'It was always in the front of my mind that, to be accepted by the management staff and my teammates, I needed to be better than everyone else in some regard, or at least to show I had something to offer. And without blowing my own trumpet, when it came to covering the ground, I felt I did make a difference.'

Was Hessenthaler pleasantly surprised how well his fitness levels stacked up for a plasterer who trained twice a week compared with full-time professionals who played and trained every day for a living?

'Put it this way, I was pleased that I wasn't getting left behind on the endurance work, but all along I thought I had a good chance of adapting well because I was doing fitness work every day in the building trade: you don't feel the grass growing under your feet when you're running up and down ladders or mixing sand and cement all day.

'I was just chuffed to be going into such a good club and joining in with some great lads. Luther Blissett was a club legend, Alan Devonshire was injured for much of that season but was still an experienced player with a fantastic track record, Peter Nicholas was a strong character, Trevor was great company, I knew Steve Butler from his time at Maidstone, and I've kept in contact with Joe McLaughlin. All these lads had been there and done it, and I looked up to them because I wanted to prove I belonged in their company.

'My first involvement with the first team was an away game at Brighton, where Steve Perryman took me along as the spare man in the squad to help me get used to the lads, how they prepared on matchdays and some of the details that go with them – like pre-match meals and the travel. It helped that we won 1-0, at the old Goldstone Ground, and Steve Butler scored the goal. As one of the lads I knew before I ever set foot in Vicarage Road that helped me settle in because, like me, his background had been non-League.

'My debut was the following Tuesday night, away at Blackburn, which was such a big moment for me that it all became a bit of a blur, but it might have been that night I was asked to fill in at right-back. To be honest, I'm not a right-back and I never have been, but if you've only been in the professional game five minutes and the gaffer asks you to help out the team – even if it's not in your natural position – you are not going to turn him down.

'And the following week we were playing Everton in the League Cup at Goodison Park, and the likes of Peter Beardsley and Martin Keown was a big step up from where I'd come from. That was a tough night, to be fair, frightening if I'm honest, although we only lost 1-0.

'But for my home debut I was relieved the supporters saw me in my best position – the one where I felt I could influence the game most – and, even better, I marked it with a goal. It was one of those chances that sat up nicely, only a few yards out, and I couldn't miss. That was a fantastic feeling: home debut, first goal and three points. From that moment, I felt I'd got the supporters on my side, and when I look back at my spell with Watford the memories are overwhelmingly positive. There were some brilliant people at the club, and they were happy times.

'Although Elton John had sold the club he was still a big fan and he came to the odd game. It felt a bit surreal to be lumping bricks around a yard one minute and then shaking hands with a superstar the next. And I couldn't get my head around this world-famous celebrity calling me "Hessy" – I was in awe of the guy, so being on first-name terms with a bloke like Elton John was like something from another world.

'On the pitch we had quality in all departments and, although we were never quite consistent enough in the League to have a real dart at promotion, we had some fantastic nights. The best of them was probably when we knocked Leeds, who were the champions of England at the time, out of the League Cup. The ground was rocking, and to come out on top after pitting your wits against Eric Cantona, David Batty, the late Gary Speed and Gordon Strachan felt like a tremendous achievement.

'We were all a bit surprised when Cantona was clean through, one-on-one with Perry Suckling, and put his shot wide when he had all the time in the world. But of the photographs I kept of my Watford career, one or two of the best were from that night.

'When times have been tough – and I'm talking about everything that's happened to me in football – it has always brought a smile to my face when I look back to where I came from and remember how much I loved being in that environment, doing something I thought I would never do, relishing the special moments I never thought would come round when I was a builder's apprentice.

'That's what drove me on when it was hard graft, when you were playing at Scarborough in the FA Cup and it was so cold I thought we were playing at the North Pole. And that's what kept you going when you came across Jürgen Klinsmann on one of those nights when everything he touched turned to gold for Tottenham, and you get beat 6-3 at home.'

That night in 1994, when Klinsmann was flavour of the month on Fleet Street, was a showcase for Hessenthaler's indomitable spirit. Manager Ossie Ardiles had built a formidable forward line at Spurs – all roof and no foundations – but they were a swaggering force with the German World Cup winner, Teddy Sheringham, Darren Anderton and Ilie Dumitrescu in their arsenal. The Hornets had scored in the first minute, missed a penalty and trailed 6-2 going into the last 60 seconds, when Running Man breached Tottenham's defences again, skipped round Spurs' Watford-born goalkeeper Ian Walker – whose father had worn the no.1 jersey for the Golden Boys in an FA Cup semi-final 24 years earlier – and made it 6-3 with the help of covering defender Gary Mabbutt's futile attempt to clear the danger.

Although the second leg at White Hart Lane was, by most estimations, a dead rubber, Watford led three times before going out 8-6 on aggregate, a glut of scoring which said much about both defences over the 180 minutes. 'It would have been very interesting if we had somehow managed to get a two-goal lead in the second leg,' says Hessenthaler. 'If I remember, we had one or two chances to make that happen, and if we'd taken one of them the crowd might have got very nervous.' As it was, Tottenham were booed off on the night and the Hornets' captain could take pride in their refusal to accept defeat, let alone a rout, over two legs as inevitable.

Hessenthaler had been awarded the armband by Roeder for fulfilling the first law of captaincy: leading by example. And three years into his speculative change of career the player himself was still full of running.

'As captain, I didn't do anything different,' he says. 'I knuckled down, and if I made mistakes I did my best to put them right. I wore my heart on my sleeve and I worked hard to earn the other players' respect. Coming out of non-League football, that was always the big challenge. To be honest, I don't think it took me long to earn that respect. For the first few days there might have been one or two sideways looks and people wondering, "Hello, who's this new fella?" But the lads soon realised I was prepared to back them up, I was ready to go to war with them and I was ready to fight to the bitter end, even when the cause seemed lost. Maybe I appreciated it more because I was a late starter in the game. You see people like Jamie Vardy, Rickie Lambert and, going a bit further back, Ian Wright and Stuart Pearce . . . they took the same route, and they took their chances as if their lives depended on it.

'Nothing makes me more sad, or frustrated, as a manager now when I see talented youngsters with the world at their feet but their careers peter out before they have even started because they don't want it badly enough. Too many kids want money first and achievement later, but their attitude means they never get as far as the achievement. My advice to kids coming through age groups now is to appreciate what they have got and make the most of it – because football is a fantastic way to earn a living.

'As captain I got the players in a huddle and said a few words, but in general I knew the smartest way to bring the best out of them was to be consistent in my own performance: do as I do, not do as I say. I left motivation to the manager, because I believe that's part of his territory, but we had a good bunch at Watford and they rallied round when the going was heavy. We were not shy of talking as a group, and when it came to team meetings I was prepared to say my bit. I wouldn't sit there mute and leave it to everyone else to let off steam.

'Steve Perryman used to have a sports psychologist coming in to talk to us as a squad. Maybe it happens all the time in football now, but 25 to 30 years ago it wasn't a common practice, and it was good to talk and open up the discussion to include the quieter lads, especially if things were not going particularly great.

'It took me a while to find my voice, because I was always conscious of having to earn respect, and earn the right to pipe up. If lads like Gary Porter, who had been at the club for years through thick and thin, stood up to make a point, you listened to it because of what they did for Watford. His opinion never fell on deaf ears. Once I felt confident enough to back my actions on the pitch with a few words, I wasn't afraid to stand up and say my piece. Maybe that helped my case when Glenn decided to make me captain.'

Hessenthaler's application was so immense, and he was so immersed in the demands of his box-to-box shuttles, that he recalls little of his 14 goals for the Hornets – save that first one against Charlton on his home debut. 'And I only remember that one because it wasn't far out, on a special day for me all round,' he jokes.

Let's jog his memory, because there were some hugely significant moments among them, notably the winner against Portsmouth in the penultimate game of the 1993–94 season, which clinched survival in the First Division (but second tier), much as Paul Wilkinson's only goal at Oxford had had the same effect three years earlier. For good measure Hessenthaler then went to Selhurst Park on the final day of term and punctured as many balloons as he could simultaneously to spoil Crystal Palace's promotion party atmosphere and championship-winning celebrations.

In recent times meetings with Palace have often been tinted with disappointment, especially at Wembley, but that was a satisfying Sunday matinee on live terrestrial TV and, all things considered, a good 'save' in terms of beating the drop. Watford's season had been disrupted by no fewer than seven red cards in the first 19 games, two of them in bandit country on the opening day, and there had always been an element of playing catch-up.

Only when the Hornets edged a breathless, madcap, seven-goal thriller at Peterborough on the run-in could the supporters dare to turn hope of survival into expectation. The loss of striker Bruce Dyer to Palace with 13 games left, in a deal which made him Britain's first £1 million teenager, had the appearance of running up the white flag, and a desultory 3-0 home defeat by Grimsby the following midweek was decorated by protesting fans storming the directors' box to register their feelings with chairman Jack Petchey up close and personal.

Throughout the upheaval Hessenthaler's graft was a reassuring turbine at Vicarage Road. Sure, there was the odd hurried clearance where composure might have served him better, but Hessy's industry was a shining light: the plasterer for whom League football was sweet home alabaster.

He's a grandfather now, and has completed almost two decades as a manager, but there has been no slacking in the standards he expects of himself or his players. He has little time for strolling millionaires whose strut is fuelled by a haughty sense of entitlement, nor can he understand the laziness of players who allow opponents to pass the ball among themselves, sometimes only five yards away, without making any effort to win it back.

'It drives me round the bend,' he says, the tone of his voice darkening conspicuously. 'When I'm watching Premier League games and I see that, it makes me mad. Sometimes I have to turn off or I end up shouting at the telly like a wolf howling at the moon. I do feel it's become too easy for players not to bother because of the finances at the top end of the game now. Personally, I don't think it's healthy for football when you see players on phenomenal money going through the motions, not even breaking sweat. Do some of them earn their wages week in, week out? I don't think they do. They get away with it, and the people they are cheating most are the supporters. Having bags of ability with a ball at your feet doesn't make you a complete footballer. You can't win football matches if the other team has got the ball and you don't make any effort to win it back.'

***

When the time came for Andy Hessenthaler and Watford to go their separate ways, their parting was unsatisfactory.

Relegation, on the final day of the 1995–96 season, had been on the cards since a ghastly 12-match winless run over the winter – Glenn Roeder lost his job as manager two-thirds of the way through it – left the Hornets with too many mountains to climb, despite the Klondike rush of 15 goals in three home games against Port Vale, Reading and Grimsby offering tantalising hope of escape.

Some of the temporary cast Roeder had drafted in, amid a frightening injury crisis and equally daunting haemorrhage of confidence, had included Kerry Dixon (a controversial signing, even on loan, given his age and previous employment), Steve Hodge, Warren Neill and Danny Hill, whose only appearance came during the 4-0 trouncing at Palace which signalled a change in the dugout. None was ever seen in a Watford shirt again.

Inevitably, relegation also led to a certain degree of housekeeping. Out went £400,000 striker Jamie Moralee, who had never looked remotely capable of filling record sale £2.3 million Paul Furlong's boots, along with long-serving defender David Holdsworth – whose twin brother, Dean, had been sold in haste to Brentford seven years earlier and Steve Harrison, the manager who sanctioned the transfer, repented at leisure.

To widespread disappointment the captain joined the evacuation, although Hessenthaler was actually in no rush to get away. Simple economics dictated that lower division football, and the near certainty of lower income streams that come with it, would require pruning of the squad, especially as owner Jack Petchey showed no inclination to loosen the purse strings, despite the return of messiah Graham Taylor as general manager, a welcome focal point of unity following the Hornets' return to the rough after 17 years on the fairways.

Although Petchey had resigned as chairman, and then from the board after the unsolicited picket of the directors' box by the delegation of unhappy patrons at the Grimsby débâcle, he still held the keys to the petty cash tin – and he was not signing any cheques to fund big new contracts, no matter how deserving the case.

Hessenthaler, out of contract, had been waiting for Watford to table a new deal, but when the paperwork materialised it did not, in his opinion, reflect his standing at the club, nor his selfless transition from blue-collar tradesman to professional sportsman. When Gillingham, 15 minutes up the road from his Kent home, offered similar terms over three years, not the 12 months Watford were offering, he makes no bones about it: he was not agitating for a move, but his head was turned.

Hessenthaler says, 'I'm not going to lie, it did hurt the first time I went back to Vicarage Road with Gillingham and some of the fans called me a "short, greedy bastard". I can't argue with the "short" part of their chant, but the rest of it was harsh. I've spoken about this before over the years, and I accept that I was a bit hasty leaving Watford at the time. But it's frustrating because most people don't know the full story and were never armed with all the facts, so maybe this is a good time to put the record straight.

'First and foremost, I loved my time at Watford. I loved the club, the players, the supporters and I owe Watford Football Club a lot because they took a chance on me where others had obviously decided that, at 26, I had missed the boat. I worked as hard as I could to establish myself in the team, to be accepted in the dressing room and to win the approval of the fans. It's for others to judge, but I think I managed to do all those things.

'But around the time Graham Taylor came back to the club, my contract was up and, whatever the constraints he was working under, the renewal I was offered wasn't something I felt comfortable about signing straight away. After nearly five years at the club, three of them as captain, I didn't think the offer reflected how much I'd given. It didn't make me feel valued, so I didn't sign it there and then.

'Graham Taylor also had this rule about players living within a certain radius of the club, and he didn't want them travelling long distances to work every day. Since I became a manager, I totally get the point he was making – I've seen big lads unfold themselves from behind the wheel of a car after spending two hours in traffic to get to training, and they are stiff as flat-pack wardrobes. But we never even got round to where I lived being a problem – I just didn't feel the terms on offer were a fair reflection.

'Charlton were interested, and at one point over that summer it looked done and dusted, but Alan Curbishley vetoed the move. They got cold feet about signing and paying compensation for a 31-year-old, which was bitterly disappointing because I thought it was a done deal. As it happens, I played another 350 games after they turned me down, so maybe I wasn't on my last legs, after all. But after the move to Charlton didn't happen, that's where Gillingham, easily the nearest League club to where I lived, came in and the transfer fee went to tribunal.

'To be fair, Watford did all right out of me in the end. The tribunal fee was set at £235,000, with bits and pieces attached, so they got nearly four times what they paid for me.'

It would be glib to accuse the Hornets of making a mistake in selling Hessenthler, just as it was a cheap shot for fans to accuse him of deserting a sinking ship. In a bilateral conundrum, neither party could look at the estrangement with 20–20 hindsight and say it was a wrong call. Within two years Watford would begin their rebound from relegation – a revival where the momentum sustained them all the way to the Premier League with a new midfield axis of Micah Hyde and Richard Johnson. And

Hessenthaler would make consecutive playoff visits to Wembley with Gillingham – the first culminating in gut-wrenching defeat on penalties by Manchester City, the sequel providing him with a happier ending. Two goals in the last six minutes of extra time against Wigan clinched an equally dramatic passport to promotion, former Hornet Steve Butler scoring the first of those goals to turn the tide in the Gills' favour.

'Yeah, one way or another, it worked out well for everyone,' says Hessenthaler. 'Watford made it to the Premier League, I made it to Wembley a couple of times and I managed to keep playing until my legs were screaming at me to stop.'

In fact, Hessenthaler is thought to hold a record among players who made the step up into professional football late in the day. Among his 616 senior appearances in three divisions, nobody has ever played more than Hessy's 551 League games after making his debut at that level beyond his 26th birthday. Just think about that for a moment – and think how far the Running Man must have run before he took the final curtain at Barnet, in a 0-0 draw with Shrewsbury, in March 2007.

Even then, when his League career was done, Hessenthaler returned to his non-League roots, joined Dover Athletic as player-manager and led them to consecutive promotions. He was three months short of his 45th birthday by the time he hung up his boots. By any yardstick, Hessenthaler's playing career was a colossal feat of endurance, and management was an obvious career path for him to pursue.

Two spells at Gillingham covering six-and-a-half years, the first four of them as player-manager, included leading the Gills to their highest-ever League finish, and his son Jake made 181 appearances for the club in midfield until he was released in May 2018 and joined Grimsby Town.

By far the barmiest, weirdest and wackiest episode of Hessenthaler's post-playing career came during his brief spell as assistant manager to Kevin Nolan as Leyton Orient slipped towards the Football League crypt. On Boxing Day in 2015, after Orient's 3-2 win against Portsmouth at the Matchroom stadium, owner Francesco Becchetti *kicked* Hessenthaler up the backside in front of the dugouts in an extraordinary move which looked less than friendly. Interviewed a short while later, Hessenthaler was a model of diplomacy, insisting, 'It probably looked worse than it was. He's a passionate guy, but it was good-natured and part of an ongoing thing between us over the last few weeks.'

Becchetti, whose short time in charge of Orient was little short of disastrous – nine managers in three years – was a demonstrative owner, but his hot temper appeared vaguely menopausal and, on reflection, Hessenthaler's interpretation of the incident is now a good deal less charitable than his initial public statement.

'It was a crazy time and, I've got to say, it didn't bring me a lot of joy,' he says. 'I've never come across someone like that as owner of a football club. At the time it happened, I didn't realise it was my own chairman putting the boot in. I spun round and I was going to throw a punch, but Paul Cook [the Portsmouth manager] got in between us and stopped me from getting involved, so I am grateful to him for that. You don't expect that sort of behaviour from anyone at the end of a football match, let alone your chairman, and I could have taken it further. I was sorely tempted to get the League Managers' Association involved, but there was a lot going on at Orient around that time and it was probably for the best that I slept on it and decided to leave it as it was. But I was a feeling a bit mixed-up when I went to bed that night. I've never come across anything like it in football. It's terrible . . . I always thought it was my job to go round kicking people!'

In a happier epilogue to his playing days, Hessenthaler became a three-times World Cup winner with England in the summer of 2018.

If it wasn't quite the full Jules Rimet, he was no less proud to win the Seniors World Cup in Thailand, beating Scotland 4-0 in the final.

'Five games in seven days is hard work in that heat,' he says. 'Premier League managers would blow a gasket at the schedule, but when you get to my age you can seize up sitting on plane for ten hours, so playing football is a real bonus – although some old habits die hard. I managed to get booked in both our first two group matches, so I was suspended for the third one. Apart from that I played every minute of every game. I lifted the trophy as captain in 2017, and this time it was [former Middlesbrough and Everton winger] Peter Beagrie who did the honours, but to win it three times on the bounce brings out the patriot in you. That hat-trick is up there with the proudest things I've done in football because you're representing your country and I was the oldest player on the pitch. Afterwards there were only two things I wanted to go with another World Cup winner's medal – a beer and a stair-lift!'

7

ROBERT PAGE

THE THIRTY-NINE STEPS

There are now 107 steps from the touchline to the Royal Box at Wembley. Only qualified mountaineers need apply.

At least the view, once victorious footballers have scaled the national stadium's north face, is worth the climb. Before a 1,000 foot arch (rising up to 170 feet above the pitch) became the shrine's most striking feature when it reopened in 2007, fans had swayed up English football's famous promenade, between the merchandise stalls and steaming pancakes of equine origin, under the gaze of iconic twin towers – and the ascent to shake hands with royalty was just 39 steps.

Only one Watford captain in the club's history, Robert Page, has climbed the victors' stairway at Wembley to lift a trophy, after the 2-0 win against Bolton Wanderers in the 1999 playoff final, which restored the Hornets to the roof garden after an 11-year absence from the top flight. That happy ending to the club's longest-ever season – 296 days from the 2-1 win at Portsmouth on the first afternoon to the wonderful denouement – also gave Graham Taylor one of his happiest days in football at a venue which had dealt him little fortune 15 years earlier at the FA Cup final or as England manager.

For every football supporter, there are weekends in our lives which remain unforgettable – the JFK moments where we can relate what we were doing, where we were living, how we celebrated, and how on earth we got home afterwards remaining a complete mystery. The day Page climbed those

39 steps to lift the Promotion Cup will stay in the hearts and minds of each Watford fan among the 38,000 who bore witness to it in person, and plenty more who had to follow it from afar, including chairman Sir Elton John, who tuned in from his concert tour in Seattle from 7 a.m.

Forgive us our Press passes, but some of us in the Fourth Estate remember the Whitsun Bank Holiday weekend in 1999 for momentous events in two sports. England were hosting cricket's World Cup that summer, and making an unedifying hash of it. Somehow, they managed to get turfed out of their own party before the official tournament anthem, 'All Over the World' (by Dave Stewart of the Eurythmics), had even been released. Unsurprisingly it did not trouble the scorers, as they say in cricketing parlance, in the top 100 of the UK charts. Even the opening ceremony at Lord's had been a dismal spectacle, with Prime Minister Tony Blair's speech audible only to those who were not disenfranchised by a prehistoric crackle on the ground's public address system.

The day before Watford's march on Wembley, I was assigned the World Cup tie between South Africa and Australia at Headingley. When Australian captain Steve Waugh (on his way to a match-winning 120) was dropped on 56 by South African opener Herschelle Gibbs, spilling the ball as he went to hurl it skywards in premature celebration, the apocryphal version is that Waugh told him, 'You've just dropped the World Cup, Hersch.' Great punchline though it was, and demonstrably true in the light of subsequent events (Australia went on to win the tournament), revisionist intelligence insists Waugh never actually said it. Oh well, never let the facts get in the way of a good one-liner.

On the return journey south, stopping off at Leicester Forest East services on the M1 for a calorific refuel, your hungry scribe was queuing for a pre-Wembley dinner of Kentucky

Fried Chicken when he felt a sharp tap on the shoulder from the neighbouring echelon of eternal optimists in an orderly line for the healthy option, Burger King.

It was former England batsman John Morris, on the retreat from a heavy defeat with Durham against Sussex at Hove, and a familiar face to scribes who had followed his escapades on the 1990–91 Ashes tour of Australia. Morris and David Gower had been fined £1,000 by tour manager Peter Lush for leaving England's tour match against Queensland on the Gold Coast, and 'buzzing' the Carrara Oval as passengers in a Tiger Moth bi-plane, to celebrate teammate Robin Smith's return to form with a hundred. Lush's anger was no doubt fuelled by the realisation that he had loaned Gower his £27 air fare.

Pretending that portions of chips qualified as one of our five-a-day fruit and vegetable rations, Morris introduced his co-passenger. 'And one day, this lad is going to open the bowling for England,' he announced. Looking up, as you would at the foot of the Shard in London, my gaze set upon a gangling 6 foot 4 inch frame who would vindicate Morris's prediction spectacularly. The young prospect was Steve Harmison, whose fast bowling would make headlines for much of the ensuing decade, notably in the 2005 Ashes series which ranks no.1 among the immense sporting contests I have covered as a wandering hack. Grievous Bodily Harmison, as I took to calling him in irreverent despatches, became a fearsome opening bowler and remains a good pal.

When you have a Wembley ticket in your back pocket it is surprising how carefully you negotiate the middle-lane hogs and motorway numpties the night before one of Watford's biggest games – certainly their most important one-off occasion since the 1987 FA Cup semi-final against Tottenham.

Pulling into the drive, home safe and sound, the hardest part for everyone connected with Watford still lay ahead – negotiating that final ridge, that hallowed flight of stairs up to the Royal Box. The true miracle of those 39 steps is that Robert Page ever got to climb them at all.

***

Where Watford needed a whirlpool, they could only manage a stagnant pond. A season of considerable promise was in danger of petering out tamely by the time the Hornets ground out an uninspiring goalless draw with Bury at Vicarage Road. And they were both lucky to get nil.

Graham Taylor's side had been one of only three teams to beat runaway champions Sunderland (who won the division by 18 points), in a match memorable for Gifton Noel-Williams' poetic chest trap and volley on the turn for the winning goal – and the brutal challenge from Paul Butler which put him out of the game for the best part of two years. Butler would get his comeuppance on a glorious Bank Holiday under a Cardiff roof seven years later, but early in 1999 Watford's form was patchier than a Dalmatian's spots and harder to cure than Nigerian left-back Ben Iroha's bunions.

The stalemate with Bury seemed to kibosh, once and for all, any lingering prospect of back-to-back promotions, and the club captain agreed the Hornets were going nowhere. 'There were eight games to go, we were something like nine or ten points off the playoff places and it looked, for all the world, as if our season had run out of steam,' says Page. 'Graham Taylor's philosophy was always based on us being the top scorers every season, and for the first half of that one we were certainly right up there with the best in our division. But every team goes through a sticky patch at some stage and, yeah, when we drew at home to Bury the going was heavy. We were almost grinding to a standstill. We could have been forgiven for thinking it wasn't going to be our year, and that there was no shame in mid-table consolidation for a side who had only been promoted the previous season. There was a two-week break until our next game, and I don't remember us doing anything special during that fortnight to make a difference, but in football you don't always need to look too hard for the solutions to a puzzle – sometimes you are galvanised by events on the spur of the moment.'

The catalyst for an extraordinary run which took the Hornets to Wembley and beyond – to the Premier League, a gilded empire which came into existence in 1992, when Richard Keys and Andy Gray, the wise men of Sky Sports, invented football – was 20 minutes of anarchy against Tranmere Rovers. Ian Grant, on the *Blind, Stupid and Desperate* website, splendidly compared the carnage with 'trying to trap a hurricane in a matchbox'. Somewhere amid the chaos, Richard Johnson and Allan Smart were sent off, etiquette around the dugouts should have been referred to WBC judges' scorecards, a feckless referee lost control and the rolling mauls of indiscipline were unfit for a family club audience before the watershed. And yet the lawlessness served Watford well: tired of trying to find their way out of the maze before closing time with pieces of string or paper trails, they burrowed their way out by dismantling the hedgerows with a chainsaw.

The first 70 minutes had been as inconsequential as afternoon tea before the apocalypse and, when David Kelly fired Rovers in front, the Hornets' hope of salvaging anything from another dreary home performance looked buttock-clenchingly grim.

But Taylor's triple substitution – at face value an act of displeasure more than tactical gravitas – yielded a response, and Peter Kennedy's equaliser at least signalled Watford's intent to go out with guns blazing instead of a whimper. Then it all kicked off: a magnificent maelstrom of indignation, violent feuds and Tranmere manager John Aldridge becoming embroiled in protracted arguments with fans behind the dugouts. He picked the wrong fight: patrons in the main stand had not exercised their wrath to such a degree for 22 years, when an officious chump named Trevor Spencer sent off Tony Geidmintis and Alan Mayes against Huddersfield and was treated to a cup of tea – not necessarily still in the cup – as a token of the fans' appreciation after Watford's miraculous 2-0 win.

A controversial penalty – from which Michel Ngonge bundled home the winner after Kennedy's spot-kick was saved – led to pockets of unrefined mayhem, with punches thrown and Kelly losing his shirt like a gambler down on his luck at the bookies. Smart's expulsion for his part in the blisters of acrimony left Watford three minutes plus stoppage time to cling on with nine men. Page believes the ordeal turned a half-decent team into a band of brothers. He says, 'I wouldn't like to say we turned it round by channelling our anger, because getting two people sent off is not normally the way forward, but it was pandemonium. In many respects, you would say two red cards brought out the worst in us – but in a strange sort of way it actually brought out the best in that team. It brought us together as a group. It reawakened our fighting spirit, and we went on an unbelievable run. Looking back, if you ask me when I truly believed that we could win promotion, and we were going to be unstoppable, that afternoon when Johnno and Smarty got sent off was the start of it all. I remember thinking, "We're going to be written off now because two key players are going to be suspended – but we've got something going here." We had nothing to lose – and nothing to fear.

'When you go into games with such a powerful feeling – not arrogance, but a belief that nothing is going to stop us – that willpower becomes a force of nature. All the players and management staff have to take credit for buying into it.'

Two days later, at promotion-chasing Birmingham, Taylor pulled another rabbit from the hat, bringing former Aston Villa winger Tony Daley into the side, and he seized the opportunity to spike the old enemy's guns in the Second City one more time with a rare headed goal which proved to be the winner. And by the time Watford completed an impressive home-and-away double over Bolton, their momentum was becoming irresistible.

'All of a sudden the top six were being reeled in,' says Page. 'We'd needed binoculars to see them disappearing over the horizon after the Bury game, but now they were creeping into view. The players believed we were going to do it; the supporters were beginning to believe we could do it. More often than not, teams who finish the season like a train, and get into the top six full of confidence and momentum, are the ones who get promoted.'

The wins kept coming. Crewe, Crystal Palace and Port Vale all fell by the wayside as Tommy Mooney caught the wave in a timely run of six goals in as many games. Although the Hornets were thwarted in the penultimate game of the regular League season by a late equaliser at Barnsley, their destiny was in their own hands at the finale against Grimsby.

If there were any doubts that promotion fever had reached intoxicating levels in Hertfordshire they were allayed by the extraordinary queues snaking along Vicarage Road more than two hours before kick-off. The last time most of us had seen thousands of people filing around the ground was in 1984, when FA Cup final tickets went on general sale.

Kennedy's crisp half-volley just before the break was enough for Watford to finish fifth, on the back of 22 points from a possible 24, and book a semi-final date with Birmingham – but only after the thrilling intervention of goalkeeper Alec Chamberlain. Twice, immediately after the Hornets had gone in front, Chamberlain produced exceptional saves – right out of the magician's top hat – to deny Peter Handyside and Kingsley Black instant replies for the Mariners.

'Alec was exceptional for us all season,' says Page. 'But when it all boiled down to win or bust, he came up trumps when it really mattered. Those saves were top drawer, not just for their technical agility but the concentration that enabled him to make them. I would have been devastated to lead out the boys that day, with all the tickertape and the party atmosphere, if it had all fallen flat. Top keepers stay switched-on and we were lucky to have a supreme professional in goal on that run-in. It says everything about the man that I'm stoked to be working with him again 20 years later – he's coaching the keepers in the Wales under-21 squad and younger age groups.'

Reaching the playoffs, in any division, serves only one useful purpose: going on to win them. Anything other than promotion means the season ends in anti-climax, and often the hangover of disappointment spills over into the following campaign – a syndrome with which Graham Taylor was painfully familiar.

In 1995, at the end of his first season as manager of Wolverhampton Wanderers – his splashdown back in club football after that ill-starred reign in charge of England – Taylor finished fourth in the First Division, as it was then known, just three points off automatic promotion. Wolves faced Bolton in the semi-finals, and it was GT's misfortune to come up against an inspired 45-year-old goalkeeper called Peter Shilton in the first leg at Molineux. Of Shilton's 1,005 League appearances in club football, he made only a couple for the Trotters – but one of them was a masterclass, restricting Wolves to a narrow 2-1 advantage, and when they lost the return leg 2-0 Taylor was denied a measure of redemption, after his disappointment with England, at the first attempt.

Four years later he would be reacquainted with Bolton in the playoffs again, but first came Birmingham in the semi-finals.

Four points from two meetings with the Blues during the regular League season suggested Watford had nothing to fear unduly, but those who lived through the epic drama of a sultry night in the Midlands will not forget it in a hurry.

Michel Ngonge's early header gave the Hornets a 1-0 lead from the first instalment at Vicarage Road. If the woodwork was unkind, denying Mooney and Nick Wright the breathing space of a second goal, Watford were also fortunate that Birmingham strikers Paul Furlong and Dele Adebola made an impossible mess of an open goal – and Paul Robinson's sending-off meant old stager Nigel Gibbs would have to deputise at left-back, his first start for seven months, for the tie's conclusion.

In any event, Brum levelled the aggregate before any nerves could settle in the second leg, and the Hornets took their fans on a white-knuckle ride like no other.

Page says, 'All the gaffer asked of us was to go out and win every game. He was never interested in playing for a draw, but at the same time he accepted there were never any guarantees that you could win by two, three, four or any preferred margin. Yes, we could have been out of sight in the first leg but, as far as we were concerned, any advantage to take up to St Andrew's for the second leg was useful. Unfortunately for us it was wiped out inside the first two minutes, and we were in for one hell of a battle.'

The 120 minutes of unbearable, gut-wrenching, high-wire tension, and the interminable penalty shootout which followed, left players and supporters alike emotionally exhausted to the point of delirium. For the 2,900 travelling Watford fans trapped inside the ground, there was no escape. It was like being forced to watch *X Factor* finalists Rak-Su regurgitating their single on the pitch during half-time at the home game with Manchester United during the 2017–18 season. They were from Watford, so you were glad when they won the competition, but their genre certainly wasn't to everyone's taste. And for those watching TV at home, there was no point in hiding behind the sofa. The anguish was just as excruciating in the darkest corner of your living room.

Birmingham were reduced to ten men when former Watford skipper David Holdsworth was sent off for two yellow cards, but the blue waves kept lapping at the Hornets' door, and the immense Chamberlain came to their rescue time and again with a catalogue of fabulous saves. Peter Ndlovu, Gary Rowett, Michael Johnson and ex-Golden Boy Furlong were all denied as the nerves jangled like a nightclub Lothario's bling. Then came the shootout. If there has ever been a finer prescription for beta blockers, cardiologists have yet to write it.

Furlong blinked first, Chamberlain intercepting Brum's first spot-kick with a strong right hand, but Watford's player of the season Steve Palmer dragged their next penalty the wrong side of a post, and when Page stepped up to the mark the equation was down to sudden death.

'It's fair to say I was not a prolific goalscorer, as the boys would often remind me over the years,' he says. 'But we had been practising penalties in training – the boss told us to pick which square of the net we were aiming for, and to go for it with conviction – and as captain I was happy to take on the responsibility. I wouldn't say I was confident as I strode forward from the halfway line, because it's not easy to feel confident when your heart's beating out of your chest, but I was definitely up for it – until I looked at the penalty spot.

'It was like a crater with a two- or three-inch dip, and when you placed the ball it nested there like a golf ball lying in a divot on the fairway. You needed a clean contact just to dig it out. And when I looked up there was one particular distraction among the hundreds of Birmingham supporters trying to put me off. Behind the goal one fan had dropped his trousers and pants round his ankles and he was sticking his bare arse towards me. He obviously wasn't very impressed with our performance on the night.

'It was quite an inviting target, but instead of putting me off, it probably sharpened my focus. I turned, walked back five yards, and concentrated on striking my penalty with as much conviction as I could muster. I wasn't going to wait for the keeper to move, and he wasn't getting anywhere near it. I think my shot took a coat of paint off the underside of the bar on its way in, but I was chuffed with the execution. I didn't look for our friend and his mooning backside behind the goal, but it turned out well.'

Have some of that and put your trousers on, mate.

When the indefatigable Chamberlain had the last word, smothering Chris Holland's weak 16th kick of the never-ending shootout, Watford were heading for Wembley. If the drama had drained every last drop of adrenalin from our systems, the celebrations were effectively hyperventilation.

'The atmosphere that night was incredible, absolutely electrifying,' says Page. 'Credit to the Watford supporters who helped us over the line, because we had our backs to the wall after falling behind in the first two minutes and we didn't give them a lot to shout about until it went to penalties. But we heard them, they lifted us, and together we just about made it.

'I was given the man of the match award, and I remember sharing it with the lads in the Portakabin changing rooms afterwards. When I say I "shared" it with them, I sprayed them with it like a Formula One driver who's just won a Grand Prix. But, as you can imagine, the players were going bananas in there.

'The changing room had been a happy place 12 months earlier, when we had won the Second Division title at Fulham on the final day, but now there were senior pros letting it all hang out. You could see how much it meant to the likes of

Nigel Gibbs, Steve Palmer, Johnno and Alec that we were going to Wembley. We had to do it the hard way, but over the course of that run-in, and the way we held our nerve, it was a fantastic time for all of us – and it was a very special 24 hours in my life.

'On the Thursday night we played at Birmingham my wife was in hospital, going into labour after being induced, because our first child was due. I couldn't be there with her at first, but she managed to hold on and the following day she gave birth to our son, Corey. Booking my first trip to Wembley and becoming a father . . . what a couple of days that was.'

***

Behind every successful team there is a network of support staff, and Watford's journey to Wembley in 1999 reflected huge credit on manager Graham Taylor and his trusted assistants Kenny Jackett and Luther Blissett.

Much of the damage caused by a decade of decline, decay and neglect between Taylor's two incarnations as messiah at Vicarage Road had been repaired, to some extent, by his intimate working knowledge of the club and his enduring, forensic eye for detail. Jackett – who had been in charge of the first team for a season before stepping back down to second in command when Taylor returned to the dugout after a sabbatical 'upstairs' as general manager – and favourite son Blissett provided reassuring umbilical cords with the glory years of 1977–87, when they were the bullion in GT's first generation of Golden Boys.

But on the road to Wembley in the 1998–99 campaign another figure was a reassuring presence, if not a good-luck charm, as Taylor branched out into unexplored tangents of medical science. Mental fitness coach Ciaran Cosgrave was known among supporters as 'the man in the pink shirt', and his distinctive dress code was an inextricable part of the scenery during the Hornets' dramatic upswing in form over the last two months of the season.

Cosgrave says his brief was to help build the players' 'mental muscle', and his pink shirt became a symbol of the competitive toughness he was trying to instil when Watford had no margin for error. 'Preparing to win in sport and in life is about gaining an edge,' he says. 'In modern sport there is very little between the top teams, but being mentally fitter than your opponent will give you that extra one per cent.'

If turning mental capacity into performance was once derided as hocus-pocus and nutty professor jargon, Watford players were soon converted by the value of Cosgrave's input. Watch the highlights reel of a memorable season and there he is on the touchline – pink shirt, black trousers, white trainers – conveying the power of positive thinking to the Hornets and, perhaps, undermining opponents as if his very presence was an illusory force of nature.

'Ciaran was at the training ground every day with us,' says Page. 'If he had turned his role into hour-long seminars or lectures, the boys might have zoned out – but GT always seemed to find the right time to bring him into our preparation for a quick chat about where we were going and how we were going to achieve it. When players hear the same voices at work every day, sometimes it keeps you on your toes when you listen to a different voice. He was certainly an influence on the group, and I remember him being there in the tunnel with us before the playoff semi-final. The pink shirt? It became more and more significant because we went on a winning streak and it became associated with us winning. The gaffer, Kenny and Luther were the main men, but Ciaran helped to make us feel unbeatable. The combination worked a treat.'

With 11 days to fill between the shootout marathon at St Andrew's and the playoff final at Wembley, one of Taylor's biggest tasks was to keep the mood upbeat, keep the engine ticking over – and keep the squad entertained. A short break abroad was quickly dismissed as an unnecessary risk of logistics and temptation to switch into holiday mode, so instead the management organised a day of go-karting as a bonding session. Their good intentions did not, however, gain the players' unqualified approval.

'A week out from the biggest game of our lives, one or two of the boys came up to me and said they were not happy,' reveals Page. 'There was no rebellion against a change of scenery, or the lads bonding on a day out, but they were worried about the possibility of crashing and missing the final through injury. No one really wanted to go go-karting, and we ended up having a conversation with Kenny and GT to ask if we could just have a round of golf instead.

'Kenny said, "What happens if one of you gets hit by a stray golf ball? There's an element of risk in everything you do." So we ended up go-karting, driving round the circuit like 20 Miss Daisies to make sure we didn't crash, and, in fact, we had a great few days together in the build-up.'

Apart from players killing time before showpiece finals at Wembley, there is a glaring anomaly football's governing bodies need to address urgently.

Clubs promoted to the Premier League through the playoffs start their summer recruitment three weeks behind their top-flight rivals. They cannot commit transfer fees and wages to new signings until they know in which division they will be kicking off the following season – and, concurrently, top players are not going to sign contracts with clubs who might be in the Championship. The jump in quality is forbidding enough; to make that quantum leap after big clubs have cleared the shelves in Harrods, leaving playoff winners to do their summer shopping at Lidl, is patently unfair.

Between 2006 and 2016, seven of the 11 clubs who climbed into the Premier League's land of milk and honey via the playoffs came straight back down again. That is the reality Watford have faced twice this century, and it was no different in 1999 when Graham Taylor led the Hornets out at Wembley – but for the man bursting with pride one pace behind him, nothing could detract from the enormity of the occasion.

'To walk out of that tunnel as captain of my club, and the events which followed, is right up there with the proudest moments of my professional life,' says Page. 'It's a photo-finish between Watford at Wembley and pulling on a Wales shirt. The Watford fans were at the far end of the stadium, so they were right in front of us as the teams came out before kick-off, and I will always remember a whole end decked out in yellow and red. That will stay with me for ever – it was a beautiful sight. I walked out holding a mascot's hand, and as soon as we emerged from the tunnel into broad daylight there were fireworks exploding all around us. It was a bit startling if you weren't expecting it, and the mascot squeezed my hand so hard I almost snapped my fingers in half. But that walk to the halfway line, in front of the Royal Box, was 60 yards of bliss. We knew roughly where our families would be sitting up in the stand and, by the time we had stood for the national anthem and shaken hands with the VIP guests, there was a moment to pick them out in the crowd and give them a wave.'

In the Second Division playoff final 24 hours earlier, Manchester City had trailed Gillingham 2-0 going into the 90th minute, only for goals by Kevin Horlock and Paul Dickov to earn them a dramatic reprieve, and they seized it in a penalty shootout. Incredible, isn't it? A club now coached by Pep Guardiola, one of only two managers in history to spend £1 billion on transfers – José Mourinho is the other – was languishing in English football's third tier in the closing overs of the twentieth century.

City's brinkmanship was a timely reminder that Watford should take nothing for granted, a message duly underlined in a nervous opening half-hour when the ever-dependable Chamberlain came to the rescue, twice denying Icelandic striker Eidur Gudjohnsen and exuding an air of assurance. Once the Hornets settled, however, they gradually became the more assertive team, and Nick Wright's eye-of-the-needle overhead kick which gave them a precious lead was a moment of magic beyond our wildest dreams.

'It was all part of the plan to rush the keeper and cause a bit of a mêlée when Peter Kennedy whipped set-pieces in towards the near post from our right flank, and we scored from our first or second corner of the match,' says Page. 'Ngonge was so keen to get on the end of it that he ended up in the back of the net, and Bolton probably thought the immediate danger was gone when they half-cleared PK's corner and it dropped over Wrighty's head. But for execution, there can't have been many better goals of its type in a playoff final. Over the keeper, over Neil Cox – who is guarding the near post and has not moved off the line – and right in the top corner. Coxy is about 6 foot 1 inch and it dipped over his head. Perfect.

'It was a bitter blow for Bolton, who probably didn't deserve to be behind at half-time on the balance of play, but it gave us something to defend. Micah Hyde and Johnno were absolute terriers in midfield that day – they hardly missed a tackle – and in the second half we played without fear.'

With their invincible man in the pink shirt transmitting positive vibes from the bench, and Bolton – relegated from the Premier League 12 months earlier – leaving more gaps as they fought to retrieve the deficit, Watford fashioned the best chances after the break, Kennedy ramming a first-time shot inches wide and Mooney's powerful header beating Trotters keeper Steve Banks but suffering the same fate.

Then, just four minutes from time, substitute Allan Smart's tenacity broke up another Trotters raid, Hyde's weighted pass released Kennedy into a vast expanse of unpatrolled pasture, and the Northern Ireland winger rolled an inviting cross along the 18-yard line. Smart, whose rudimentary tackle had set up the breakaway, ran 40 yards to meet Kennedy's pass, drilling his shot into the bottom corner without breaking stride.

As revealed in *Tales from the Vicarage* Volume 5, some of our celebrations were so enthusiastic that we strained our intercostal muscles in the outpouring of euphoria, and it required an industrial quantity of local anaesthetic – served in a pint glass – on Watford High Street later that night to soothe our discomfort.

Manchester City's improbable comeback the day before briefly tempered the giddiness, and reminded the Hornets' huge following not to take anything for granted, but Bolton's body language betrayed them. They were cooked.

Page says, 'The last 30 seconds of that game were out of this world: the best feeling you can ever experience on a football pitch. One of the Bolton players – I think it was Per Frandsen – had a dip from about 30 yards, and I remember "Chambo" actually cheering with joy as it sailed harmlessly over the top. I turned to the ref, Terry Heilbron, and asked him how much time was left, and he told me once the ball had been retrieved, and the goal-kick was in the air, that he was going to blow.

'That was the first time, in the whole match, that I allowed myself to look around and to take it all in – the sights, sounds and feeling of winning at Wembley. It's hard to explain the relief and joy of a moment like that, especially when we had seemed a million miles away from it when we were 1-0 down at home to Tranmere eight weeks earlier. You have to cherish it, drink it in and soak it up in the knowledge that you might not get another chance to play at Wembley – and, of course, the year after we won promotion, they knocked it down.'

And those 39 steps to the Royal Box?

'It's the sweetest climb you can make as a player. By the time you get to the top, everyone is shaking your hand, even though you don't know who most of them are. And then you catch sight of the directors, who are full of the joys, and we are sharing the moment together. But I only had eyes for the trophy, and the yellow and red ribbons attached to it – because every schoolboy who has ambitions of becoming a footballer dreams of doing what I was about to do. I picked it up, gave it a quick kiss, showed it off to 38,000 fans and passed it along the line for each player to hold aloft. Anyone who tells you they have never dreamed of going through that experience is lying.

'I'm so glad Graham Taylor, after all the cruel luck he suffered with England, got the chance to go back to Wembley and lift that Cup. I think it meant more to him than he ever let on at the time, and I clocked Tom Walley's reaction after the final whistle because he was a massive influence on my life, both as a footballer and as a man, after one of his scouts in Wales had recommended me to Watford at the age of 11.

'You climb those steps, you collect your medal and, when you win a ticket to the Premier League, you never want the day to end. If I could bottle that feeling I would be a multimillionaire. It's the best way to go up, but it's also the most horrible way to fall short: I tasted the other side of the coin four years later in the playoff final when Sheffield United lost 3-0 to Wolves at Cardiff. We were three down at half-time and it was game over. That was the worst feeling in the world.

'But, looking back, I still take enormous pride in the way we made that step up with Watford. I remember the gaffer walking off the pitch by himself at Wembley, because he had to do a live TV interview with Elton in the tunnel, and turning to look at the sea of yellow banked around one end of the stadium. He said there were 38,000 Watford fans in heaven – and his players were in heaven, too. All the players and staff went back to Sopwell House for a party with their families that night. There were a few pairs of dark glasses on the open-topped bus tour of the town the following day!

'The spirit we summoned over the last two months of the season was a powerful force. We were total outsiders for promotion before we embarked on that run to get in the playoffs: the odds would have been against us when Birmingham scored after two minutes of the semi-final, and Bolton had stacks of Premier League experience in their team at Wembley – we had virtually none. But what we achieved shows how far you can go when you have good professional people around you, a winning mentality and strong voices in the dressing room to provide direction and purpose.

'Although I made my debut for Watford at what is now Championship level, I had to establish myself in the first team at lower levels – and I wanted a taste of the Premier League. I wasn't prepared to let other people take it off me, and fortunately I was surrounded in that dressing room by teammates who shared that sense of pride.

'Not many teams make the jump from the third tier to the Premier League in consecutive years. Norwich did it under Paul Lambert, Nigel Adkins won back-to-back promotions at Southampton, and Manchester City followed in our footsteps the next year, but it's not a common feat.

'I remember signing my new contract in Graham Taylor's office when we were in the Second Division [what is now League One], and we spoke about his five-year plan to restore Watford to the top division. He did it three years ahead of schedule, if you like, which was a mark of the man's genius – and I don't use that word lightly.

'Whatever lay ahead for us in the Premier League, it meant the club could invest in better facilities, invest in the training ground, invest in the squad and give us a platform to build for the future.'

Page's wise words would be wasted on Taylor's successor Gianluca Vialli, whose house was built on sand.

**

Promotion, promotion, player of the season. Watford were relegated, at the first time of asking, on their return to the aristocracy, but Robert Page completed an enviable hat-trick of sorts. 'That's a proud stat for me to have against my name, even if the season didn't unfold the way we wanted,' admits Page. 'I must have told the kids a thousand times, and they must have switched off for about 999 of them.'

The Premier League was an unforgiving environment for the Hornets, although there were some memorable scalps among the disappointments. There was boyhood Liverpool fan Tommy Mooney's winner at the Kop end to stun Anfield, Allan Smart's supreme finish and Caledonian celebration against Chelsea and, if there was an accolade for goal-line clearance of the season, Page's miraculous preservation of three points at home to Bradford was in a class of its own.

When Gareth Grant raced clear, rounded Watford keeper Chris Day and had the goal at his mercy, the Bantams were odds-on to rescue a point. Out of nowhere, or so it seemed, Page raced back and slid at full stretch to hook Grant's goalbound shot off the line: 'Nobody likes losing football matches, and unfortunately we lost too many that season, but it was my only experience of Premier League football and, for me personally, it was like playing an FA Cup final every week. To beat Liverpool at Anfield, and to turn over Chelsea was satisfying – and for the supporters to recognise my efforts as player of the season was the icing on the cake. I didn't score many goals in my career, so stopping them at the other end is how I used to get my kicks. I was happy to let the boys further up the pitch steal all the glory and take all the headlines, so for me that clearance against Bradford was the equivalent of scoring. It was my job – defending is what defenders are supposed to do, it's what I was taught to do from an early age.'

Like so many of Watford's home-grown assets over the last 40 years, Page has reason to be thankful for his football upbringing and the tutelage of Tom Walley, the juniors coach who won the FA Youth Cup with the Hornets in 1982 and reached another final three years later. Walley enjoyed conspicuous success scouting his homeland, unearthing strikers Iwan Roberts and Malcolm Allen from his network of contacts in Wales in the 1980s – and Page rolled off the same conveyor belt.

'I was recommended to Tom as an 11-year-old, and from that age onwards I would spend most of my school holidays at Watford as part of their academy set-up,' says Page. 'At that time Graham Taylor was coming towards the end of his first spell at the club, but he had set a huge emphasis on making sure schoolboys and youth-team players on the club's books were looked after in lodgings with impeccable hosts. [Taylor once used his matchday programme notes to advertise for potential landlords and families who could offer schoolboys and apprentices on the club's books comfortable accommodation.] With the gaffer and Tom running the show, parents knew their sons would be well looked after. When I was going back and forth between Watford and Wales I would stay with a lovely couple, John and Brenda Booker, who made me feel as if I was being put up in a four-star hotel. For a young lad moving away from the valleys it could have been an intimidating experience, but it was a real home from home. I could see why Watford had such a good reputation as a family club – because you were made to feel part of an extended family.

'At 15 I signed schoolboy forms and a year later I was proud to be offered an apprenticeship. Kenny Jackett was the youth-team manager at the time – another thorough, decent man;

a strong character who was always straight with you. I made my first-team debut away at Birmingham as an 18-year-old when Glenn Roeder was the manager, although it was Kenny who later appointed me captain, and I was always proud to be entrusted with that role when I was only 21 or 22.

'My only regret as captain was missing out on clinching the Second Division title at Fulham on the last day. I had suffered a dead leg a week or two earlier, so I was sat in the stands – but I was on the pitch, with everyone else, when the final whistle went. Unfortunately the Football League had taken the trophy up to Preston, where they obviously expected to present it to Bristol City, who were top of the table going into the last round of fixtures . . . but Bristol City lost and we overhauled them by winning at Craven Cottage.'

That season had included a glorious contrast spanning four days in November, when Page found himself playing for Wales in a prestigious friendly international in midweek – and, on his return, geographically the shortest away trip Watford have ever made for an FA Cup tie at another League club.

'From Brazil to Barnet,' he says. 'That was an unreal experience, going from pretty sultry conditions in Brasília to a grey, drizzly afternoon on the slope at Underhill. We lost 3-0 in Brazil, and on the plane coming back I could sense a bloke in the row of seats behind me just across the aisle, staring at me. He would peer over the top of his newspaper – like a private detective in a really bad film, and have a good look – then bury his head back in the pages whenever I turned round because I could feel his eyes burning the back of my head.

'In the end I resolved to find out what it was about me that he found so fascinating, so I leaned across the aisle and said, "Hello, can I help you?" This chap stared at me again, looked back at his paper and then exclaimed, "It's you!" He showed me a photo in the paper he was reading – and there I was, going up for a header with Rivaldo the night before. We had a laugh, shook hands and both of us were pleased the mystery was solved. After that I could recline in my seat and look forward to playing Barnet – where we had a poor first half and nearly made a mess of it before we fought back, coming down the slope, to sneak through 2-1.'

That double-take at 36,000 feet was not the only brief encounter Page recalls fondly from a halcyon era of his career. Confined to barracks one year, with a busy festive schedule preventing him from nipping home to see his family in Wales, Page trained as required on Christmas Day before resting up in the north Watford digs where he lodged for some time in his transition from youth-team player to first-team captain, with another hospitable couple, David and Christine Rickman.

'They looked after me so well, they were my surrogate family,' he says. 'I had been upstairs in my bedroom for a couple of hours, watching *Robin Hood, Prince of Thieves* on TV, when Christine called me down for some Christmas dinner before I went off to link up with the squad at the team hotel ahead of our Boxing Day game. [If you haven't seen the film, Alan Rickman steals the show as the Sheriff of Nottingham; Robin Hood's American accent is less convincing.]

'I came down for a bit of roast turkey, and there in the kitchen was David's brother – the late, great actor Alan Rickman – who had come round to join us for the meal. I was probably a bit star-struck because all I could say was, "Merry Christmas – I've just been watching you on the telly." Never mind being the only Watford captain climbing those steps to lift a trophy at Wembley – I'm sure I must be the only Watford captain who's ever sat down to Christmas dinner with the Sheriff of Nottingham.'

8

NEIL COX

There was a time when Neil Cox's career appeared to be blighted, as if he walked under ladders as a rite of passage, broke mirrors for fun and every day of the month was Friday the 13th.

From being dropped on FA Cup final day to relegations, losing a playoff final and the unbeaten start which turned into a blowout, Cox took more trips down Misery Lane than a Samaritans helpline volunteer.

Even when he fought back from being cast as excess baggage – once forced to train with the reserves, he was later appointed club captain at Vicarage Road – Cox soon found himself on the frontline of sandbags and storm defences as the waves of fiscal catastrophe lapped at Watford's door. When the collapse of ITV Digital, a television deal which turned out to be exactly as it appeared – too good to be true – left a black hole in the Hornets' finances, it was Cox who brokered a 12 per cent deferral of the players' wages which saved the club from oblivion.

By any yardstick, the response of Watford's players to adversity reflected only credit on them. From the autumn of 2002, when the financial outlook appeared bleak, manager Ray Lewington presided over a triumph of dwindling resources and a distortion of logic. By leading the Hornets to two major semi-finals in as many years, against prohibitive odds, Lewington's team earned as much affection as any promotion could generate. And for Cox, all the frustration and disappointments of an unfulfilling start to his time at Vicarage Road melted into a golden hue of respect from the supporters for galvanising the dressing room in times of hardship – and, eventually, making sure his teammates were paid back every penny of the wages they deferred.

Cox may have fallen out with his chairman along the way, but he will go down as the captain of Cup fighters who proved a cut above at Watford.

By the time he was 28 Cox had played in the top flight for four clubs, won half a dozen England under-21 caps and featured in a League Cup-winning side at Aston Villa. He made 248 appearances between 1999 and 2005 for the Hornets, where he stayed longer than any other club in his playing career. And when turbulence came calling at Vicarage Road he was almost a veteran among riders on the storm, going back to acrimony in the Middlesbrough camp hours before a major letdown at Wembley in 1997.

'It was a difficult time for Middlesbrough,' he says. 'We had lost the League Cup final against Leicester after a replay, and the week before the FA Cup final we had been relegated on the final day of the season. We only went down because of the three points the club was deducted for failing to turn up at Blackburn after the squad had been absolutely decimated by illness. There was a flu epidemic and we didn't have enough players left standing to fulfil the fixture. It was a heartbreaking way to go down, drawing 1-1 at Leeds and seeing little Juninho sat on the pitch in tears afterwards. If we had won that afternoon we would have stayed up – but that no-show at Blackburn cost us big time.

'So the FA Cup final was a big thing for us, a chance to salvage something from all the disappointments, but in the build-up there was a big doubt about Fabrizio Ravanelli's fitness because he was getting intensive treatment for a hamstring injury.

We had such a good spirit, and we fought so hard over 54 games, to achieve something that season that I was prepared to speak my mind – too much for my own good, as it turned out. I always got on really well with the manager, Bryan Robson, and he always encouraged people to have their say at team meetings, but on this occasion it cost me my place.

'Ravanelli had not trained all week, and yet all of a sudden he was fit to play at Wembley. There had been enough speculation about his fitness, so maybe I should have kept my mouth shut. But on the morning of the game we had a bit of a set-to at breakfast – let's just say we had a frank exchange of views – and I was the one who paid the price. When the team was announced, I wasn't in it. I wasn't even on the bench. I wasn't even in the dressing room before the game.'

Ravanelli, it transpired, had taken exception to an interview in the *Daily Star* in which Cox had suggested Danish striker Mikkel Beck should start at Wembley and gambling on the fiery Italian striker's fitness was a risk too far. While Boro were lining up for a squad portrait in their Cup final suits and sunglasses, the glowering 'White Feather' adopted the red rag and threw a punch at Cox. Boro midfielder Robbie Mustoe told *FourFourTwo* magazine, 'It turned into the most awful final preparation for the biggest game in most of our lives. In the team photograph you had Ravanelli basically trying to reach across players to have a fight with Neil. There was so much crap – even on the way to the game, Rav was shouting at Neil at the back of the bus.'

Robson had arranged for stand-up comedian Stan Boardman to provide in-flight entertainment on the coach ride to Wembley to keep the mood light. It turned out to be one of the toughest gigs of his career. Middlesbrough lost 2-0, and four days later Cox was sold to Bolton for £1.5 million. 'Look, the manager had to make a decision, and Ravanelli was such an important

player because he'd scored 31 goals for us that season,' says
Cox. 'Once Rav and I had fallen out, and I had been left out
of the side altogether, me not being in the dressing room was
probably the right way to go. As it turned out, the game went
away from us pretty quickly – Roberto Di Matteo put Chelsea
in front after 42 seconds and Ravanelli's hamstring gave way
after 20 minutes.

'Hindsight is a wonderful thing, and I'm not usually the sort
to go around saying "I told you so", but the fact is I was right.
I felt the club let him get away with it a bit: I would say wanting
to play in a major final without training all week was a liberty,
but it's water under the bridge now. I never got to play in an FA
Cup final but, like I say, the proof of the pudding was there for
all to see.'

Reaching two Cup finals, losing them both and being
relegated because of a points deduction was a lot for Cox to
swallow in one season on Teesside, but his hard-luck story had
only just begun. Twelve months later Bolton – christening their
shiny new Reebok stadium after 102 years at Burnden Park –
were relegated on goal difference, with the tin lid once again
supplied by a 2-0 defeat against Chelsea.

The Trotters' baptism of their new home proved both
controversial and costly, and Cox recalls, 'When we played
Everton in our first game at the Reebok, Nathan Blake "scored"
with a shot that hit the underside of the bar and TV replays
showed it landed two feet over the line – but it wasn't given.
The game finished 0-0 and, although we didn't know it at the
time, the two extra points we should have taken would have
kept us up.'

On the last day of term at Stamford Bridge, Bolton
needed only to equal Everton's result against Coventry to
ensure survival, but Chelsea – preparing for the European
Cup Winners' Cup final three days later – were a tribute to
professionalism, despite some of their own fans wanting to

lose and end Everton's unbroken 44-year run in the top flight. A minority greeted goals in the last 18 minutes from Gianluca Vialli and Jody Morris with good-natured pantomime villain boos, and Bolton were condemned to a tearful fate by a 1-1 draw at Goodison Park.

Little did he know it, but Cox's hard-luck story at Bolton had another disappointment in store. The following season, another trip to Wembley rewarded him only with more heartbreak – at Watford's expense.

The Hornets had beaten Colin Todd's side home and away during the regular League season, and the Golden Boys stormed into the playoffs on the back of 22 points from a possible 24, but Bolton – still packed with Premier League experience from the side relegated 12 months earlier – looked slight favourites on paper.

Not for the first time on the home straight towards promotion, Watford were indebted to Alec Chamberlain's sharp reflexes as the Trotters made the better start, but once Nick Wright had opened the scoring with an acrobatic masterpiece, poor Cox began to absorb a familiar, sinking feeling again. 'I had a great view of Nicky's wonder goal – because it dipped over my head into the top corner,' he groans. 'And when I joined Watford a few months later, they didn't let me forget it.

'I remember 1999 well because Bolton only just missed out on automatic promotion and the disappointment probably caught up with us at Wembley. We thought we could control the game if we managed to get our noses in front and we made a fast start, but "Chambo" produced a couple of great saves from Eidur Gudjohnsen early on and Watford grew in confidence. They had been on a great run and, deep down, I think everyone knew it was the kind of game where the first goal would be huge – unfortunately for us, Nicky pulled that overhead kick out of nowhere and we were left chasing the game. To be honest, we didn't often look like turning it round.

We knew Watford could hurt us on the counter-attack, and they had better chances to make it 2-0 than we had to equalise before Allan Smart put the game to bed. On the day, the better team won in the end – they had more fight and deserved to go up. As difficult as it is to watch another team celebrating at Wembley, I remember thinking it must be the best way to go up: you climb those stairs, you lift a trophy, you pick up a medal, you do a lap of honour and you wave to your family in the crowd. For beaten sides it's a sickener, but for the winners it's the perfect day.

'I went into the Watford dressing room afterwards to congratulate the boys personally because I was brought up to respect the opposition and be gracious in defeat. I wished them luck in the Premiership, told them, "Enjoy every minute of the experience and I'm sure you'll be fine." I was good friends with Graham Taylor because I had dealt many times with his dad, Tom, when I started out at Scunthorpe, where he was a sports journalist on the local evening paper. Neither of us realised what was in store the next season . . .'

***

Early-season optimism was draining away faster than bathwater when the plug has been pulled out. Amid the 10 defeats in 13 games there had been glorious snapshots for the family album, notably Tommy Mooney's winner at Anfield, where Graham Taylor presented his former rival in international management, Gérard Houllier, with a bottle of Château Lagrange and the Liverpool boss probably needed it to drown his sorrows after Watford's shock 1-0 victory.

And there was a richly deserved 1-0 win against Chelsea, where Smart's expertly finished goal and debutant Nordin Wooter's twinkling footwork hinted at moments of brightness amid the one-way traffic. But when Bolton Wanderers accepted Watford's £500,000 bid for Neil Cox in November 1999, the writing was not just on the wall for the Hornets: it was trailed in plumes of smoke across the sky.

Cox joined his fourth Premier League club – after playing in the top flight with Aston Villa, Middlesbrough and Bolton – knowing the odds were stacked against Watford staying up. To an extent, his hand was forced. He had reservations about signing up for more potential disappointment on the pitch; and to a larger extent, he had misgivings about uprooting his family. Cox had one young daughter, and his wife was expecting their second child.

It says everything about his application, and much about his contributions in a yellow shirt, that by the time Cox and Watford went their separate ways six years later he had turned a sequence of personal setbacks in football – serial misfortune on an industrial scale – into the best of times.

Cox was not the most gifted player to wear the hart's antlers. Nor, if truth be told, was he always the most popular among the supporters. But when the club's tailspin, beginning with Premier League relegation and then acceleration towards the abyss, threatened Watford's very existence, he lit the path towards survival. And providence rewarded them with sporadic – but memorable – success against the forbidding odds.

'Behind the scenes, Bolton were having financial problems. Colin Todd had left the club and Sam Allardyce came in with a new set of ideas,' says Cox. 'Big Sam was very straightforward – a few of us would have to go out of the door to make way for changes to the squad. I got called in to say Watford had made a bid, the club had accepted it and Allardyce was letting me go. All of a sudden I was on the train south to discuss terms, which was a big issue because my daughter was one year old and another baby was on the way. To live in a hotel, even for just six weeks while we found somewhere to call home in Bushey, was never going to be easy.

'But I had seen quite a lot of Watford – obviously I had a great view of them getting promoted the previous season – and I always felt there was a certain warmth about the club. Around the time when they won the Fourth Division title, Elton John turned up to watch them at Scunthorpe's Old Show Ground, and the songs home fans were singing about him were not repeatable – and then there was the Graham Taylor connection. We went to the same secondary school in Scunthorpe [High Ridge School has now been renamed the St Lawrence Academy] and, like I said, I got on well with his dad. When I was breaking through into the first team at Scunthorpe Tom Taylor once told me, "You will end up playing for my son one day." And he was right – before Watford, I played for Graham at England under-21 level.

'It was a big thing for me to go and talk to Watford, not only because it was another opportunity to play in the Premier League but because I thought I would play at centre-half again, which I considered my best position. For one reason or another I had spent a lot of time at right-back with Bolton and Middlesbrough, but I didn't see how I was going to get a game there at Watford. They already had Nigel Gibbs, a club legend, in that position and Graham had started the season with Des Lyttle in the side.'

As it turned out, Taylor preferred to use Cox as a full-back, but even a Las Vegas croupier's shuffling of the pack, in any permutation, would not have saved Watford from the drop in 2000. They went down 12 points from the safety line, and Cox finished on the winning side in only three of his first 22 appearances for the Hornets. They were relegated with Sheffield Wednesday and Wimbledon, whose ten men had beaten Watford 3-2 on the opening day of the season thanks to a horrid Richard Johnson own goal. In the Vicarage Road tunnel afterwards Dons coach Terry Burton – who would later provide distinguished service in Watford's backroom staff under Ray Lewington – had celebrated their unlikely win by gleefully admonishing journalists who had tipped them for relegation. He was less ebullient when their fate was sealed with a 2-0 defeat on the final day at Southampton.

Appearances can sometimes be deceptive in football, and just as Wimbledon's premature euphoria in 1999 proved to be a mirage in the desert, Watford's barnstorming start to the following season was the precursor to crushing anti-climax – and the king's second abdication.

When they took 39 points from a possible 45 for starters, and remained the last unbeaten club in all four divisions, it looked as if the Hornets would rebound into the top flight at the first time of asking. Cox contributed four goals to the 15-match unbeaten run, including a pair of identikit headers against QPR, a fine chip at Taylor's old club Wolves and a lung-bursting 90-yard run to pop up on the far post – where a left-winger, not a right-back, might usually appear – to finish Wooter's mazy run and cross against Birmingham. That last goal crowned a special baptism for my four-and-a-half-year-old son, paying his first visit to Vicarage Road, and maintaining his admirable sense of occasion. He had been born, around the opening titles of *Match of the Day*, in a propitious alignment of events when Watford beat Port Vale 5-2 and a heathen tribe lost 4-0 at Birmingham on the same day. That night, in celebratory mood, yours truly filed his match report of David Connolly's hat-trick and Devon White's pair of goals for the *Daily Mirror* from a payphone in the maternity unit at Wycombe General Hospital.

There are several theories about the reason for Watford's collapse of form in the 2000–01 season. On the back of that unbeaten run, the Hornets lost seven of the next eight games, and even the respite of a 3-3 draw with West Bromwich Albion, and the relief of Tommy Mooney's late equaliser, was tempered

by the loss of a two-goal lead. Some believe Watford were
simply 'rumbled' and opponents worked out a way stop them.
Others point to Taylor's growing disenchantment with multiple
agendas in the boardroom – a far cry from his first decade at
the club when he called the tune and Elton John played it on
the piano. And there was, undeniably, an inexplicable loss of
form in certain cases. Norwegian goalkeeper Espen Baardsen,
who had arrived during the close season in a record £3.5
million job lot from Tottenham with midfielder Allan Nielsen,
morphed from a towering physical presence into an Edward
Scissorhands tribute act of fumbles and shrinking confidence.

Cox, however, attributes the volte-face of results to fatigue.
By Christmas, he felt the Hornets were running on empty.
'After being relegated, the gaffer took us to the Royal Navy's
HMS Raleigh training base at Torpoint in Devon for a week
in pre-season, and we got absolutely run into the ground. I've
got no problem with maximising your fitness levels, because
you need plenty of fuel in the tank to get through a gruelling
46-game season – the gaffer wanted us to be the fittest team
in the League, and to show we meant business – but we just
burnt out. When we started losing games around November,
we trained incredibly hard to try to stop the rot – but the harder
we trained the more we were getting beat. It was a vicious circle
because our legs had gone. The boss believed in playing his
strongest side every week – again, no problem with that in
principle – but nobody was rested and some of the lads were
on their last legs with half the season to go. The more we lost
games, the more we blew up. That season was the hardest I've
ever been worked, by miles. Graham Taylor was renowned for
his attention to fitness, and his record as a manager speaks for
itself, but I felt we were overcooked that year.'

Watford's patchy form in the second half of the campaign
sent Taylor into a short-lived retirement – he would resurface at
Aston Villa in 2002 – on the back of five wins, five draws and

10 defeats in their last 20 games, bearing out Cox's observations about their staying power.

If Taylor's decision to walk away, after the Hornets turned their supercharged start into a disappointing ninth-place finish, gave supporters a chance to send him into the sunset with a warm send-off at the last home game of the season against Tranmere, the changing of the guard was unsettling for Cox. To this day he maintains that Taylor advised his successor Gianluca Vialli to give Cox a wide berth because he was a dressing-room agitator. But in Taylor's autobiography, published posthumously in late 2017, the outgoing messiah appears to suggest he was merely doing the new manager's bidding for him, saying, 'Before I left, it became apparent that the new manager had a clear idea who he did and didn't want to keep, and that he didn't fancy having to tell the players he was rejecting that they should move on. I felt the least I could do was to sit down face to face with the players the club no longer wanted and be straight with them, even if it really wasn't my responsibility to do so.'

Either way, when Vialli moved into the hot seat, Cox found himself banished to train with the reserves as excess ballast in a squad soon bloated by expensive refurbishment.

'It wasn't just me who was told I wasn't wanted,' says Cox. 'Robert Page was told from the outset he was surplus to requirements, which must have been hard for him to take as club captain, and Peter Kennedy was another one who was moved on. My understanding is that Graham Taylor told Luca, "These are the players you need to keep and these are the ones you might have to release" – and mine was one of the faces that didn't fit. We didn't find out for sure until later on, when the squad met Luca and his staff, exactly what he was thinking, and we were told the news by Terry Byrne, the general manager. I have no problem with Luca, he was good as gold about it. As a professional footballer, you know that when a new regime moves in there will be changes and you just get on with it.

Most of the lads who weren't wanted moved on pretty quickly, but I stayed on because Watford wanted a big fee for me. One or two clubs were interested but nothing ever came of it, so I just kept my head down and worked hard. I didn't have a problem training with the reserves because you never know what's around the corner in football and you have to be ready to step up when required.

'Sure enough, that's exactly what happened. We had a couple of injuries and when I picked up a call from a number I didn't recognise, and a voice speaking English with a thick Italian accent asked me to link up with the squad at Wolves, I thought it was a wind-up. But it was the boss, and I ended up playing nearly 40 games that year, playing at centre-back – my best position – with Filippo Galli, who was a class act, even at 38 years old.

'I got on well with Luca, and I like to think I won him over by knuckling down when I could have made a fuss. His style of football was easy on the eye but our results were inconsistent, and one day he pulled me aside, over a round of golf, to ask my opinion. I told him we needed to get the ball forward a bit quicker, because we had the quality to do more damage in the final third. But my team talk obviously went down well – three days later he got the sack!

'That was when a few chickens started coming home to roost about the club's financial position, and Ray Lewington took over, knowing the squad was going to be decimated and he would have to slash the wage bill by around 75 per cent.'

***

When the numbers started to crunch, the gap between solvency and ruin read like a ransom note. Watford had already gone £2 million into the red after handing Gianluca Vialli more than £6 million to replenish his squad, with a Premier League parachute payment and a £2.8 million share of the ITV Digital fortune earmarked to cover any shortfall. But when the TV deal turned out to be payable on the 12th of never, and the Hornets were saddled with an annual wage bill approaching £17 million, the balance sheet was not just under pressure: it was collapsing like a sumo wrestler's deckchair under the strain.

Shipping out some of Vialli's unimpressive recruits – the gilded Ramon Vega springs readily to mind – would make a dent in the £9.5 million Watford needed to raise in two years to ride out the storm, and just nine months after buying the freehold of Vicarage Road for £750,000 the club was forced to sell the ground again.

Yet when all the cost-cutting and fundraising had been totted up, there was still a £1.9 million black hole in the £9.5 million required to satisfy the bank managers and book-keepers. Chairman Graham Simpson and chief executive Tim Shaw had raised in excess of £3 million between them but, in terms of the club's financial health, it was like trying to fit a junk-food addict's waistline into a supermodel's size-zero jeans.

After winning four and drawing three of their first ten League games – punctuated by atrocious scenes in a Worthington Cup débâcle, where Lewington admitted the enduring hostility between Watford and their unloved neighbours from over the border had caught him by surprise – the directors went cap-in-hand to the players. The club, they warned, may not have been able to survive as a going concern unless the squad deferred a percentage of their wages – or, in effect, agreed to take a pay cut. Cox, installed as captain by Lewington, and goalkeeper Alec Chamberlain, the Hornets' delegate from the PFA players' union, were assigned as the links between dressing room and boardroom.

'The situation, as it was presented to us, looked bad,' says Cox. 'We wanted to get the PFA involved, and they said they would send someone down to help, but lots of other clubs were in the same boat as us and the cavalry never arrived. I walked into a meeting with the chairman, Terry Byrne and the gaffer to be told, "Sorry, but we need all the players to take a pay cut." Just like that. For some of the boys who were on Premier League wages, maybe trimming five or ten per cent off your wage packet was not going to make a whole world of difference to your living standard, but for younger lads on the fringes of the squad it was a big deal. The boys got their heads together and said we would take an eight per cent wage cut – but when I went back with the offer, the chairman's response left me a bit stunned: "Sorry, not enough." I had to go back and tell the players, "We've got a choice: either we can defer 12 per cent of our wages, or we don't get paid at all." As you can imagine, there was a lot of unrest – this was late September, and in the run-up to Christmas, with all the expense involved for those with young families, not being paid was not an option. I didn't like going into team meetings and effectively asking to take money off people. As I saw it, that wasn't part of my job. I had only just been made captain and I was left in the lurch. As well as dealing with the players, Alec and I were fielding calls from about 20 agents, and we really needed the PFA to help us out. In the end, I went back and told Mr Simpson we would agree to defer 12 per cent of our wages – but we wanted our money back if the crisis eased, or the club came into some unexpected income. Throughout the whole process Ray was an absolute trooper and he told me, "Whatever you decide to do, I'm right behind you." He took us out for meals to keep the squad tight, and the night before we played at Sheffield United, when we sat down together in the hotel, Ray said, "I'm not sure who's going to pay for this" and I replied, "It will have to be you, gaffer – we've just taken a pay cut and we're all skint!" That was just good-natured banter, of course, but I'll never forget his pre-match

team talk at Bramall Lane. Sometimes managers will try to fill
your head with Winston Churchill or Chinese warlords, and
your eyes will glaze over if it's not the right occasion for it, but
Ray got the message spot-on that day. He told us, "We've had
a week from hell, people have lost money hand over fist, so
you've got nothing to lose: just go out there and play. Go out
and show the people what you are all about, as footballers and
as men. Walk tall and be proud – because if you come back in
here with three points, the supporters will be proud of you and
I'll be proud of you."

'We could have felt sorry for ourselves, but we produced
a performance which was a proper reflection of that group's
spirit and solidarity. We weren't going to let anyone steamroller
us. It might have been after that Sheffield United game, but
we were on the coach heading back down the M1 after an
away win that autumn and Sir Elton John [who was now the
club's honorary life president after stepping down as chairman]
overtook us, winding down his window to give us a thumbs-up.'

The team who returned from Bramall Lane with three points
on 28 September 2002 did not reach the FA Cup final, play in
Europe or finish runners-up to Liverpool in the League. But
they will always command the respect of fans who appreciate
pride in the shirt more than money in the bank.

When former Hornets striker Wayne Allison gave the Blades
an early lead, Watford didn't curl up their toes, cut their losses
or sulk. The response belongs, perhaps, in the club's top 20
finest wins of the last 40 years – not necessarily for its artistic
merit, although there were spells of admirable football, but for
the sheer tenacity and refusal to wallow in misfortune.

When Micah Hyde, who had not looked out of place in the
Premier League under Taylor, sent Heidar Helguson through
on goal and Phil Jagielka intervened, at the expense of a red
card, Cox slammed the resulting penalty beyond Paddy Kenny

as if he was releasing all the pent-up frustration of a difficult week's negotiations with the chairman.

Helguson, darting to the near post, made it 2-1 before the break, and although the Hornets also finished with ten men, as Hyde collected a second caution in the late siege, Watford held on stoically. In adversity Lewington's side won five out of six games following the wage-deferral agreement, banking enough points to keep them safely cocooned in mid-table when their League form became patchier either side of Christmas.

They set off on the road to redemption early in 2003, when Cox and the players discovered that an FA Cup run was the cure for all pay cuts. After negotiating a potential booby-trap at lowly Macclesfield, and a superb display against top-flight West Brom – Helguson's late winner meant Albion keeper Russell Hoult's blinding save from Cox's fiercely struck penalty was immaterial – they edged past Sunderland, anchored to the Premier League seabed, in front of 3,500 travelling fans on Wearside, to reach the quarter-finals. Tommy Smith's twice-taken penalty was controversial both in its award and referee Mike Dean's insistence on the sequel, but the Hornets deserved their luck.

'You could sense an atmosphere around the club,' says Cox. 'We didn't set out in the third round expecting to reach the last four, but the players had a right go and the fans got right behind us. We absolutely battered West Brom, and afterwards I remember thinking, "We've got to keep this going, we're on to something here." Not a lot was going our way in the League, but the club had not budgeted for a long Cup run and the penny dropped: this was a chance to get our money back.'

The home quarter-final against Burnley was not a classic, but there have been few happier days, and few larger crowds at Vicarage Road this century. Smith, badly injured in a car crash barely three weeks earlier, made a prodigious recovery to make the starting line-up and scoop the crucial opening goal from close range before Stephen Glass dipped a glorious free-kick over the wall to settle all arguments.

For Cox it was arguably the high watermark of his six years at Watford. 'The pitch was awful, and as a spectacle it probably wasn't the most thrilling game that's ever been live on TV,' he says. 'But it was a full house, there were balloons flying everywhere and the atmosphere was electric – tense at first, but once we had gone in front, it was happy hour. Really memorable. Really special.

'My only regret about that run is the semi-final at Villa Park. Southampton had not been to a major final for 20-odd years and all the pressure was on them, but some of our lads froze and there were one or two selection issues.' (Influential midfielder Allan Nielsen was only fit enough to start on the bench with Smith, who was miffed to be left out for Michael Chopra following the on-loan striker's four goals in a remarkable 7-4 win at Burnley eight days earlier.) 'I never got to play in an FA Cup final – I had been dropped on the morning of the game by Middlesbrough six years earlier and with Watford we just couldn't make it over the line. But that run was worth something like £2 million to the club in extra revenue, which was good news for the lads who were owed 12 per cent of their wages for the previous seven months.'

Later that year Cox would go into bat again on his teammates' behalf to lobby, respectfully, for the backdated pay they were owed. Always a reluctant shop steward, even if he was not shy about offering an opinion, he did not intend to fall out with Graham Simpson, but evidently he felt the dressing room's goodwill gesture was not returned with sufficient tact by the chairman.

'I had a bit of uncertainty around that time. You don't expect the chairman to thank you for taking Watford on a lucrative Cup run with flowers and chocolates, but the boys wanted their money back and, from what I was hearing, there was now enough in the pot for the club to honour their side of the deal. I went to see the chairman and he said to me, absolutely deadpan, "I'll pay you back in full, but I can only give the others half their money." I remember looking at Terry Byrne and asking, "Are you taking the piss?" Mr Simpson insisted he was only joking, but that's when the chairman and I had a bit of a ding-dong, and after that I always felt he wanted to sell me.

'Fortunately, Ray Lewington didn't want to let me go and I think he may even have offered his resignation, as they were having arguments about me. I was happy at the club, working with a manager I trusted and a bunch of players who had got on with it when their pay was reduced, so instead of rocking the boat I felt the best solution was to give up the captaincy for the good of the team in the long run.'

Back in the trenches, Cox and Watford marched on Wembley again in the 2004–05 campaign – this time under lights – with a hugely enjoyable run to the Carling Cup semi-finals. After grinding out a laboured win against Cambridge, a convincing 3-0 success at Reading and a penalty shootout triumph after 120 barren minutes at Sheffield United, the Hornets completed the south coast 'double' with emphatic home wins against Southampton and Portsmouth. Helguson's volley on the run in a 5-2 romp against the Saints was sublime technique. And the ultimate team effort to knock out Pompey, also then in the Premier League, was further evidence, if any was needed, that the higher the opposition's quality the more Lewington's coaching brought out the best in his team. In the *Sun* Dave Kidd described Vicarage Road as a 'roaring fortress' on the night Helguson and Bruce Dyer put Portsmouth to the sword 3-0.

In the two-legged semi-final against Liverpool Steven Gerrard was the difference. The England midfielder, who would go on to lift the European Cup four months later in the so-called miracle of Istanbul, scored the only goal at both Anfield and Vicarage Road, but another Cup run gave Cox – whose relationship with chairman Simpson was now beyond repair – more reasons to appreciate Lewington's resourceful management.

'We played really well to put Southampton and Pompey away,' recalls Cox. 'And the games against Liverpool, especially the first leg at Anfield, were fantastic experiences. We gave as good as we got up there, and probably deserved to bring them back to Vicarage Road on level terms, but I stuck out a leg when Gerrard's shot might have been hitting the post, or even going wide, and turned it in. And although Liverpool shut down the game at our place we should have had a penalty when Jamie Carragher fouled Heidar in the box, but for some reason Mike Riley didn't give it. It was disappointing to go out in another semi-final but, mentally, it's the biggest hurdle of all in Cup football, and it took a player of Gerrard's class and quality to make the difference. Liverpool beat Juventus, Chelsea and AC Milan to win the Champions League that season. We can be proud that we pushed them all the way.'

For Lewington the end of the road in the League Cup effectively signalled the end of his tenure as manager. Eight points from the next nine games in the Championship was enough for Simpson and the board to press the panic button, and Cox was not happy to lose his biggest ally among the management.

'I was angry at the way Ray was treated,' he says. 'He had been forced to slash the wage bill, was given very little money to bring in new players, and he managed us through the pay cuts. He would have kept us up, and it was a poor decision to let him go, but the players knew something was up. We were playing Preston and when we got to our pre-match hotel, the gaffer's name was not on the guest-list. He thought it was a bit strange, and from his reaction you could smell a rat. Sometime later I was told Aidy Boothroyd was at the Preston game, which we lost 2-0 and sealed Ray's fate – if it wasn't sealed already.

'Watford have had some terrific managers down the years, and the people who took them into the Premier League take a lot of the credit, but I don't think Ray Lewington got the plaudits he deserved. He had absolutely no money to play with, and yet he kept the club in the Championship and took us to two semi-finals. Elton John obviously thought he did a fantastic job – because when he played a concert at Vicarage Road that summer Ray and his family were allocated front-row seats, bang in the middle of what is now the Upper Graham Taylor stand. I know exactly where he was sitting because I was sat right next to him. I thought it was nice when a group of fans on the pitch below spotted Ray and serenaded him with a chant of "Lew-ing-ton, Lew-ing-ton" as a measure of respect.'

Cox – who, when his playing career wound down, moved briefly to Portugal and worked in property development, with a bit of scouting on the side – was among the old guard shipped out by Boothroyd in July 2005. He had no qualms about his treatment from Lewington's replacement as manager, even when he was made to train with the apprentice professionals. Cox suspects his card was being marked from higher up the food chain, but three weeks into pre-season he sealed a free transfer to Cardiff.

When he took his first steps in management Cox hooked up with his former Watford and England under-21 teammate Neal Ardley at AFC Wimbledon in 2012. He had tipped off Lewington about Ardley's availability as a player ten years earlier, and they became stalwarts of the squad who took the pay cut on a promise of jam tomorrow.

Jam? For a player whose Watford career was blighted by ill fortune at first, it is not a back-handed condiment to suggest Neil Cox played a captain's innings when the club was close to collapse.

9

GAVIN MAHON

THE RUMBLE IN THE TUNNEL

Sunlight was bursting through the skylight in the Millennium Stadium's closed roof, as if in celestial approval of the comprehensive dismantling of fallen giants.

One half of the venue was a riot of yellow, as 27,000 Hornet pilgrims turned the excursion into the largest long-distance migration of Watford supporters in the club's history by far. In the directors' box, Leeds' famously cantankerous chairman Ken Bates was a portrait of grumpiness. Those of us who had been banned from Stamford Bridge by the great Captain Birdseye lookalike seven years earlier when Chelsea was his constituency – in fairness, comparing Bates' programme notes with the merits of fertiliser is not necessarily a compliment – momentarily empathised with the great man's distress. And then thought better of it. Next season we would be going to Manchester United; dear old Ken would be taking his show to Colchester United.

When the tickertape showers had subsided, the laps of honour were complete and 40,000 ashen emissaries in white had begun their crestfallen retreat towards Yorkshire, we finally managed to drag ourselves away from the scene of triumph: a thoroughly satisfying, life-affirming, utterly wonderful triumph. As we shuffled out into the streets of Cardiff a refrain acclaiming Aidy Boothroyd as a football genius reverberated along the River Taff. And good old Aidy, swept along by the euphoria and the praise deservedly cascading his way after directing an

unlikely charge to promotion, accepted the accolade at face
value. Within a couple of years Boothroyd would leave Vicarage
Road with Watford pretty much where he found them, flirting
with the rapids at the wrong end of the Championship.

But as of 2018 he remains one of only three men to lead
the club into the top flight, along with the canonised Graham
Taylor and Slaviša Jokanović, the inspired Serbian who
built an empire by popping in for seven months. And when
Boothroyd burst through that skylight into the Premier League
in the Welsh capital, the Hornets executed his well-laid plans to
perfection – starting with an almighty racket in the tunnel which
reduced their opponents to proverbial rabbits in headlights, and
gratifyingly they never emerged from their trance.

Watford captain Gavin Mahon recalls, with delicious clarity,
the manner in which Leeds were spooked before a ball was
kicked in the playoff final – and how Kevin Blackwell's side had
rubbed the Hornets up the wrong way the night before.

'We were staying at a different hotel from our wives,
girlfriends and families,' he says. 'Entirely by luck, and not
through espionage, some of our partners booked into the
Leeds team hotel, and we were receiving feedback that they
fancied their chances. I was told a couple of the Leeds players
got into a lift with a Watford player's wife and told her, "This
time tomorrow, you are going to be feeling sad – sorry about
that." And there were apparently one or two of them walking
round the hotel as if they owned the place. I've no idea if that
was actually true, but that was the information coming back to
us and it was just what we wanted to hear. Perfect motivation.'

Before the semi-final first leg at Crystal Palace, Boothroyd
had delved into his repertoire of mind games and put the names
of his first-team squad in a hat. Each player drew a name and
was required to stand in front of his teammates extolling his
colleague's virtues. It sounds like the kind of gimmick he might

have learned on his football management course at Warwick University, but for stoking egos before a defining match of the season it was a masterpiece of positive thinking.

In the lucky dip, Mahon pulled out Ashley Young's name. Initially rejected by Watford as a schoolboy because of his matchstick legs and skeletal physique, Young had fought heroically to salvage his dreams of a career in professional football. In 12 months on Boothroyd's watch he had progressed from bit-part and occasional understudy for Paul Devlin on the right wing to rising star. Young's dead-ball delivery, not least his ability to lash 25-yard free-kicks into the top corner, became a feature of the Hornets' relentless embarrassment of bookmakers who had chalked them up as relegation favourites in the 2005–06 campaign.

Mahon says, 'You might look at it in the cold light of day and dismiss it as a stunt, but I could see what Aidy was trying to do. Psychologically, how are you going to feel if a teammate who goes through the same sweat and graft as you stands up in front of the whole squad and tells them how important you've been? You're going to feel ten feet tall. We had come to a stage of the season where nine months of hard work now boiled down to three games, and anything that gave you an extra boost – even if it was just mental stimulation – was a good idea in my book. I spoke for two or three minutes, saying how proud I was of the way Ashley had developed into a match-winner for us, how he was a dedicated professional who had never given up on his ambition, and was always wanting to stay behind for extra training to work on his game. I said he had a great attitude for such a young lad, he was a future international, and this kid could well go right to the top.

'After I spoke, one of the lads looked at me and said, "I wish you'd drawn my name out of the hat." And, of course, with the benefit of hindsight, I got it right about Ashley. He's had a fantastic career and he's done Watford proud as a home-grown international footballer.'

The semi-final went absolutely according to plan: textbook, clockwork and a nice punch-up when Palace were beyond redemption. Marlon King gave Tony Popovic a guided tour of south-east London; Young whipped one of his signature free-kicks over the wall, bending it into the top corner beyond Gábor Király, Palace's Hungarian keeper in pyjama bottoms; and Matthew Spring adding the garnish with an emphatic finish. Oh, Springy, Springy, he used to make you shudder but he's all right now.

By the time Boothroyd and Palace defender Fitz Hall – who would join the Hornets six years later in the first wave of recruits in the Pozzo era at Vicarage Road – had a minor disagreement over a throw-in during the reassuring banality of the second leg, it was all over bar the judges' scorecards under Queensberry Rules.

'We didn't get much joy against Palace in the two League games earlier that season,' recalls Mahon. 'But Marlon loved backing into defenders, rolling them and the physical battle. Before the semi-final he kept saying, "I'm going to run this guy into the ground." And he was as good as his word. For the second leg, Aidy had told the players to keep our discipline: no red cards, nothing that could undermine our chances in the final . . . and then he went and picked a fight with the biggest bloke on the pitch! Later in my career I ended up playing with Fitz at QPR and we used to have a good laugh about it.'

***

Ten months before leading his team out at the Millennium Stadium, with upwards of £34 million Premier League loot at stake, Boothroyd had famously assembled the Hornets squad for their first pre-season team meeting by arranging the chairs in the seating plan of a bus. Sat in the driver's 'cab', he turned to his nonplussed players and announced, 'This is my bus to Premiership – who's coming with me?'

Mahon admits the gathered assembly was unsure if their manager was acting out a comedian's charade or whether he was being serious. 'Yes, we looked at each other as if to say, "Is this guy for real?" After all, we had only stayed up with not much to spare at the end of the previous season. Heidar Helguson's winners at Stoke and Rotherham proved the difference between survival and going down, so to talk about winning promotion seemed a bit optimistic.'

While Boothroyd's raging positivity and can-do attitude was not misplaced, former chairman Sir Elton John's intervention in the summer of 2005 was critical. The Rocket Man had agreed to play a concert at Vicarage Road during the close season – dress code yellow – with the club claiming the projected £1.3 million proceeds would go towards the 'ring-fenced' fund for redeveloping the antique main stand. The ring-fence, it soon became apparent, was riddled with holes and was unfit for a chicken run, but in mid-concert Sir Elton dropped the proverbial bombshell. Between numbers on his playlist, and in front of 25,000 witnesses, he revealed that he had insisted on all the profits from the gig being handed to Boothroyd to strengthen his squad. 'Let's get behind the new manager,' he said, and the huddled masses roared their consent.

Armed with considerable spending power where his predecessor Ray Lewington's budget had been buttons, Boothroyd went out and signed Marlon King, Darius Henderson, Malky Mackay, Clarke Carlisle, Matthew Spring, Jordan Stewart – whose transfer fees, as if by magic, came to £1.3 million in total – and brought in promising goalkeeper Ben Foster on loan. This was not an arbitrary trolley dash: it was the retail therapy of a manager who knew the fastest way to improve a team was to strengthen the spine.

'I'm not going to lie: the players were surprised when Aidy got the job,' says Mahon. 'I knew he had been a coach at West Brom and Leeds, and that he was ambitious – nothing wrong with that – but he wasn't a name on everyone's lips.

'One thing you can say about Aidy is that he's a brilliant talker. I imagine he interviews really well because he can talk for Britain – and he'll do it convincingly. One of his biggest attributes was the way he spoke to us, and got us all pulling in the same direction straight away. Maybe he wasn't everyone's cup of tea but he had that winning attitude, that winning mentality. He obviously wanted to make a name for himself, and he ruffled one or two feathers, but once we were all aboard Aidy's bus it took us places pretty quickly.

'He was very thorough, very dedicated and looked into every detail – how fit we needed to be, how to see out games if we were 1-0 up with 20 minutes to go, how to protect a lead if we were down to 10 men, diets, nutrition, hydration and setting points targets for each block of six games. He left no stone unturned.

'Although some of the work on the training ground was repetitive and a bit tedious he drilled us and drilled us until it became second nature. And if we hit our points target he came up with ways to reward us, like taking the squad out to lunch.

'Once our season was up and running we knew that teams were not going to run through us, and I was chuffed that Aidy wanted me to be his captain because there was no lack of experience in the squad he built. Malky had won promotion from the Championship with Norwich and West Ham in the two previous seasons, and he was proper captaincy material, but Aidy trusted me and, in return, I trusted him.'

If early results were a little hit and miss, Boothroyd's bus soon picked up speed. If there had been any doubts about the players believing in their rookie manager's buoyant outlook they were dispelled by the fightback at Derby County on the

August Bank Holiday. Clarke Carlisle celebrated his late winner by running straight towards the dugout with teammates in hot pursuit, and Boothroyd was soon submerged beneath a rolling maul of euphoria. Watford were not just fuelled by a unity of purpose: they meant business.

Six years after Graham Taylor's side had been cajoled towards the chequered flag by the Man in the Pink Shirt, mind coach Ciaran Cosgrave, another sports psychologist was aboard Boothroyd's Routemaster. Keith Mincher, a qualified coach, had been appointed manager of Carlisle United in the summer of 1999 – a vintage summer for English football, as any Hornets fan will attest – but resigned, amid the mild turbulence of former Manchester United entrepreneur Michael Knighton's control, without taking charge of a game.

Mincher's encouragement supplied perfect backing vocals for Boothroyd's cheerful soundtrack. 'Keith was brilliant, whether he spoke to the lads individually or as a group,' says Mahon. 'A lot of the players confided in him and he seemed to know all the shortcuts to bring out the best in us.'

Goalkeeper Foster, who won his first England cap during his two seasons on loan at Vicarage Road, concurred with his captain's praise for Mincher. 'I did a lot of work with Keith in my first year at Watford,' he told the *Independent* in 2006. 'He gave me so much more confidence in myself as a goalkeeper. He helped me to deal with mistakes better. Now I feel if I make one, as all keepers do, I can move on. I can deal with it and learn from it.'

Boothroyd made one dreadful mistake in the summer of 2005 – disposing with the services of one-club Watford legend Nigel Gibbs from the backroom staff he inherited with a pathetic, perfunctory footnote on the club website, bundling him out of the door without even a carriage clock. Gibbs deserved better for 24 years of service. It was, mercifully, offset by promising performances on the pitch, and his players taking to the new voices in their midst.

One of Boothroyd's psychological gadgets was to form a circle of chairs and ask each player about his role and analyse the contribution of his main sidekick in the team. Mahon recalls, 'I had to speak about playing in central midfield, what the guy next to me was doing well, what he could do better to help me out – and then he had to do the same.

'Some players at other clubs might take offence, and it would turn into a slanging match, but we had strong characters who could take constructive criticism on board, and we would work on it in training. When our talking shop paid dividends, and we put our plans into action in games, it was very satisfying to do it by the book. I remember when we won away at Luton around the New Year, we were 2-0 up before half-time and we had spoken about taking the heat out of the game and running the clock down. They didn't like us winning on their patch, and I don't think they enjoyed the way we did it, but we executed our game-plan perfectly. That was the game where Malky scored with an inch-perfect toe-poke, because it crossed the line by about an inch. But it made all the extra work on the training ground worthwhile, especially the sessions where the drills were not always enjoyable and you're thinking, "Come on, I need to pick the kids up from school," or whatever. It was all done for a reason.'

By the time Watford welcomed the old enemy – and their reduced following, after the lawless prelude to a Worthington Cup tie four years earlier – back to Vicarage Road with five games of the League season remaining, the point from a 1-1 draw effectively guaranteed the Hornets a place in the playoffs.

Then Boothroyd arranged an innovative postscript to the Easter Monday win against Ipswich, asking the 16,721 crowd to stay behind for a mock penalty shootout in front of the Rookery, to help the players prepare for the tension of a possible trial by spot-kicks in the playoffs in front of a live audience instead of sterile rehearsals on a deserted training pitch. As we later discovered, the ritual proved obsolete, but it was another snapshot of a manager covering every base and trying to give his players every possible advantage.

Watford's win at Selhurst Park in the semi-final first leg was up there with the best away days in the twenty-first century. After a couple of close calls in a tense opening 45 minutes, Boothroyd's tactical literacy came to the fore as Henderson's physical presence was sacrificed for an extra man in midfield and the Hornets took an unassailable three-goal advantage back to Hertfordshire.

After each goal – King rolling his defender and swivelling to shoot in off the post, Young's boomerang free-kick and Spring's soaring finish into the top corner – the celebrations were tempered by Mahon tapping his temple and reminding his teammates to remain focused on getting the job done.

'It was just about the perfect away performance – clean sheet, pick them off with three clinical finishes, no lapses of concentration or discipline,' says Mahon. 'I had a front-row view of Youngy's free-kick because I was in the wall, leaning on one or two of the Palace defenders to help them enjoy it as well. He scored one like it at Plymouth in our first away game of that season, he did it again up at Leeds, and he's still doing it now. Watford fans should not have been surprised by the free-kick he scored for Manchester United at Vicarage Road [in November 2017] because we all know where he learned to do it.'

After leaving Watford, for a then record £9.75 million, in January 2007, Young went on to win England caps, the title, FA Cup and League Cup winner's medals with United and play in a World Cup semi-final. For a time, he also acquired a reputation for going down too easily to win cheap free-kicks and penalties, but Mahon never saw any evidence of Young resorting to the dark arts with the Hornets. He says, 'To be fair, "Ash" would get sliced down every week for us in the Championship and he would always be the first to jump back up when he was fouled. He never dived for Watford – all I saw was a kid who was rejected by the club at first and worked incredibly hard to convince them he was worth a shot. I don't remember him winning a single free-kick or penalty by making a meal of anything – if Ash was on the deck, it meant someone had kicked him. With him and Marlon up front we always felt there was a bit of magic in our locker.'

There was definitely magic in the air when Boothroyd pitched his big top in Cardiff on Sunday 21 May 2006. Just as he had made sure his players were up and about by 7.15 a.m. to ensure they were fully switched-on and awake in every sense for the away leg at Palace, the Hornets manager went for the early bird option again before the playoff final. To break up the 12-day countdown to Watford's date with destiny, he took the squad down to Wales six days before the game, checked into the same hotel where they would be staying the night before taking on Leeds, and after a training session on the Tuesday morning the punters enjoying a guided tour of the Millennium Stadium included an excited coach party from the WD18 postcode.

'I wanted everyone to get a feel for the place, to get used to the size of it,' says Boothroyd. 'When you pull up outside a ground for the biggest game of your life, you don't want to be stepping off the coach and asking, "Which way are the dressing rooms?" And you don't want the players to go out and look at the pitch thinking, "Wow, this place is massive" when they should be in the zone and tuning in on the right frequency – so I persuaded the chairman it would be a good idea to go down the week before, have a good look round the place, get the holiday snaps out of the way and then get down to the important business of winning a football match. When the day itself came round I wanted us to play the game, not the occasion. I think we got it spot-on.'

Psychologist Mincher, who had just returned from a holiday in the Himalayas, was well placed to address a final team meeting about climbing mountains, and as Watford prepared for their Everest moment, they announced themselves in the tunnel with impressive bombast and bravado. Like every other aspect of a memorable day, it was all part of the plan.

Mahon says, 'Aidy always wanted us to get going in the tunnel before kick-off, and we didn't need any excuse to turn up the volume for a playoff final. We were quite a noisy team by nature and we had some big characters in that dressing room who knew about intimidation and how to make it work in your favour. It was all carefully planned – the devil was in the detail.

'During the League season, whenever we played away the boss insisted on us trying to make it feel like it was a home game. It was a siege mentality. He wanted us to take over every ground we visited. When the coach pulled up outside the players' entrance, he wanted us to get off the bus in a certain manner – not just drifting off one or two at a time, but all together in a pack, looking like a team who really meant business. Backroom staff would hang around in the tunnel and the corridors in their Watford coats, and we would put Watford posters on the dressing-room door. We would go out to warm up together, come back in 15 minutes before kick-off together and do everything in military unison. Aidy wanted to let the other team know Watford were in town – we were there in your faces and you couldn't get away from us.

'As captain, I was happy to do the manager's bidding, if you like. I was the link between Aidy and the players, and I loved all that psychological warfare. It wasn't everybody's cup of tea, but that's exactly what we were trying to achieve. We were rocking up on somebody else's turf as if we owned the place, and they didn't like being forced out of their comfort zone.'

Although the Millennium Stadium was a neutral venue, neither their own territory nor behind enemy lines, Watford were by now proficient in the art of making themselves at home. Familiar with the scenery after their works outing to Wales the previous week, the players were eager for the rendezvous with their prey.

Ten years earlier, Boothroyd's playing career had been curtailed by a badly broken leg when he was playing for Peterborough against Notts County. The other player involved in the challenge, no malice intended, was Shaun Derry, who would be playing for Leeds against the Hornets. But there was a keen, almost ravenous interest among Boothroyd's players in the other players who would be lining up in the tunnel with them.

Mahon says, 'An hour or so before kick-off, the two captains went to the referee's room to shake hands, exchange teamsheets and go through a few basics: no dissent, play to the whistle, that sort of thing. As I was leaving the changing room to go and see Mike Dean, who was in charge that afternoon, Marlon King was telling me, "Please, please, *please, PLEASE* come back and tell me Paul Butler is playing – because I'm going to run him ragged, I'm going to run him into the ground."

'No disrespect to Butler, who was an experienced defender, but we knew he had been racing against the clock after a month out with a calf injury, and if he was selected there was a fair chance he would not be completely match-fit. When I came back from the referee's room, Marlon was waiting for me by the door, like a dog waiting to ambush the postman. Sure enough, Butler would be playing at centre-half for Leeds, and I had never seen Marlon look so excited. He was right up for it.

'The last thing I remember, before we went out into the tunnel ten minutes before kick-off, was Aidy asking Bob Oteng, our kit man, to give the last pep talk. Bob was very good at speaking, a good motivator, and it was a different voice for the boys to hear after they had been listening to the captain, a bald git with a Brummie accent, all season.'

Then it was tunnel time. Up in the stands, Watford fans could not see what was going on in the bowels of a cavernous maze where, among other things, scenes of Doctor Who's reunion with Daleks had been shot on location and, in hindsight, the Daleks might have been more mobile than Leeds' back four that day. But viewers tuning in to Sky Sports could see the Hornets' mind games unfurling in all their premeditated glory.

Mahon says, 'Fans have often told me they thought Leeds were beaten in the tunnel that day, and to an extent I have to agree with them. I was at the front of the line, because I had to lead the team out, but I could hear Jordan Stewart shouting the odds behind me. Jordan was a great lad – he instigated a lot of the stuff in the tunnel, and when the boys responded he would shout even louder and at a higher pitch. Jay DeMerit got stuck in, Ben Foster was pretty vocal and Malky Mackay was a top professional who knew all about winning promotion from the Championship. Out of the corner of my eye I could tell the Leeds boys were wondering what the hell was going on.'

Striker Henderson shares his captain's view that Leeds were taken aback, if not actually disarmed, by their noisy opponents. He told watfordlegends.com, 'We played out that situation in our minds beforehand so we knew exactly what we were doing and it gave us the upper hand. The Leeds lads thought we were crazy and had lost our marbles, but it was all play-acting. The plan was simply to make as much noise as possible to show how focused we were on the game and how up for it we were. It was very intense in the tunnel, but a good feeling to be there.'

Just as they were the biggest noise in the tunnel, Watford dominated the match itself. DeMerit's flying header, from Young's wicked delivery, was gold dust for scriptwriters charting the rise of the American backpacker picked up from the Hornets' non-League neighbours Northwood in exchange for a set of playing kit two years earlier.

The Hornets' second goal owed more to luck than finesse, but who cares? James Chambers' shot looped off Eddie Lewis's attempted block, hitting a post before the rebound crept apologetically over the line after a helpful ricochet off Leeds keeper Neil Sullivan's back. If you rehearsed the manoeuvre another thousand times on the training ground, none would produce the same outcome. When Derry's clumsy challenge felled King in the box, Henderson – released by Leeds as a 16-year-old – stepped up to settle all arguments from the penalty spot, and all that remained for Mahon was to lift the trophy.

Unlike Wembley – the national stadium would reopen 12 months later after a £750 million facelift without any meaningful access improvements – there was no staircase leading to the Royal Box. The trophy and medals were handed over from a hastily constructed rostrum on the pitch, with tickertape guns firing yellow and red streamers into the air and the sponsors handing out colour-coded t-shirts for the victorious players to become walking billboards, an unnecessary intrusion on their triumph.

But as Watford saw out the game with no alarms, and our watches ticked round to Premier League o'clock, Mahon allowed himself the luxury of drinking it all in and basking in the satisfaction of a job well done. 'As a footballer, you need to be mentally tough to cope with the big occasion and prove you deserve to perform at the highest level,' he says. 'This was our chance, and we grabbed it with both hands. When you get to a final, winning is all that matters. I had been to the Millennium Stadium once before, with Brentford in the LDV Vans Trophy in 2001, and finished on the losing side. That was never going to happen again.

'Even now, people ask if we were nervous and, honestly, I couldn't tell you. Your heart-rate might be going through the roof, but what we brought to the party more than anything else was the desire to make it happen. Even the substitutes stayed right on it – they came out after half-time fired-up and we made ourselves heard in the tunnel again. The night before the game, one of the last things that went through my mind before I drifted off to sleep was that, out of everyone on that pitch and 70,000 people in the stadium, I could be the one getting my hands on the trophy as the winning captain. And when I woke up the following morning, it was the first thing that came into my head. It was the perfect state of mind – positive, full of good vibes, no negativity – and, as a team, we took that confidence onto the pitch.

'It was only when the final whistle went that I thought Aidy should lift the trophy with me. He'd invested a lot of trust in me as his captain, and if it wasn't for him there probably wouldn't have been a bunch of lads in yellow shirts having the time of their lives and looking forward, in most cases, to their first taste of the Premier League.

'Such is the pressure of professional football these days that you are often playing for your manager's job, and he isn't going to pick you if he can't trust you to carry out his plans, or if he doesn't think you've got his back. If I remember correctly Aidy was first on stage to collect his medal, and I was the last one up there. I thought, "A lot of this is down to that man and he deserves to share the moment." So I called him over. He told me to grab it, so I gave the trophy a kiss and then we lifted it, one hand each. We'd started the game by making a noise in the tunnel – and we finished it with a party in the dressing room. Happy days. Great memories.'

Watford were relegated at the first time of asking, but they were rarely embarrassed and a somewhat fortuitous run to the FA Cup semi-finals sustained the supporters' optimism until the fat lady was clearing her throat. In truth, the writing was on the wall after just two games, when the Hornets had just one point to show for giving a decent account of themselves at Everton and largely outplaying West Ham in a 1-1 draw at Vicarage Road. At Goodison Park the decisive goal proved to be a penalty awarded against Chris Powell when the ball hit him in the face, a farcical and ominous foretaste of the luck Boothroyd would endure in the Premier League.

Fortune also deserted Mahon when, better late than never, Watford's 4-2 win against Portsmouth on Easter Monday was garnished by his only goal of the season, a thunderous left-foot shot beyond ex-Hornets keeper David James. It came too late to be included in the official shortlist for the club's goal of the season, which is a pity, because it would have been a certain winner. Such was the dearth of viable candidates for the accolade that Henderson's winner from the penalty spot at West Ham was among the contenders.

But if Boothroyd was down on his luck in the penthouse, he was the author of his own misfortune as Watford squandered an eight-point lead at the top of the Championship the following season. The manager's fidelity to 'caveman' football won few admirers, and his recruitment featured a crop of duds, notably £3.25 million record signing Nathan Ellington. As Watford's flying start was unravelling, midway through the campaign Mahon was informed he would be surplus to requirements – a surprise after six years of reliable chugging through the Hornets midfield – and he signed for QPR.

'Aidy has since apologised to me and admitted he made a mistake,' says Mahon. 'I bear no grudges – I wanted to try to win a second promotion in three years, but he had his reasons for letting me go, so something had to give. I played more than 200 games for Watford, and they got their money back on me when I left, so I like to think I gave them decent value. After we reached the Premier League there was a lot of hype around Aidy, and talk of him being a future England manager, which was understandable. Maybe his mistake was buying into it.'

***

Graham Taylor awarded Gavin Mahon his first professional contract as a teenager at Wolves after he had progressed through the youth-team ranks. Nine months after Taylor was removed from office at Molineux with indecent haste – and his homing instincts had restored him to the heartlands where his star never waned – he tried to sign Mahon again as Watford, newly-relegated to the third tier, began planning for the long haul back to English football's upper slopes.

'Graham had moved "upstairs" for a year as general manager, and I came down to meet Kenny Jackett, who had taken over running the first team,' says Mahon. 'But I was only 19. I just felt I would be moving away from home too soon, and I wanted to play more locally in the Midlands, so I joined Hereford on a free transfer instead. Within two years Hereford had been relegated out of the Football League altogether and Watford had won promotion back to the Championship. It was a harsh lesson in making sure you choose the right path when your career's at a crossroads.

'We should never have gone down with that squad at Hereford – we had Tony Agana (once of Watford), Nicky Law and Trevor Matthewson, who came with bags of experience – and the boss was Graham Turner, who was the previous manager at Wolves before Graham Taylor. We should have had the know-how to stay up.

'Drawing with Brighton on the final day of the season, where we needed to win and they only needed a point to stay in the League, was one of my worst experiences in the game, because I was sat in the stand, unable to do anything to prevent it, but it also stood me in good stead. After going through something like that you never take anything for granted again in football. People say being relegated out of the League is the unkindest drop of all – and they are right. It was a horrible feeling.'

Chastened, but not destroyed, by his experience at Edgar Street, Mahon rebooted at Brentford, winning promotion in his first season and establishing himself as a muscular, consistent performer under a decent young manager named Ray Lewington.

Proficient and knowledgeable, Lewington left the Bees to become Watford's reserve team manager as part of Gianluca Vialli's regime, but he was soon reunited with Mahon. Six years after Taylor had first tried to bring him to Vicarage Road as a promising teenager at Wolves, Mahon became Vialli's last signing at Watford before the collapse of ITV Digital and the emergency reduction of the Hornets' unsustainable wage bill brought the Italian's unlamented reign to an end after just 12 months.

For the second time, Watford had chosen the successor poorly when Taylor abdicated his throne. In 1987 Dave Bassett – a credible candidate on paper – chose the wrecking ball where only feather dusters or a lick of paint was required, and Vialli's expensive tastes in the transfer market yielded little value for money and even less affection among the supporters. Italian defender Filippo Galli's commitment and competence were beyond reproach, and Marcus Gayle was more of a success at centre-back than the centre-forward role for which he was ostensibly signed, but the likes of Ramon Vega, Pierre Issa and Patrick Blondeau were only acquired tastes once other clubs had acquired them. In a moment of pure black comedy,

Issa was even dropped from his stretcher by first-aiders when he was carried off against Charlton in a League Cup tie.

Little did he know it at the time but the capture of Mahon, for an initial £150,000 fee, would be Vialli's parting gift to the Hornets, so let us be thankful that, late in the day, he got something right. In truth, the deal was based substantially on Lewington's recommendation, but the player had no hesitation in making the switch.

'Ray had told me, two or three months before, that I was on Luca's radar and to keep my standards high,' recalls Mahon. 'Some of his high-profile signings had struggled to adapt to life in the Championship and he was looking for players better suited to the competitive nature of the division. Sure enough, after Vialli came to watch a game at Griffin Park and the clubs had agreed terms, I was invited over to his house in Hampstead.

'I walked into his front room and there was this legend who's won just about every trophy in football from the Champions League downwards, and with him is his assistant Ray Wilkins, one of the most recognisable faces in English football for the past 30 years. We had a chat for 45 minutes about Watford, his expectations of taking them back into the Premier League and how some of the players he had brought in hadn't worked out.

'Three years earlier I'd played non-League football for a season at Hereford United – which did me no harm because it kept me humble – and times were so hard that they were paying some players cash-in-hand because they couldn't afford to put it through the books. Now here I was being asked to sign for one of the best in Europe. I'm always thankful I had the hunger and the desire to dig deep and work my way back into the League, and I had to do it the hard way, but after being knocked down it felt like this was my payback.

'I used to go to school, play in the same school team and at county level with Ian Ashbee. He had to graft his way to the top as well after being sold to Cambridge and then captaining Hull all the way from League Two to the Premier League. Two lads from the same neck of the woods, two careers which appeared to be going down dead ends, but both of us made it to the top flight. We weren't Pelé and Maradona, but we grafted and we got there.'

Mahon got on well with Vialli and, like others, felt he was let down by players whose commitment to the cause did not match their bank balances. After setting up Gayle to score in a 2-0 win at Crystal Palace on his debut, and a run of half a dozen matches in the side, Mahon's Watford career stalled as the manager was binned after a season and he missed half the 2002–03 campaign through injury.

'My form wasn't great at first,' he concedes. 'I was getting a few groans from the terraces, which makes it even harder, but that was where playing non-League proved so valuable. You develop quite a thick skin when you can hear the cutting remarks from a couple of blokes behind the goal in a crowd of only a few hundred. It toughens you up mentally. I knew that once I got fit and played regularly in the right position – central midfield – I would be able to contribute.'

Although Mahon often found himself used a stop-gap in various positions, including right-back, his return to fitness coincided with the Hornets reaching two major semi-finals in three seasons despite Lewington, left to pick up the pieces from the extravagance of the Vialli experiment, being forced to slash the wage bill from around £15 million a year by more than two-thirds.

'You would struggle to find anyone in football with a bad word to say about Ray. He is one of the most down to earth, decent blokes you'll ever meet,' says Mahon, who flourished under Lewington's tutelage to such an extent that he was voted player of the season in 2004. 'Ray was such a likeable guy that everyone got on with him. No ego, no hidden sides to his character. He had this aura about him that made you want to play for him. I knew Sean Dyche would make an excellent manager because he created the same vibe.'

Mahon played in every round – against Macclesfield, West Brom, Sunderland, Burnley and Southampton – as the Hornets reached the FA Cup semis in 2003, bowing out with a narrow 2-1 defeat against the Saints at Villa Park. Mahon's contribution to the run was not always spectacular but often valuable, including a last-gasp clearance off the line to deny the Baggies an undeserved replay and an assist in the goalmouth scramble leading to Tommy Smith's opener against the Clarets. He came to regard the semi-final as a missed opportunity rather than an honourable defeat, saying, 'You don't get many opportunities to play in an FA Cup final, and we weren't that far away. I found myself up against Chris Marsden, who was known as "the Crab" when we were youngsters at Wolves because he was never going to skin you for pace, although he had a left foot like a wand. I remember joking with him in the first few minutes and telling him not to try to run me, and he replied, "OK, I won't skin you as long as you don't kick me." There wasn't a lot in it, and we felt a bit harshly treated to find ourselves 2-0 down. Marcus pulled one back with a few minutes left, but there wasn't enough time for us to mount a late charge. It's one of the few regrets in my career that we didn't find that extra five per cent on the day.

'But it was a great run which made the club a lot of money they hadn't expected, and there were some real highlights, like Stephen Glass being told he was being given a free transfer in the week before the Burnley game and then sticking that free-kick in the top corner. It wasn't a classic, but Stephen could produce moments of quality which set him apart. I thought he could have had a better career, but that left foot had something extra when you needed it.'

Watford's other run to the last four under Lewington was in the Carling Cup two seasons later, when they completed the south coast double over Southampton and Portsmouth before bowing out to Liverpool, a Steven Gerrard goal in each leg of the semi-final proving decisive.

'We had some top, top professionals and they came to the fore under the Vicarage Road lights on that run,' says Mahon. Lads like Neal Ardley and Heidar Helguson were outstanding, and I enjoyed going up against Gerrard in the semi-final. We played really well up at Anfield in the first leg, where there wasn't much to choose between the teams on the night, and we stayed in the tie for a long time at home as well.

'Those Cup runs brought the best out of Ray as a coach – we knocked a few Premier League teams out in both of them – because he knew how to get the best out of people, but he wasn't afraid to rip your head off if he thought you were slacking. He could go through you like a dose of salts when the mood took him. You could always tell when he was angry or uptight about something because he would bite so hard on his lip he would make it bleed. It was a bit like that villain Le Chiffre in the James Bond film *Casino Royale*, whose eye used to bleed when he was under pressure. When Ray was raging he used to draw blood.'

When Mahon left Watford in January 2008 he moved only 20 miles down the road to Queens Park Rangers – but at times it felt like he had been transported into a parallel universe. Unwittingly he became a TV star when QPR were featured in a BBC documentary *The Four Year Plan*. Rangers' excitable joint owner Flavio Briatore had ordered sporting director Gianni Paladini to leave the directors' box and petition caretaker manager Gareth Ainsworth to send on Mahon. The former Watford captain's cameo proved a masterstroke – Mahon came off the bench to head the winner against Cardiff – and Briatore, his tactical genius now established beyond dispute, was a portrait of righteous anger.

'That was a strange one,' laughs Mahon. 'We had a couple of wealthy owners [Formula One magnate Bernie Ecclestone was another] and it seemed one of them wanted to have a say in everything from team selection to substitutions. I think Flavio had actually wanted me to start the game, but I'd just been out for two or three weeks with an ankle injury and there was no way I could have lasted the 90 minutes. That's why Gareth put me on the bench in the first place, but Flavio came up to me afterwards and said, "I told you – I know what I'm doing." He used to ring me at two o'clock in the morning to ask me what I thought of the manager, or ask me to explain why I thought we could beat Wolves at home but lose to Burnley. He invited me to his office, just across the road from Harrods, and it was a bizarre feeling to be sat in this room as he asked me about various players and managers. For whatever reason, he seemed to trust me, or value my opinion, but that's another story – I could write a whole book on it . . .'

10

JOHN EUSTACE

GHOSTBUSTER

According to baffled Watford manager Aidy Boothroyd it was like a confirmed sighting of an alien UFO spacecraft landing on Earth. And given dear old Aidy's dabble in Bluetooth headset technology (for communication between dugout and directors' box), nobody was better qualified when it came to calling occupants of interplanetary spacecraft on an unexplored wavelength.

To those of us in the stands on 20 September 2008, being asked to swallow a 'goal' that was no more authentic than Father Christmas, the tooth fairy, the Easter bunny or the man in the moon, was indeed the stuff of another galaxy. The day John Eustace was debited with an own goal in a 2-2 draw with Reading at Vicarage Road was more far-out than Pluto.

If there has ever been an occasion when vocal cords and larynx have been more strained by booing the officials at a Watford match, few of us can recall it. The infamous 'ghost goal', awarded to Reading in error by referee Stuart Attwell on the catastrophic advice of his deluded linesman Nigel Bannister, was quite simply a profanity. A grotesque miscarriage of sporting justice. An urgent prescription at Specsavers. A hideous miscalculation of geometry. And an insult to the intelligence of fans who paid to witness it.

To say Eustace remains incredulous about the imaginary goal being attributed to him is a huge understatement. To their eternal shame, the Football League and the Football Association have made no effort to amend the record books by deleting the Hornets midfielder's name from the scoresheet.

Remarkably, it would be another five years before the authorities were dragged, kicking and screaming, into the twenty-first century with the introduction of goal-line technology, a field in which cricket and tennis had left football trailing in a Jurassic age and the likes of Eustace short-changed. All that is left now of a ridiculous episode at Vicarage Road is footage which will become a monument to controversy as it gathers dust in the archives.

Of course, Eustace was not the first player to be treated poorly in incidents where officials' judgements had been compromised by pink elephants obscuring their vision, and he wasn't the last. Back in 1980 Crystal Palace striker Clive Allen's free-kick, arrowed into the top corner against Coventry at Highfield Road, rebounded into play off the metal stanchion. When a goal was not awarded, the decision was laid open to nationwide ridicule on *Match of the Day* later that night. Allen protested to Coventry chairman Jimmy Hill, normally a high priest of progressive change in English football, that the goal should have stood, and he was disappointed when the chinny one advised him simply that it wasn't a goal because the referee's decision was final.

Astonishingly, almost 30 years later, the same kind of nonsense was still happening to Palace. In 2009 on-loan forward Freddie Sears fired home from close range at Bristol City, but his crisp finish hit the metal frame inside the goal that pins the net to the turf, around four feet behind the line. Like Coventry's defenders in the instance of Allen's disallowed goal, City players momentarily looked crestfallen – until they realised the officials had missed what was obvious to everyone else in the ground, and, somehow, they escaped. Palace manager

Neil Warnock, who never settles for flower arrangement when volcanic incandescence is available, was understandably miffed.

But Allen and Sears were both robbed in instances where the ball had crossed the line between the posts; Reading's ghost goal at Vicarage Road, on the other hand, never went within six feet of the target. Hard as we might try to understand what Attwell and Bannister *thought* they saw, it is still difficult to comprehend how they reached their crackpot conclusion.

The notoriety does not define Eustace's contribution to Watford's history, but it has followed him like the parrot on a pirate's shoulder. That he became such a respected captain, revered both in the dressing room and the stands, was perhaps the least he deserved for his five and a half years of service. But it did define Attwell's reputation among Hornets supporters. Subsequently, whenever they disagreed vehemently with a referee's decision, they would rebuke misguided officials with the chorus, 'Are you Attwell in disguise?' It would be almost six years after his blunder made *News at Ten* before he was let loose on another Watford match at Vicarage Road, a 1-1 draw with Burnley, which passed mercifully without controversy.

Attwell will go down in our little black books with Roger Milford, the coiffured jobsworth who cost Wilf Rostron the chance of a lifetime to lead out Watford at the 1984 FA Cup final with a cruelly unfair red card in bandit country. [He robbed the Hornets of a semi-final place two years later, falling gullibly for Liverpool striker Ian Rush's issues with gravity and awarding an unjust penalty with Watford leading 1-0 just four minutes from time.]

If Attwell's and Bannister's phantom supplied the tin lid on an eventful first eight months with the Hornets for Eustace, it was another sign that the tide was going out on Boothroyd, whose grand design to regain top-flight status at the first time of asking had come up short the previous May.

'We had been going through a patchy start after the disappointment of missing out on promotion the previous season,' says Eustace. 'Reading had just been relegated from the Premier League but Steve Coppell had kept most of their best players, and it looked a tough game on paper. All of a sudden it became a whole lot tougher.

'Ten years later, I still can't make head nor tail of it. I don't spend my evenings beating myself up about it or watching replays, because it's not one of my happiest memories. But the worst part is that we still don't really know how, or why, the officials got it so wrong.'

Watford's task, against one of the pre-season favourites for promotion, had suffered an early setback before moon-gazers had even adjusted their telescopes, let alone spotted the alien landing. Goalkeeper Mart Poom was forced to retire hurt with a dislocated shoulder after just three minutes, with rookie Scott Loach – whose only previous appearances for the Hornets had been in the Carling Cup against Bristol Rovers and Darlington the previous month – summoned from the bench for what would become an unforgettable League debut.

For Poom, an experienced Estonian international, the peep-show turned out to be his last game for the club. And after recovering sufficiently to win his 120th cap against Portugal nine months later, he retired from competitive football at the age of 37. But for Loach, what happened next was a baffling introduction to the Championship. 'It still annoys me. The first thing I had to do, on my League debut for Watford, was NOT to pick the ball out of my net, if you know what I mean,' he told the *Daily Mirror* in 2017. 'You'll have to ask the ref and his linesman what they thought they saw, because I haven't a clue. But you can certainly say it was a baptism of fire.'

If you have never seen the ghost goal, don't take my word for it. Treat yourself on YouTube or any online search engine. Years from now they will still be including it in compilations of football bloopers. You couldn't make it up. Well, not unless your name was Attwell or Bannister.

Eustace says, 'We were under the cosh, defending a corner from our left flank. I think John-Joe O'Toole contests it at the near post but he doesn't get a touch, and as it comes into our six-yard box I manage to block it and bundle it behind off my hip, three or four yards wide of the post. It's gone out of play before Noel Hunt hooks it back into the box and Scott fingertips André Bikey's header against the bar – which was a brilliant save, but the whistle has already gone and everyone's running back towards the halfway line. As far as I can tell, nobody is claiming anything – every single player believes it's a Watford goal-kick or the ref's seen an infringement.

'The next thing I know, all hell's breaking loose and he's awarded a goal. Aidy got sent to the stands for making his feelings known, and I think he even got a letter from the FA, but when you are on the receiving end of something that's so clearly wrong I defy any manager to sit there with arms folded and say nothing.

'It was a young referee who was highly regarded as the next big thing: he was being fast-tracked towards games at a high level, and he's got to be bold enough to make big decisions. I get that. But what happened to me was ludicrous.

'Between them, I don't understand how officials can get it so wrong. I know a referee may be misled by his assistant, but we all know the facts. The ball never never crossed the line between the goalposts. He should have awarded a corner, not a goal.'

Bannister explained his blunder was the result of an 'optical illusion' from his patrol in the south-west corner of the ground, but it was more like a mirage in the desert. His view could not have been compromised by squinting into the sun, which was at his back. And it has never been adequately explained by the officials how they concluded a goal was the rightful outcome when it was a *Reading* player who hooked the ball back into play after it had crossed the dead-ball line. Why would Noel Hunt be trying to prevent the ball from going into the net if it had crossed the line between the Hornets' posts?

Before Loach could restart the match from his six-yard line, it was evident something was amiss. Attwell had joined Bannister in conference on the touchline, and suddenly there was a picket of yellow shirts, led by captain Jay DeMerit – this parody of common sense happened before the armband was passed back to Eustace – growing anxious.

One Reading player, Republic of Ireland winger Stephen Hunt, Noel's brother, joined the discussion and, when Attwell sparked uproar in the stands by signalling a goal, his celebration looked hollow at best and downright disingenuous at worst. 'I'm not sure why he was lobbying the ref,' says Eustace. 'You'll have to ask him if he was pleading with Mr Attwell not to award a goal. Strangely enough, when I got sent off in what turned out to be my last-ever League game, for Derby at Ipswich in 2015, Stephen was right there in the referee's ear again. Let's give him the benefit of the doubt . . . I like to think he was pleading my case.'

Noel Hunt – the player who should have been credited with scoring, if anybody – gave his version of events to talkSPORT radio five years after the flaw show, and admitted he *did* celebrate when Attwell awarded a goal.

'I'm not going to lie, when the referee stopped it, I did celebrate, but Stephen was arguing that it wasn't a goal. I was saying to him, "Shut up, Stephen, get back to the halfway line." I admit it was naughty of me; I was naughty at the time. After the Thierry Henry incident (where the Republic of Ireland were cheated out of a possible place in the World Cup finals by the France striker's infamous handball in a playoff) we were talking about it and I asked him [Stephen] if he would have done the same thing, and he said he probably would have done, so I'm not taking all the blame. But a few months later we were on the end of the Henry thing, so we got a taste of it on the other side.'

Suitably outraged, Watford players surrounded Attwell and Bannister to beg for an urgent review of a stupendously bad decision. Although their protest did not conform with the requirements of the Football Association's 'Respect' campaign – a worthy initiative confronting verbal and physical abuse of referees from grass-roots levels upwards, which had been launched only six weeks earlier – it was not violent or threatening in tone.

Attwell should have sensed something was seriously amiss, but his reaction was to wave away the dissenters and brandish yellow cards at O'Toole and Jon Harley with bogus authority. Watford went in at the break 1-0 down, and when Attwell was informed in the tunnel of video footage he might wish to review as a matter of priority, his response was abrupt. By then, he would have been well aware that home supporters had bees in their bonnets, if not entire swarms, from the cacophony of booing. But in a three-sided ground, where the condemned main stand was now a corrugated graveyard and a monument to dilapidation, for once the cauldron of noise did not disperse into the atmosphere. This time, the patrons' anger was intense, and it wasn't going away.

As Eustace recalls, Watford were so fired-up by the sense of injustice, it was the catalyst for them to play with more gusto, more purpose, more zeal after the interval. Not necessarily with more polish, you understand, but the fans were up in arms and the players' renewed fervour reflected the communal sense of grievance.

'Up until the "ghost" goal we had been second best,' admits Eustace. 'But the anger we felt gave us a desire to get hold of the game and play really well. Sometimes it's amazing what a bit of resentment can do for a team if you channel it in the right way.'

Tommy Smith, turning sharply after a sustained outbreak of pinball in the box, rifled a deserved equaliser as Reading, pinned in their own area, finally cracked under relentless pressure. And seven minutes later O'Toole, exchanging passes with Will Hoskins, took the return in his stride and fired an excellent angled finish left-footed into the far corner beyond Marcus Hahnemann before leaping into the Rookery to share his jubilation with the 14,761 crowd.

Watford were within three minutes of a memorable win, if not poetic justice, when Eustace was adjudged to have fouled Shane Long at the expense of a penalty, and Stephen Hunt tucked away the resulting spot-kick. Long celebrated Attwell's decision with the air of a striker who had 'won' the decision, rather than the home player conceding it, and notably the Reading substitute had overrun the ball out of play.

But after the nonsense of the ghost goal, Eustace simply did not have the energy to contest another highly debatable decision. At least this one was subjective and, even if Hornets fans did not agree with it, they could understand why it had been given. The penalty was barely a footnote in the post-match inquests – after the ghost goal, it would have been like ignoring the dead body in a murder scene and complaining about the state of the carpet.

Boothroyd, who was well qualified to talk about mysterious objects from outer space after favouring a direct approach based loosely on falling meteorites the previous season, raged, 'I've never seen anything like it. A mistake like that is like a UFO landing on Earth. I went to see the referee and, in fairness, he's only going on what the linesman says. He's working in a team, and if someone is in his ear telling him "it's a goal" I suppose he's got to give it.'

Only the most impermeable heart would have denied the Watford manager his exasperation, and after just one clean sheet in the next eight League games, with 14 goals shipped in six home matches, the axe fell following a 4-3 home defeat by Blackpool in heavy rain, the Hornets having led three times.

Reading boss Coppell, always one of the more cerebral managers with a dry sense of humour, presented a straight bat this time. He said, 'When the whistle went I wondered what it was for, as I could not see a foul. Everyone trooped back to the centre circle and then it became obvious the referee had given a goal. After speaking to Noel Hunt it was clear the ball went out of play well wide of the goal.'

As the phone-in lines and chat-room message boards went into meltdown, some Watford fans were critical of Reading for not allowing their opponents a 'walk-in' equaliser once the magnitude of Attwell and Bannister's folly became apparent.

And intriguingly, 48 hours after the event, Coppell even offered to replay the game. (No thanks, Steve, we'll take the point.) But his stance on applying the laws of football remained unchanged: 'Let's get this clear. The responsibility is not with the opposition to right a wrong. It is up to the officials to get it as right as they can. It's like cricket: do you walk or not if you've nicked one behind? As a renowned opening batsman, I used to walk, but it's a hypothetical question. If the referee had come and told me at half-time that they'd cocked it up, I don't know whether I would have let Watford score.'

Eustace was understandably aghast when he saw the ghost goal debited to him as an own goal and, quite rightly, Watford made representations to football's governing bodies to have it attributed elsewhere. Their polite enquiries fell on deaf ears.

'That was the final insult,' says Eustace. 'I understand it's a bit embarrassing for the FA and the Football League to change their records, but look at it from my point of view: who wants a goal like that on their slate? Not me, thanks. The fairest solution would have been to disallow the "goal" in the first place, but if the referee and his assistant weren't going to change their minds, the simplest thing would be to credit the last Reading player to touch the ball with it.'

In 2018 English football conducted its first experiments with Video Assistant Referees (VAR) as an extra layer of authority to deal with controversies, with the main focus on simulation, red-card incidents and penalty decisions. Worryingly, rules governing the intervention of VARs make no provision for optical illusions, ghosts or UFO sightings, although the most-ignored law of all in football – common sense – suggests Attwell would have referred to colleagues monitoring video evidence in a bunker if such an option was available.

It is fair to say VARs have had teething troubles on a par with root-canal treatment, even at the 2018 World Cup final, and the system's early evidence has left Eustace wary of its influence on the ebb and flow of games. 'We have the technology in place to get the big decisions right,' he says. 'Remember, the officials only get one look at every incident in real time. However we get there, the most important thing is that we arrive at the right decision – but it's crazy that mistakes are still being made, even when the VAR system is available. We need referees to use their skill and judgement at every level. We just don't need the ghosts.'

A decade later, Eustace is just about over the chagrin of an unfathomable mystery. Attwell is still at large on the Premier League list of officials, and no stranger to controversy, but Bannister – the real phantom of the soap opera – has disappeared from prominent service on the touchline. In my 36 years of scribbling notes and writing about football, the ghost goal remains an unparalleled tribute to every prankster who has scared friends, relatives or strangers by appearing in the dark with a white sheet over their heads.

Back in 2005, some of the touring Australian cricket team, staying in Lumley Castle before a one-day international against England at Chester-le-Street, were spooked by tales of a murdered fourteenth-century aristocrat's ghost roaming the corridors of their accommodation. All-rounder Shane Watson was so scared by things going bump in the night that he left his room and asked to sleep on teammate Brett Lee's floor, and the England players were quick to turn his discomfort into comedy gold on the pitch. Fast bowler Darren Gough taunted Watson, raising his hands to his ears and mimicking a ghost, although it didn't save England from a comprehensive defeat. Gough's trolling was quite funny, but there was nothing amusing about the apparition wrongly debited to Eustace as an own goal.

***

Watford were top of the League and on course for a swift return to the top deck in the week John Eustace joined the Hornets from promotion rivals Stoke City, early in 2008. They fell short for a variety of reasons – notably a minimalist, one-dimensional playing style which manager Aidy Boothroyd only modified when it was too late – and it would be another five years before they knocked on the penthouse door again.

Two owners later, as the club absorbed the disappointment of another near-miss with the Premier League in 2013, Eustace moved on with his reputation so enhanced that he departed effectively with an open invitation to return as a member of the coaching think-tank. There was no playing contract on the table, as injuries had severely restricted his contribution to the Pozzo revolution's overture at Vicarage Road. But head coach Gianfranco Zola had been so impressed with his captain's professionalism, especially in the finer arts of preparation, that he had left the door ajar for Eustace to join the backroom staff.

Determined to exercise his prerogative, and extract every last drop from his playing career, Eustace opted for a move to Derby County, but his affection for Watford has not diminished in the intervening years – and our admiration for his honest toil, and occasional gem, is reciprocal.

'The moral of the story, in terms of my time at Watford, is that the Championship is very hard graft – and you don't always get what you want out of it,' he says. 'When I left Stoke, where I had a really good time, as far as I was concerned I was jumping out of the frying pan and into the fire, from one promotion contender to another.

'I had gone through a tough couple of years, missing a lot of games through injury, but in the final year of my contract at Stoke I had managed to string about 25 games together, and in different circumstances I would have stayed there for longer. When I tried to get a new contract the club was very reluctant to offer me anything more than a short-term deal because of my medical history, and they wanted me to prove my fitness over a period of time before they would commit to anything longer.

'Watford, who were top of the table, were prepared to offer me security, which is exactly what I wanted. In the week after I signed we won three games on the bounce – Wolves, Ipswich and Leicester – and it looked like I'd hit the jackpot. Then we hit a sticky patch, drawing lots of games we should have won, and we lost momentum, even though I still don't think we played badly.'

Eight points clear at the top in October, Watford's lead had been eroded from the moment Middlesbrough recalled on-loan winger Adam Johnson, and their confidence was punctured by a chastening 3-0 home defeat by West Bromwich Albion in a top-of-the-table clash. In the background, striker Marlon King – whose goals had been such a key influence in the 2005–06 promotion campaign – was eyeing a move, record £3.25 million signing

Nathan Ellington was struggling to raise a gallop and Boothroyd's assistant Keith Burkinshaw parted company with the Hornets just before Christmas for unspecified 'family reasons'.

Burkinshaw, who had been a critic of Watford's direct football under Graham Taylor when the Golden Boys upset too many apple carts among the metropolitan elite 25 years earlier, had been a supportive sounding board for Boothroyd on the road to playoff glory in Cardiff and the unsuccessful battle against relegation from the Premier League which followed. But the man who won two FA Cups and the UEFA Cup as Tottenham manager could not sustain unqualified enthusiasm for Boothroyd's primitive route-one approach. Increasingly, in games crying out for the precision of a surgeon's scalpel, Watford were turning up with a caveman's club. By the end of the January transfer window the promotion charge had been slowed to a crawl by just 14 points from a possible 42.

The arrivals of midfielder Eustace, defenders Leigh Bromby and Mat Sadler, plus on-loan Fulham striker Collins John supplied a badly needed transfusion of fresh blood, and the three consecutive wins which greeted Boothroyd's new recruits promised renewed momentum. An infuriating sequence of seven successive draws, however, knocked Watford off the no.1 spot, out of the automatic promotion places – and they only scraped into the playoffs on goals scored after a nervy 1-1 draw with ten men at Blackpool on the final day.

Defensive paralysis, in a costly opening 20 minutes, left the Hornets 2-0 down at home to Hull in the playoff semi-final first leg, and there was little hope of retrieving the deficit once Eustace had been sent off – wrongly – by referee Kevin Friend with half an hour remaining. The red card was overturned and Watford, with a reconfigured formation and more enlightened approach, scored first in the return leg on Humberside before a shocking equaliser drew the sting from their fightback.

Rudimentary as Boothroyd's so-called 'hoofball' may have been, it is fair to say luck was an evasive ally for Watford on the run-in towards anti-climax.

Eustace had been sent off in the 0-0 draw with his former club Stoke by Rob Styles, a referee who invariably left his calling card at Vicarage Road (always red); Darius Henderson had a goal chalked off against Crystal Palace which proved costly; and when the playoff home leg against Hull was goalless, Danny Shittu met Jobi McAnuff's corner with a towering header, only for Friend to be the sole man in the entire ground to spot an infringement.

'It was a horrible way to finish the season,' says Eustace. 'We didn't get any luck and the gods never smiled on us. We absolutely battered Hull, and I've absolutely no idea why Danny's goal was not allowed to stand. We were good front runners – once ahead we had never lost that season, so it was a crucial decision. And we were well on top until I was sent off, which took the wind from our sails. Hull had an experienced team on the pitch and they "managed" the game very well. I didn't do anything to deserve a red card, but the incident happened in front of their bench and maybe the ref got sucked into their antics. Yes, the red card was rescinded – but the damage was done. It's like getting a refund if your summer holiday is cancelled: you're not out of pocket because you get your money back, but you still miss out on the tan.

'We surprised them a bit by changing our shape in the second leg. We had a sniff when "Hendo" gave us an early lead up at their place, and we were well on top again until we conceded a very sloppy equaliser right on half-time. After that, we were done.'

For the second time in seven years Watford had led the Championship going into November, only for their results to fall off the proverbial cliff and the season to end in disappointment and recrimination. When Boothroyd's time was up at Vicarage Road six months later, and Chelsea's highly rated young coach Brendan Rodgers replaced him, it looked as if Eustace would be surplus to requirements as well.

'Brendan came in with a whole new crop of ideas – and the only problem for me was that he didn't see me as part of the way he wanted to play,' says Eustace. 'I had to leave on loan, and I ended up at Derby. I have no axes to grind with Brendan, I understand how it works. When new regimes move in they come with their own principles and they want to bring in their own people. That's the nature of football, and I was fortunate that another Championship club was keen for me to help them out, so I managed to keep the engine ticking over. I was still keeping an eye on Watford from a distance, because obviously I had a lot of friends there, and towards the end of that season they played some fantastic football. The only disappointment for me was that I really wanted to be part of it. I only scored one goal in that loan spell at Derby, and inevitably it was against Watford on the last day of the season.

'You can see why Brendan has gone on to be a top manager. Within five years of him getting his first job he came within a whisker of winning the title at Liverpool, so credit to Watford for giving him his big break.'

Rodgers, perhaps mindful of an approaching financial storm, jumped ship after just 193 days. When the Hornets turned to another rookie manager – Malky Mackay – as his replacement, it brought Eustace back into the fold and led to his reinstallation as captain.

He says, 'I felt I had unfinished business at Watford, so when Malky took charge and said he wanted me to be part of it again I jumped at the chance. There were a few problems behind the scenes with cutting the wage bill and players being sold to balance the books, but I was happy to be involved again.'

In the firesale to maintain solvency – or at least manageable levels of debt – Tommy Smith, Mike Williamson and Tamas Priskin were sacrificed, leaving a young squad to cope with the demands of a two-faced pitch. Up until Christmas, when the surface played true, Watford unfurled some decent stuff, never more so than on a famous Monday night in front of the live TV cameras against QPR, when Lloyd Doyley memorably broke his goalscoring duck for the Hornets on his 269th appearance in senior football.

But when the trampling hoofmarks of 20-stone prop forwards turned to lunar craters – Watford shared their ground with rugby tenants Saracens, whose £500,000-a-year rent was income too valuable to turn down – the pitch became a barely passable obstacle course. Inevitably results suffered, and Mackay was grateful for Eustace's unwavering leadership and positive outlook.

When a grim eye injury to central defender Jay DeMerit (a piece of grit lodged beneath his contact lens, scratched the surface of his eyeball and required revolutionary graft surgery to repair the damaged cornea and save his sight) left the American on the sidelines for three months, Eustace was the obvious choice as captain, a job originally handed to him by Boothroyd.

If taking responsibility is a mark of leadership, Eustace had set himself apart from the crowd in 2006, when he forked out £40,000 of his own money to have career-saving surgery on a torn knee cartilage in the United States. And when he was given a clean bill of health to resume playing he joined fourth-tier Hereford, where his grandfather Ken had made one appearance in goal during the 1949–50 season, to prove his fitness.

For the next three years at Vicarage Road Eustace compensated for any lack of pace with his positional sense, organisation and eye for goal. 'We played some great stuff under Malky and I felt we were very underrated,' he says. 'He was left with a young team and they did him proud. If we had been able to keep a large part of the group he inherited together you never know what we might have achieved. In Malky's second season we went on a couple of runs that had a real streak of quality about them. We won at QPR on a Friday night in December, outplayed them on live TV, and we were the first team to beat them that year. Danny Graham was in the form of his life and we looked a decent side.'

When Mackay was headhunted by Cardiff, and Sean Dyche stepped into the breach, the Hornets struggled initially, but winger Michael Kightly's arrival on loan from Wolves was the genesis of a marked upturn in results. For Dyche to finish 11th in his first year as a manager, with mysterious owner Laurence Bassini dealing him only a finite hand in terms of recruitment, was a stupendous achievement – and a foretaste of his conspicuous success at Burnley.

Although it ended in undeserved defeat, one highlight of Dyche's reign was Watford outplaying Tottenham in an FA Cup fourth-round tie, where Eustace gave a masterful performance in exalted company. Spurs manager Harry Redknapp turned up at Vicarage Road straight from the dock at Southwark crown court, where he was in the middle of standing trial on tax evasion charges. He was acquitted on all counts by jury, but Tottenham's 1-0 win was floodlit robbery and 'Arry knew he was bang to rights on that score. 'How we won that game, I'll never know,' admitted Redknapp. 'If Watford played like that every week they would be top of the League – they were fantastic. Eustace was outstanding, he ran the game.'

Redknapp was taunted by the Rookery's mischievous chorus of 'stand up if you pay your tax' but he was gracious enough to seek out the Watford captain afterwards and deliver his tribute personally. 'Harry was very complimentary when he spoke to me, which was top-class of him,' says Eustace. 'I remember joking with him that there were still a few days of January left and it was not too late if he was interested in a transfer deal for me. He took his medicine from the fans in good humour that night.'

A change of ownership at Vicarage Road led to a new head coach and, by common consent, the football served up by Gianfranco Zola's team in the middle part of the 2012–13 season was some of the most gorgeous entertainment of any era in the club's history.

Injury restricted Eustace to only a handful of appearances, but one of them was the 4-0 defeat of Huddersfield on a wintry January afternoon illuminated by Cristian Battocchio's first goal for the Hornets, a sumptuous move of 12 passes involving six players, including the club captain.

Dozens of fans had answered the call to clear the pitch of snow hours before kick-off, and Fernando Forestieri's cameo from the bench was pure cabaret, one challenge dumping him face-down in snow piled behind the touchline. But the move leading to Battocchio's goal – started in his own half by Eustace – was the biggest talking point, and evidently one hack was so excited his match report in the *Daily Mirror* was of questionable taste: 'Sexy football is an honourable virtue, but Cristian Battocchio's first goal for Watford was pure pornography – belts off, trousers down, back of the net.'

But it was, by any yardstick, joyful to watch. If a move of such extravagance had been completed by a deft finish from the boot of Ronaldo, Messi or Bale, we would never have heard the last of it. Eustace recalls, 'I was desperate to be part of that side. Franco was a magnificent player in his day, and for a spell the football we played that season was a reflection of his career. In that Huddersfield game I came off the bench and got a little taste of his philosophy in action, but unfortunately I was injured for a lot of the time. Although I was physically fit for the playoff final against Crystal Palace, in all honesty I was not match-fit. Much as I would have preferred to play in such a big game, we had a strong squad and I had no divine right to walk back into the team. At Wembley I would have been happy to do the ugly side of the game, which I enjoyed doing, and leave the finer arts to the other lads, but it wasn't our day.

'I did enjoy helping out with the younger players in that group. Although I wasn't able to make my presence felt on the pitch very often because of a back injury, I took great satisfaction in helping some of the youngsters to improve.

'And it was typical of the man when Franco sat down with me towards the end of that season and said, "We can't offer you a playing contract, but if you would like to join the coaching staff, we would like you to stay and the door is open." That was a huge compliment, and if I had been a couple of years older I'm sure I would have jumped at the opportunity because the club was close to my heart for five years, through all the ups and downs and the ghost goal.

'But at 33, I felt I owed it to myself to give it one more shot as a player. You are a long time retired, and I wanted to drain every last drop from my legs before committing myself to coaching. Watford is a fantastic club, they looked after me great, and I would love to go back there eventually. To leave Vicarage Road with the door ajar, and the possibility of picking up almost where I left off, speaks volumes for Watford's class.

'Where I would fit in now is a good question – they have been in the Premier League for three years already, and they are doing great. They have built a good squad, the ground looks fantastic and they are well on the way to establishing themselves at that level. But I'm just grateful that when the time came to move on – and I carried on playing for another two seasons at Derby – we parted on the best of terms. That means a lot in football.'

When *Tales from the Vicarage* caught up with Eustace, he was leading Kidderminster towards the playoffs in the National League (North) and making a decent fist of his first job in management before joining QPR as former England coach

Steve McClaren's assistant. There was also a tidal wave of fawning in the mainstream media about an overhead kick with which Cristiano Ronaldo scored for Real Madrid in their 2018 Champions League quarter-final win against Juventus.

No arguments in this parish: it was a tremendous goal, with stunning technical execution in such a high-profile game. But was it any better than Wayne Rooney's winner in the Manchester derby in 2011? Or Trevor Sinclair's spectacular effort for Queens Park Rangers against Barnsley, which won the BBC's Goal of the Season award in 1997 ahead of David Beckham's pitching wedge from inside his own half against Wimbledon? Or, dare we ask, was it better than Eustace's overhead kick against Coventry – on Aidy Boothroyd's first return to Vicarage Road as a visiting manager – in August 2010?

On social media one Watford fan called Ronaldo 'a Portuguese Eustace', and the man himself laughs, 'Tell Cristiano it looks a lot better when you hit it from 20 yards and it dips into the far corner. As as soon as he can do one of them, I'll get back to him!'

What a player. What a captain. What an overhead kick. And, Stuart Attwell, what on earth were you thinking?

11

TROY DEENEY

ELTON'S GREATEST HIT

He was signed from the proceeds of Sir Elton John's concert at Vicarage Road in 2010. Watford manager Malky Mackay staked the lot, around £550,000 after overheads, on a single player. Sir Elton's back catalogue spans six decades, and he has sold upwards of 300 million records around the world, but buying Troy Deeney for the Hornets may be his greatest hit.

Six months before the arrival of their new forward from Walsall – one with a fair, but unspectacular, strike rate for the Saddlers in English football's third tier – Watford had flirted with financial ruin. They were minutes from going into administration, Mackay joining office staff in an agonising vigil before the storm passed. In the early days of the 2009–10 season a fire sale of the club's most marketable players, including Tommy Smith and Mike Williamson, had been required to stop the bank manager throwing a strop, and all they could afford in return were cut-price bargains and loans.

One was striker Danny Graham, a £200,000 bargain teed up by Mackay's predecessor Brendan Rodgers, and another smart deal was hatched to bring in Manchester United's highly rated attacking midfielder Tom Cleverley on a season-long loan. Mackay had long been on friendly terms with United godfather Sir Alex Ferguson, who crossed paths with his father in Scotland at Queen's Park in the late 1950s, and he managed to reach an agreement for Cleverley's services – even though

Watford could not afford the full £300,000 loan fee. Fergie told him to pay half up front and the rest when cash flow permitted.

Sir Elton was saddened to see his beloved club living virtually hand-to-mouth, and his concert at the Vic was unashamedly subtitled 'Playing for Players'. Much as his previous gig at the stadium had financed Aidy Boothroyd's unlikely promotion campaign five years earlier, this one gave rookie manager Mackay's squad more firepower – and his name was Troy.

'I like to think Watford didn't do badly out of the deal,' says Deeney. 'But I wonder if Sir Elton kept the receipt!'

One of the former chairman's best-selling albums was called *Captain Fantastic and the Brown Dirt Cowboy*. We await news of the cowboy's progress, but Elton's largesse did not just deliver a striker who would break the 100-goal barrier for Watford; Deeney would become a Captain Fantastic with his own hotline to a superstar.

'It was surreal to get a call from Sir Elton, a couple of days after we won promotion, when I was in the car with my mum,' he says. 'Obviously she was buzzing as well, because this guy is a legend, so for him to be phoning her son was a bit mad. Considering I had never even met him before he came to open his own stand, I thought that was a nice touch, and I remember he rang me again after we beat Arsenal. His boys have been mascots on a matchday, I know he still follows every kick – whether he's at our games or not – and my nan won't hear a word against him. It was her 70th birthday a couple of years ago, and I sent him a cheeky email to say, "I've never asked you for anything in the past, but is it possible to do something for my nan?" Sure enough, he sent her a birthday card and a signed CD, and I thought, "You'll do for me."

'He did a concert at Walsall, and at the end he thanked them for being a wonderful audience and added, "Thanks for Troy Deeney." I wish I had been there to catch the moment on camera. When a superstar of his magnitude gives you a namecheck like that, or sends you an email wishing you all the best for the season, it's just nuts, when you think about it. But it speaks volumes for the guy.'

In truth, Deeney's first day as a Watford player was, in many ways, inauspicious, and it did not remotely suggest a born leader of men had fallen their way. The Hornets had been cast as sacrificial stooges in the opening League fixture of the season at Norwich on a Friday night, but Mackay went back to his old club and burst the promoted Canaries' bubble expertly. For Deeney, it was all a vaguely disconcerting blur. He says, 'That was a very eventful day, and when it was over I was homeless – not sleeping rough, but it was one of them days where you end up wondering, "How did I get here?"

'I woke up as a Walsall player, and I was due to report for training as usual at 9 a.m. but I got a call to say everything had been agreed with Watford and they were hoping to include me in their squad. Next thing I know, I'm on my way to meet them at Beaconsfield services on the M40, and I signed my contract in a Shell garage – so Watford could process the paperwork in time to beat the deadline – and I was on the bench at Norwich that night. Most people pop into a Shell garage for a bit of petrol, a sandwich or a bottle of pop; I was signing for a club who were spending the whole proceeds of an Elton John concert on me. Good luck with that one, Troy.

'The lads played really well at Norwich that night – we won 3-2, and I came on for the last half-hour, but I was running around like a headless chicken and I didn't even know my teammates' names because there was no time to get acquainted. I knew Danny Graham [who scored twice at Carrow Road] was "DG", and I figured John Eustace would answer to "Skip" if he was wearing the armband, but I had to keep whistling at

Lee Hodson when I wanted the ball because I didn't know his name.

'Once I knew who everyone was, I soon figured out we had some decent quality in that squad, although the bench at Norwich was so young I was almost a veteran at 22. But you would never have watched me that night and thought, "Yeah, he's a keeper – he's going to be the club captain for five years." I wasn't quite ready for that.'

As it happened, Deeney didn't even make it to his hotel bed at the end of a long, bewildering day. When Watford's team coach made it back to the club's London Colney training ground from East Anglia shortly after 1 a.m., director of football operations Iain Moody was assigned to deliver the new recruit to his overnight accommodation.

Moody, multi-lingual and a trusted ally of manager Mackay, was a safe pair of hands who could spot the chancers and charlatans among the genuine grafters. He also understood the mechanics of football, and he made sure Deeney was able to grab a few hours' sleep ahead of the squad's recovery session – even if the outcome was not what either of them expected.

'The club had arranged a hotel for me in Hatfield, only ten minutes away from the training ground,' says Deeney. 'But when we got there it was about 1.30 a.m. and nobody was answering when we rang the buzzer. I don't know if the night manager had sacked off my room, but we hammered on the door and nobody wanted to know. One way or another, there was no room at the inn.

'Fortunately, "Moods" had stayed on the case and offered me his spare room, so I spent my first night as a Watford player crashing out on the operations manager's sofabed – which was very good of him, by the way.

'I was still very naïve at that point, and in this day and age I don't think I would have slept in a stranger's house, no matter how trustworthy he was and no matter how late it was.'

Mighty oaks from little acorns grow, and as Deeney admits, his chaotic start to life at Vicarage Road did not suggest he would become a long-serving player, a centurion among the club's goalscorers, a captain among foot soldiers, a talisman and, yes, a legend.

By the time Javi Gracia was installed as head coach in January 2018, Deeney had served under 11 different managers. Along with the returning Adrian Mariappa, who had taken in the sights of Reading and Crystal Palace for four years after signing off as player of the season in 2011–12, he was the only surviving link between the class of 2010 and the Pozzo era.

And he is still none the wiser as to how the captaincy fell into his lap, two years after his release from prison, because it is a job he neither coveted nor chased. It was only when Manuel Almunia, the playoff semi-final penalty hero of *Do Not Scratch Your Eyes* minus 17 seconds, retired suddenly in 2014 that the armband passed to Deeney almost by assumption.

'I always seemed to be captain when Manu wasn't playing,' says Deeney, who often led the side out when Almunia missed 18 games through injury in two seasons. 'But nobody actually gave me the job. There was never a conversation when I was told, "Right, you are now the captain." It just *happened* when Beppe Sannino was in charge, but there was a lot going on behind the scenes around that time, so it wasn't highest on anyone's agenda.

'When Manu left, we did pre-season, and in every game I was captain. It was a bit like schooldays – you know, "You're the oldest one, so you're captain" – and next thing I know it's the first game of the season, Bolton at home, and there's an armband with my kit in the dressing room. Nice one, cheers for that. It changes your matchday preparation a bit, because you have to go and see the ref beforehand and stuff like that, but nobody made a big deal of it.

'I never asked to be captain, I never demanded it. I never thought I should get the job: it just came my way, and it's probably for the best that it happened like that, because it wasn't a huge upheaval. And when I took it on, I was lucky enough to have played for some really good captains, so I knew it came with extra responsibilities. Coming up through the ranks at Walsall, Michael Dobson was a really good pro – limited in ability, and I don't mean that in any way disrespectfully, but he did everything right. He was always early for training and the last to leave, just a model professional.

'Then "Moons" [Tommy Mooney] came in, and as well as being a great captain he also had the people skills: he always had time for a laugh, but when it was time to work, you got stuck in. And when I rolled in here, I was in a side led by John Eustace, an absolute legend of a man. I have nothing but respect for him. He used to drive me to work from Birmingham, because we're both from the Midlands, and he did his level best to keep me on the straight and narrow when I probably wasn't in the best frame of mind to wear the shirt at that stage of my career.

'He took a lot of time out for me and I've always appreciated that. He could have decided, "This kid's a dosser, he's not worth the effort" and left me well alone, but he was a top professional and a top man.'

As we have established elsewhere in these pages captaincy is often an overblown, overstated job in football. Apart from leading the side out, tossing a coin, choosing ends and hoping the mascot isn't taller than you, it is a largely symbolic role. It is not as if a captain picks the team, decides the formation, chooses the tactics, makes substitutions or throws the teacups at half-time. Unlike cricket, where Test matches can hinge on the captain's bowling changes, field settings and nuances of instinct, football matches are seldom, if ever, settled by accomplished academics in the field stroking their beards and making autocratic decisions without the coach's blessing.

But somewhere, somehow, in his incarnation as a reformed character after spending the summer of 2012 in a postcode nearer HMP than WD18, Deeney acquired the stature of a leader, not just a follower.

Maybe it was the playoff goal against Leicester which elevated his reputation among supporters into a different orbit; perhaps it was his 25 goals in the disappointing season which followed; or was it, simply, that he provided reassuring continuity during the breathless turnover of coaches and players at Watford?

Each transfer window, the bids would come in, principally from Burnley, Leicester and West Bromwich Albion, and each time, owner Gino Pozzo and executive chairman Scott Duxbury would conclude the bidders could never match the value the Hornets put on their captain – because it could not be expressed in pounds sterling nor any other currency.

In the promotion season of 2014–15, and subsequent years when Watford were fighting to establish themselves in the Premier League, Deeney was worth more than any arbitrary sum. More than any armband.

Unless you had seen his career at Vicarage Road go from scrap to bullion; unless you had lived through the club's near miss with administration in 2009 and discharged bankrupt Laurence Bassini's hissy-fit over the keys to the club safe, you could not hope to understand the bond between a town and its leader.

How fitting that Leicester should chase his signature, in the summer after their 5,000-1 shots won the title, because it had been Deeney's dramatic goal in the play-off semi-final that gave Watford fans the greatest single moment in the club's history – and sent the Foxes into mourning simultaneously.

When Anthony Knockaert went down, with high marks for artistic licence and none for subtlety, under Marco

Cassetti's escort deep into added time in May 2013, and referee Michael Oliver pointed to the spot with that look-at-me flourish only Premier League referees can effect, some of us had seen it all before.

Two weeks earlier, in a winner-takes-all promotion clash on the last day of term in League One, Oliver had awarded Brentford a penalty in stoppage time for an unfathomable offence. Same theatrical flourish – and, incredibly, same outcome. Marcello Trotta, who had earlier been uninspiring during his walk-on part on loan at Watford, smashed his penalty against the bar, Doncaster broke upfield and scored the winner that sent them up as champions while Brentford, consigned to the play-offs, missed out on promotion.

Apart from Oliver and his linesmen, this observer may have been the only person who also witnessed the sequel at Watford 15 days later, and his cardiologist has been on speed-dial ever since. As we know, from watching it daily on YouTube since May 2013, if Knockaert had converted his unjust spot-kick, Leicester would have gone to Wembley in an Armageddon of controversy. But when Almunia came to the rescue, and the Hornets broke upfield for Deeney to hammer that unforgettable winner on aggregate, there was not just a 17-second gap between abject despair and euphoria.

That was arguably the moment when Deeney passed into the pantheon of Watford legends. Even Graham Taylor's magic carpet rides – five promotions, Europe, the FA Cup final and partying at Wembley like it was 1999 – could not compete with the explosion of joy Deeney's defining goal detonated.

On any other day it would have made more headlines, or bigger headlines, but on that Sunday English football was drowning in the sycophantic fawning over Ferguson's passing-out parade as he took charge of his final match as Manchester United manager.

The memories of a miracle are still there, however, on the worldwide web for us to rewind and enjoy. Among the must-see clips is Sky Sports News reporter Johnny Phillips losing it on the gantry during the invincible drama and footage from student digs as a Leicester fan's hope morphs into anguish and his flatmates dissolve into howling laughter.

That goal consecrated Deeney's relationship with Watford's loyal support and was probably the reference point for Pozzo every time he dismissed bids of up to £30 million for his captain at the drop of a hat. Any striker who averaged 20 goals a season over a four-year period was going to attract his fair share of vultures, and nobody at Vicarage Road could blame Leicester for hoping Deeney might sign up for a Champions League adventure, even if it was only from the bench or making a token start against Smorgasbord Rovers. In fact, you could only admire their judgement.

But Troy's value to Watford down the years has been more than goals, tucking away the odd penalty and Sky Sports commentator Bill Leslie's immortal *Do Not Scratch Your Eyes* line. Whenever a head coach came and went, it was Deeney who rallied the dressing room. It was Deeney who provided the umbilical cord between inner sanctum and the Rookery, a reassuring presence on the pitch when supporters might have been alarmed by the relentless pace of change. It was Deeney whose programme notes from the captain's table were down to earth after a famous win and defiantly upbeat when defeat came calling. And it was Deeney who lifted spirits after the Championship title slipped from Watford's grasp in the last minute of the season by grabbing master of ceremonies Jon Marks' microphone and bursting into song when many fans felt like bursting into tears.

In a momentous era there were times when Deeney was almost the *de facto* manager of Watford – not in terms of picking the team or dictating the tactics, but in conducting the mood music in the changing room with statesmanlike authority.

Take, for instance, a 72-hour period in early 2017, beginning with the Hornets being knocked out of the FA Cup at Millwall on a Sunday lunchtime (with a performance so derisory that head coach Walter Mazzarri should have been ashamed of it instead of spouting blinkered nonsense about the better side losing). And yet, out of nowhere, defying all admissible logic, on the following Tuesday evening Watford went to the Emirates and beat Arsenal 2-1 in foul conditions with a display ticking all the boxes: passion, aggression, flair and dynamism as they surged into an early two-goal lead; then backbone, discipline, guts and willpower to withstand the Gunners' inevitable fightback. Deeney scored what turned out to be the winner that night, but his contribution ran much deeper than simply leading the line and pouncing from six yards when the rebound from Étienne Capoue's solo slalom and shot fell his way.

He did not quite pin some of his teammates against the wall and threaten to hang them from the away dressing-room clothes pegs, but he did fire them up in no uncertain terms. Deeney knew he would be representing the players at Hornets messiah Graham Taylor's funeral the following day, and before kick-off at the Emirates he told them he would not tolerate having to spend the service with head bowed in embarrassment. As club captain he wanted to take his place among Taylor's grieving family and the A-list cast in a packed St Mary's parish church with no lingering awkwardness about the previous night's performance. The players took Deeney's message on board spectacularly.

'It's fair to say me and Mr Mazzarri never really got on eye-to-eye, but I told him I'd take care of that team talk,' he says. 'To be fair, he gave us a good briefing at our team meeting in the hotel before we left for the stadium. No complaints there.

But from about four o'clock onwards I was getting into people, firing them up and letting them have it – "You'd better be f****** on it tonight" – and I remember we were absolutely flying in the warm-up. It was pissing down, a horrible night, but the quality of our warm-up was unreal. Sometimes you get that sense, a gut feeling that the boys are really up for it, and when we went in for the last talk before the game itself, you wanted to keep the intensity going. Don't let them off the hook. I remember shutting the door and saying to the gaffer, "I've got this." He must have seen the fire in my eyes because normally he would insist on having the final say, "No, no, no, no," and there would be a confrontation. But, for some reason, he let it go, and fair play to him. He let me get into the lads one more time because there was this huge occasion for the whole town that I was attending the following day – I think it was only me and Lloyd Doyley who were representing the players – and I told them straight. I said, "Look, if I'm going to this funeral tomorrow, I'm going there knowing we've given everything tonight. Everything. We could lose 5-0 if they are too good for us on the night, but we are going to go out there and bust our bollocks – because if we don't, you're all coming with me."

'Thankfully, we played really well and deserved to win. I was proud of the team that night, and I was proud to represent them – on an incredibly sad occasion for everyone connected with Watford – the next day. I think there was even a picture of me and Walter having a hug after the final whistle at Arsenal, which shows something special was happening!

'I don't want to make it sound like I was helping him out because he didn't know what to do. That would be unfair. But he was very "old school" in his approach – normally he couldn't be told what to do. His way was the only way, and he had some success in Italy [Mazzarri won the Coppa Italia with Napoli in 2012 and finished runner-up in Serie A the following year], which you can't ignore.

'But on that night at Arsenal I got involved because it was like, "I know this place and I know what to expect." Two days earlier we had played at Millwall in the Cup. The team he picked was a disgrace and I told him as much. He didn't show Millwall enough respect, and then he sends me on in a token effort to save it. We had our issues, and that was the hard part of being captain. There were times when you wanted to tell it like it is, but you tell a different story to keep it on-message and say, "We'll get it right," knowing full well it might not turn out that way.

'To be fair, we got it right against Arsenal away. It was nice to go there and win two years running, because we did them in the Cup [under Quique Sánchez Flores] the previous year.'

Graham Taylor's funeral was, inevitably, a sad day to reflect on a great man's life, but Watford Football Club handled the arrangements immaculately and Deeney had no reason whatsoever to look sheepish when he joined the congregation to pay his respects. He had always called GT 'Mr Taylor' out of courtesy, because he was the Hornets' acting chairman when Deeney signed for Watford in August 2010, and he simply never grew out of the habit.

As it transpired, Arsenal manager Arsène Wenger – who had always admired Taylor as an opponent and as a dignified standard-bearer for football – was the one who had to keep his head down. To his eternal credit, Wenger showed up for the funeral, the last man in the church before the cortège arrived, even though Watford must have been the last place on earth where he felt like showing his face hours after a damaging defeat. It reflected nothing but credit on him.

And BBC commentator John Motson, who recited a personal tribute to Taylor from his long-time chairman Sir Elton, even ad-libbed his own line as a postscript: 'What a way to go out – Arsenal 1, Watford 2.'

***

It has always been in Deeney's nature to call it as he sees it. When you have played for an entire Head Coaches XI at a single club, and served more than half of them as captain, you are entitled to have a bit to say for yourself – and on your teammates' behalf.

There is little point in asking Deeney to arrange them in a league table of merit, or to award each of them marks out of ten, because in most cases the circumstances and the squad at every manager's disposal was different. But at various stages Malky Mackay, Sean Dyche, Gianfranco Zola, Beppe Sannino, Óscar García, Billy McKinlay, Slaviša Jokanović, Quique Sánchez Flores, Walter Mazzarri, Marco Silva and Javier Gracia have all had reasons to be grateful for Deeney's influence at Vicarage Road. McKinlay, whose tenure lasted only two games, was the only one who did not have the chance to pick (or drop) Troy, because he was recovering from a hamstring injury.

The only one with whom he did not get on was Mazzarri. 'I tried to be respectful, as I always am, but then there were times when I was scoring, the team was winning and next game I would be on the bench,' Deeney told BBC Radio 5 Live. 'I asked if I'd done something wrong and it was, "No, you've been great." I asked for an answer but it never happened. He also tried to sell me in the January window, which I didn't like, so I asked if I was available to be sold and was told, "No, we need you, you're the captain" – and the next thing he is still trying to sell me behind my back. As captain it became really difficult to relay the message you know you should to players who are not in the team, keeping them focused, when I probably wasn't fully focused myself.'

On and off the pitch, Deeney has adopted a forthright approach to captaincy and seldom, if ever, has he regretted his trenchant opinions in hindsight.

'I would say I've always been outspoken, and prepared to speak my mind, without shying away from hard work,' he says. 'Those things don't make you a leader on their own, but in the season when we went up, and there were four managers coming and going, we had a lot of things going on behind closed doors. We couldn't agree bonuses, players were refusing to train, that kind of stuff.

'Even when there have been bigger personalities and bigger names in the football world, I think people just respect that I've always been prepared to tell the truth – good or bad. If I believe in something, I'm not going to go down without a fight. The respect has probably built from that. Over the last three or four years a lot of the lads have been happy for me to get on with it and fight on their behalf because they know I want what's best for them, and not what's simply best for Troy. I like to think that if you have a reasonable conversation with me, you'll get a sensible outcome.'

Balancing his role as a powerful voice in the dressing room with a robust yet mobile approach to leading the line on the pitch, many of Deeney's happiest moments in a Watford shirt have been adorned with the captain's armband. Certainly there is no shortage of eligible footage for the highlights reel.

Chilling – if such a thing was possible in the summer heatwave of 2018 – in the sunshine at Watford's University College training ground in London Colney, he sifts through the back catalogue of memorable games and seminal moments: '*That* goal against Leicester, of course. Winning promotion is one, definitely. Not just getting over the line, but the way we did it, and then going down Watford High Street and sharing the moment among our fans. That will always be a highlight, along with the first game at Everton the following season.

'It hadn't really dawned on me what it was all about, and why we'd fought so hard to get up in the first place, until I walked in the away dressing room at Goodison Park, and you see the Premier League badge on the shirt sleeve of our kit. And then you walk through the narrow corridors to the tunnel, and it's full of cameras and microphones, and you think: "Now we're in the big time. This is what all the hard work was about." It just hit me like a wave.

'But I've got to say the whole promotion year was special – not because I was captain, but the four managers we went through for different reasons, and all the nonsense that came with it, mainly from outside the club. I scored 21 goals and contributed 11 or 12 assists, so I played my part in going up. When I look back, it will be a collection of moments in time that stand out – Brighton, Everton, scoring my first Premier League goal at Stoke . . . scoring at Wembley [in the FA Cup semi-final against Crystal Palace] was cool, although it would have been even better if we'd won or turned up for more than ten minutes.

'For some reason, scoring twice against Villa stands out in the memory – the home game, not the winner at the Holte end – and another one is that Huddersfield game in the Championship where we were down to ten men after Gabriel Tamas got sent off but we managed to win 4-2. Games like that – where our backs are against the wall but the crowd swings behind us, and you come in afterwards thinking, "Yeah, we dug that one out by fighting together" – that's when you feel the rewarding side of captaincy. We all put our nuts on the line to win that.

'Strangely enough, Beppe left the next day, even though we were second in the League at the time, but that underlines what I was saying earlier about stuff behind closed doors that the fans don't see. There were so many niggly little episodes, always an argument going on somewhere. You come into work and you're thinking, "What's it going to be today? Who's going to be arguing (with Beppe) this time?" Never a dull moment.

'Then he leaves, Óscar García comes in, and we're going to play a completely different brand of football because of the way he played at Brighton, and all of a sudden he has a heart attack, or a heart-related problem. He was only in charge for a few games. I played in the first couple of them before I did my hamstring at Blackpool, where I let Matej Vydra take our penalty for the winning goal to get him off the mark. He owes me a few quid for that!'

The 'experts' had a field day as Watford rang the changes – not all of them by design – in that extraordinary 2014–15 season. García was forced to step down on health grounds, his coaching lieutenant McKinlay was gone in the blink of an eye, and even Jokanovic looked on shaky ground when four consecutive defeats – including a limp one against Cardiff on the day Graham Taylor christened his eponymous stand – left the Hornets outside the top six. Even Sir Elton John, speaking at a tennis event to raise funds for his AIDS foundation, admitted he was getting 'a little bit worried about the manager'.

But holding the fort, keeping his focus trained on football, was Deeney. And when the horrid cycle of losses broke with a five-goal hammering of Fulham at Craven Cottage on a Friday night, it was the captain who led the way with a hat-trick.

'Everything just snowballed into a season where we had four managers but we ended up going where we wanted to go, and among all the changes there were some proud moments. Because of my personality, when I come out of football and step back, I'll look back at that season and realise that was some rollercoaster. Was I proud to be captain of that ship? You'd better believe it.'

Promotion was secured by a white-knuckle ride: a 2-0 win at Brighton in the lunchtime kick-off, and Watford learned they had made it to the promised land as the team coach pulled into the training ground on their return from the south coast as news of rivals Norwich and Middlesbrough dropping points in the 3 p.m. kick-offs filtered through.

Less than enthused by a goalless draw between West Bromwich Albion and Liverpool that afternoon – it wasn't as exciting as it sounds – the man from the *Daily Mirror* received early intelligence of the players celebrating among their flock in the town centre and rushed back from the Hawthorns with indecent haste to find them. Deeney, briefly escaping the giddiness to conduct a live radio interview on *talkSPORT* in a sheltered corner under the ring road flyover, was the first person I stumbled across before admiring the choral society's songbook from outside the Colombia Press. As you do.

On any Saturday night, Watford High Street is a melting pot of humanity, but the communal partying of players and fans spoke volumes for the bond between a football club and its lifeblood. In the early days of Gino Pozzo's ownership at Vicarage Road Watford had been accused by reactionary elements of Fleet Street of standing for everything that was wrong in football.

Pull the other one – promotion was built on a model of unity, and Deeney was a cornerstone of that togetherness. When remembrance was the nation's keynote on the centenary of the First World War breaking out, the Hornets' stunning Poppy Day mosaic, an initiative driven by the core 1881 fans group, set the standard. By the time Premier League football was restored to Hertfordshire Watford had a shiny four-sided ground for the first time in our lifetime, with stands named after grandees Taylor and Sir Elton, instead of three sides and a corrugated graveyard. And when supporter Nic Cruwys, a milkman from Hemel Hempstead, was beaten to within an inch of his life by pond life in Wolverhampton after the 2-2 draw at Molineux, the shock felt by players and supporters alike became a powerful galvanising force. The hashtag #ForNicForPromotion became a catalyst to get the job done. Deeney was on hand to present Cruwys with a complimentary season ticket when the lifelong fan was invited to the training ground after a painstaking recovery.

Watford, the club that stands for all that is wrong with football? You're having a laugh – that season, they were the club who got it right. And Deeney was the heartbeat of it all.

When he contributed 15 goals and nine assists to the Hornets' comfortable survival in the top flight, he was the club's first captain since Pat Rice, 32 years earlier, to win promotion and extend the Hornets' residence among the gilded elite beyond a single season. Deeney's attributes also took him to the brink of an England call-up – a phenomenon he revisited early in the 2018–19 season, with supporters of rival clubs backing his case this time.

Apart from Luther Blissett and John Barnes, the only other Watford player who had won an England cap on the back of his performances for the Hornets was goalkeeper Ben Foster, who made his debut against Spain at Old Trafford in 2007 during his exemplary loan spell from Manchester United. In 2016, Deeney was unfortunate that when the national team's head coach, Roy Hodgson, came to run the rule over him in a goalless draw with Bournemouth, he was ineffective in a deeper, withdrawn role, dutifully obliging Sanchez Flores's tactical requirements. In October 2018, when another Watford player finally won an England cap, coming off the bench against Spain to run down the clock in Seville, the honour fell to midfielder Nathaniel Chalobah - deserved recognition after a year wrecked by injury.

But Watford's Troy story was big news, and he was now a household name. We refrained from borrowing the 'captain, leader, legend' mantra from a London club because of its connotations with full-kit photobombing, but Deeney had sizeable credit in his adopted home and further afield.

After giving considerable thought to establishing his own charitable fund, and how to launch it effectively, he came up with the Troy Deeney Foundation.

Through playing football, he has given his own children a start in life that he never had when he was growing up on the sprawling council estate of Chelmsley Wood in Birmingham. Deeney has never claimed to be a perfect role model, and sometimes the headlines have been quick to remind him, but there are admirable intentions behind a mission statement to break down barriers in society and give kids with learning difficulties or life-limiting illnesses opportunities to lead fulfilling lives.

'When I look back at how the foundation came about, it would have been very easy for me to do it in Birmingham – close to my roots, keep it local, get a few pats on the back from the neighbours,' he says. That's why a school in Watford, Garston Manor, became his first project.

'Although I don't want to be crude about it, I'm not from round here. But this is my town now: I've kind of inherited it. This was my way of giving something back. Garston Manor represented me, and the values I was looking for, which was key. It's a fantastic school, and not only because of what they do for the kids. When you see children with autism, learning difficulties or some sort of illness, their pain threshold for bullshit is very, very low. As soon as you walk through the door, they look at you and think, "Who are you? What do you want?

And why are you here?" So I cut to the chase and say, "Hi, I'm Troy and I've come to help your school out." They looked at me and said, "You want to help *us?*" But that's how it was.'

Deeney's inaugural venture in philanthropy even brought about a change in the inscription on his match boots. 'Some of the boys are Watford fans. I gave one a pair with "autism" on them to raise awareness,' he told Henry Winter in an interview with *The Times.* 'I used to have my kids' names on my boots, but now it's "autism". That's not me trying to be an angel or a saint, because I'm not. I'm just trying to do something right.'

The baron of charity's maiden voyage raised £40,000 and Garston Manor enjoyed an extensive refurbishment of its play areas. Meanwhile, the connection between a town and its football club captain was reinforced like spaghetti western drifter Clint Eastwood's poncho by a lead sheet in *A Fistful Of Dollars.*

Despite public conjecture about Deeney's private life in October 2018, it would be disingenuous not to acknowledge the monumental contribution of his wife, Stacey, to the foundation's Garston Manor success, and during our interview he was fulsome in his admiration of her tireless admin, admitting, 'I just put my face to it, which is probably not the face you'd want – I've got a big head and teeth like a shark, but so what?'

Troy also concedes he could not have conceived his foundation, nor executed its first enterprise, without the kudos of captaincy to underpin his exploratory donation to social welfare. 'It could never have been a success without having the town of Watford behind me or the characteristics I've got,' he says. 'There's so much crap swirling around on social media I tend not to advertise on it. I had to rely on people knowing I was coming from a genuine place, and fortunately the people of Watford saw my objective for what it was.'

When Deeney gets the chance to reflect on his time at Watford he may care to reflect on a pivotal spell in his life where he flirted with oblivion but emerged as one of only five players to score a century of goals for the club to date, joining an exclusive set with Luther Blissett, Tommy Barnett, Ross Jenkins and Cliff Holton.

He can survey the gap between the stupidity of affray – for which he lost three months of liberty, to repent at leisure – and the goodness of a reformed character who set up his own foundation and gave a school a new £40,000 playground. He can survey the distance between the raw striker who signed for the Hornets in a petrol station and the captain who became the undisputed standard-bearer for his club. Never the head coach, but often the boss.

'I'm not bigging myself up here, but I'm pretty good at sussing out a squad,' says Deeney. 'From reaching the Premier League onwards it's all about the characters around you. When you work with someone like Valon Behrami [who had an outstanding World Cup for Switzerland in 2018], you don't have to take him on. He knows the drill, we both get it, we're both pretty rough characters. You tend to wok out who's onside. In that first year in the Premier League, the dressing room was almost run by a mini-committee – top lads like Ben Watson, Valon and "Gomey" [Heurelho Gomes] – and I would just oversee it, if that makes sense. Ben was fantastic for us that year because he was in and out of the team, so if people who didn't play on the Saturday were sacking off a Sunday session, he would deal with it or let me know. Miguel Britos was an asset as well because he could speak Spanish and Italian. Once the 25-man squad is settled, certain players will keep an eye out, and if there's anything they can't deal with, they come to me.'

As well overseeing established lines of communication within the squad, Deeney has never lost sight of his wider responsibilities as captain, notably his interaction with the public. Always last off the pitch, win or lose – and often without his boots – after thanking the fans for turning out, his post-match comments have rarely slipped into bland platitudes. Sitting on the fence was never his style where uprooting the gateposts and dismantling the panels was an option.

Those bonds of trust, he says, were built on honesty: 'I don't want to sound like I'm just prostituting myself here, but I just tell the truth. Good and bad. I've never known how people can put up a front for so long in football because it's quite tiring. When we've played poorly, I've not been afraid to come out in public and admit we were shit, because we're all football fans, we've all got an opinion and we all know whether the game we're watching is any good or not. It makes me laugh when footballers go on Twitter after they have lost and say, "Great to make my debut, disappointed with the result, but the fans were great." Do me a favour. If the fans were that good you wouldn't have to thank them. They probably booed you off and wondered why the hell the manager has signed you. Everyone wants to be loved in football, but let's not pussyfoot around.

'I'm sure that not everyone in the game – especially certain sets of fans – likes me, but I like to think they respect me, because I don't fob them off.'

So does Deeney ever regret his famous '*cojones*' comment about Arsenal following his match-turning impact from the bench (and the Gunners' palpable lack of steel) in Watford's 2-1 win at Vicarage Road in October 2017?

'No. If I'm going to be honest, and say what I feel, I've got to take the rough with the smooth. Hindsight's a wonderful thing, and I might have been better off just saving it for the boozer afterwards, but I don't ever regret it. If I'm out in London now, opinion is split 50–50. I get Arsenal fans coming up to me and saying, "That *cojones* comment was out of order, but fair play for saying what you think." Others will tap me on the shoulder and say, "Good on you, Troy. I've been saying that for years." I think Arsenal had been on a decent run until we beat them, so I was the first one to come out and say it, and one or two people piled into me. But when they lost at Brighton, Swansea, Bournemouth and others, it was all right then. A few weeks down the line, when they kept losing, it was safe for experts like Merson [former Arsenal forward Paul Merson, now a Sky Sports pundit] to come out and say, "They have the quality but they lack the fight" – in other words, he was saying exactly what I was saying, and it gave others a licence to repeat it. People used it as a pretext for saying Arsène Wenger should go as the Arsenal manager – but I never said that. I've got nothing but respect for Mr Wenger. He built the Invincibles, one of the greatest football teams we've ever seen in this country, and he was the last of a dying breed. You will never get a manager who stays at one club for 22 years again at that level.

'I just gave an honest opinion, and if a few people don't like it, tough. It's even raised the stakes and built a little rivalry with Arsenal. If that puts a bit more pressure and expectation on me, the players and the management to raise our levels, is that really a bad thing? It doesn't help when I miss a penalty at the Emirates and it turns into a f****** long day. But I got up next morning and realised I'm not dead yet. Onwards and upwards.'

TALES FROM THE
VICARAGE

Brilliant, original stories about Watford FC
by journalists, fans, former players and managers

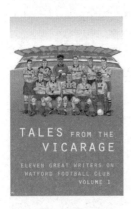

Tales From The Vicarage Volume 1

The first book in the series features former
Vicarage Road player David James, former
managers Brendan Rodgers and Malky
Mackay in addition to editor Lionel Birnie
and writers Simon Burton, Olly Wicken,
John Anderson, Adam Leventhal,
Andrew French, Tim Turner, Oliver Phillips,
Kevin Affleck and Stuart Hutchison.

Tales From The Vicarage Volume 2

The second book includes contributions
from former players Luther Blissett, Danny
Graham, Paul Wilkinson and Nigel Gibbs plus
editor Lionel Birnie and writers Mike Walters,
Andrew French, Ian Grant, Paolo Tomaselli,
John Murray, Adam Leventhal, Matt Rowson,
Olly Wicken, Miles Jacobson and Mike Parkin.

All books in the series are available now from
www.talesfrom.com

Tales From The Vicarage Volume 3: The Interviews

The third book is co-written by Lionel Birnie and Adam Leventhal and features interviews with eleven ex-Watford names – former managers Sean Dyche, Aidy Boothroyd and Ray Lewington and former players Craig Ramage, Nick Wright, Micah Hyde, Ronny Rosenthal, David and Dean Holdsworth, Tommy Smith and Paul Furlong.

Tales From The Vicarage Volume 4

Our fourth volume, edited by Lionel Birnie, features contributions from Troy Deeney, Marco Cassetti, Ikechi Anya, Jonathan Hogg, Fernando Forestieri, Tommy Mooney, Gifton Noel-Williams, Allan Smart and John McClelland.

Tales From The Vicarage Volume 5

Volume 5 comprises interviews with former managers Quique Sanchez Flores and Beppe Sannino and former players Tony Coton, Lloyd Doyley and Clarke Carlisle with contributions from editor Lionel Birnie and writers John Anderson, David Harrison, Stuart Hutchinson, Peter Jenson, Ciro Scognamiglio, Paolo Tomaselli, Kelly Somers, Olly Wicken and Mike Walters.

All books in the series are available now from
www.talesfrom.com

Tales From The Vicarage Volume 6

The sixth volume is entitled Rocket Men which tells the story of the only four players to have played in all four divisions for Watford as they rose from Division Four to One in the late seventies and early eighties. The Rocket Men were Luther Blissett, Ian Bolton, Ross Jenkins and Steve Sherwood. The book also includes a foreword by John Barnes.

All books in the series are available now from
www.talesfrom.com